The Keys to Learning

Unlocking Your Brain's Potential

Michael R. Melloch

Five Dog Books

Five Dog Books

First Edition

ISBN 979-8-9888292-1-8

For Lyn and Kate

In memory of my parents, Ray and Lottie

Table of Contents

Preface...8

Chapter 1: The Human Brain 10

Chapter 2: What is Learning? Mental Models, Creativity and Solving Complex Problems...26

Chapter 3: Memory and Spaced Study 39

Chapter 4: Your Study Environment...................54

Chapter 5: Interleaving..58

Chapter 6: Incubation..66

Chapter 7: Testing 72

Chapter 8: Purposeful Practice 81

Chapter 9: Specialize or Build a Latticework of Mental Models? 93

Chapter 10: Engage All Your Senses...................98

Chapter 11: Sleep 104

Chapter 12: Mindset...122

Chapter 13: Self-Control and Grit......................130

Chapter 14: Nutrition 148

Chapter 15: Exercise 175

Chapter 16: Meditation and Breathing 186

Chapter 17: Concept Point Recovery 195

Chapter 18: Relationships...................................201

Chapter 19: Summary...213

Epilog..217

Bibliography 218

Appendix A: Brain Energy Calculations 241

Appendix B: Boolean Algebra and Digital Circuits *243*

Appendix C: Problems from Chapter 6 .... *250*

Suggested Reading *252*

About the author *253*

Acknowledgment *254*

Review Request *255*

Preface

I joined the faculty as an Assistant Professor of Electrical Engineering at Purdue University in 1984. I always felt I was a good teacher, as evidenced by my teaching evaluations and comments from students. But at a large public research university my major emphasis was on research. That changed with two events. The first was my daughter becoming a student at Purdue University in 2006. The second was when I became Associate Head for Education for my department in 2007, a position I held for 13 years. Both these events gave me an increased sense of responsibility to the education mission, especially the undergraduate education mission, of the university.

The position of Associate Head for Education came with release from teaching, which is common with most administrative positions at a large university. However, I was inspired to continue to teach. My inspiration was Henry Yang who used to be Dean of Engineering at Purdue. For a brief time in 1990, I served as an assistant dean for Henry, before he took the position of Chancellor at the University of California at Santa Barbara (UCSB). Henry was unlike any other administrator, especially at such a high administrative level. Henry continued to do research, supervise graduate students, and teach undergraduate classes! When I was at UCSB for a meeting, I dropped by the Chancellor's office in the off-chance Henry was available to say hello. He was and after a brief conversation he suggested we could continue talking for a few minutes if I would walk with him to the class he was teaching! What other university president or chancellor has such dedication to undergraduate education?

My increased responsibility to undergraduate teaching led me to receiving all the teaching awards possible at the department, college, and university level. I especially value the awards that are solely determined by students.

In my quest to improve my teaching, I started to read books and papers on the learning process. I realized that we are still learning how people learn, but there are things that have been discovered, and known, about the learning process since at least 1885. I was surprised to learn the roles that nutrition, exercise, sleep, mindset, and meditation can play in learning. To better your learning is a way of life. I was never taught any of these things and from talking with students I have observed few have. I started to present seminars at the undergraduate and graduate level for the students in my department summarizing the things I had found out about learning. I received very positive feedback from the students that confirmed students are not being told about the learning process and how your way of life effects your ability to learn. My motivation for this book is to consolidate what I have learned in one place for students, teachers, and life-long learners.

Chapter 1: The Human Brain

At 3 pounds (1.4 kg), the human brain is about 2% of your body weight. Yet your brain uses 20-25% of the oxygen you breathe and of your body's glucose, your fuel supply. (Details of brain energy calculations can be found in Appendix A.) Without oxygen and glucose to the brain, you will become unconscious in less than 10 seconds. This is why a fighter pilot, who pulls out of a dive too fast, will black out. The pilot's heart is no longer strong enough to overcome the centrifugal force to continue pumping blood depriving his brain of oxygen and glucose.

The brain is very fragile compared to other body organs. If you were to hold a brain, it would feel like jelly because of the large amount of fat comprising the human brain. The brain is encased to protect it. The skull is made up of layers of thick bones. Between the skull and the brain are several sheets of membranes called meninges that further protect the brain. The brain is then immersed in cerebrospinal fluid (CSF), a colorless liquid that shows up as dark areas on magnetic resonance imaging (MRI) scans. The brain essentially floats in the CSF, further protecting the brain during impacts.

Besides protecting the brain structurally, there is the blood-brain barrier that keeps harmful substances—toxins and bacteria—from reaching the brain. The blood-brain barrier was discovered in the late 19th century by Paul Ehrlich. When Ehrlich injected dye into the blood stream of a mouse, he found the dye in all the mouse's organs except the brain and spinal column. Similarly, if the dye was injected into the spinal fluid, it would only end up in the brain and spinal column but not in any other organs. In the 1960s, microscopes were powerful enough to see that the blood-brain barrier is a dense web of capillaries that screens out what can cross into the brain, preventing these bad actors from entering, but allowing substances the brain needs to pass through. Some of the substances that are allowed to pass into the brain are water, oxygen, proteins, some fats, glucose by a transport protein, and vitamins.

Your brain consists of neurons and glial cells. For about 50 years it was believed that there were 10 times as many glial cells as neurons in the human brain. But many recent studies have discovered that the ratio is drastically different, with the ratio of glial cells to neurons being slightly less than 1:1 [1]. (Maybe the long-time incorrect belief that neurons represented only 10% of cells in the brain led to the popular, and incorrect, statement that humans only use 10% of their brains.)

When we think about thinking, it is the neurons that come to mind and electrical signals flowing between neurons. The structure of a neuron is illustrated in figure 1.1. Neurons are gray. When you hear a reference to gray matter associated with the brain it comes from the gray color of the neuron cell bodies. The human brain contains about 86 billion neurons.

A figure of 100 billion neurons is often quoted as the number of neurons in the human brain. It is still the figure you are likely to find if you perform a search, or read most books about the brain, especially those before the work of Suzanna Herculano-Houzel. As a neuroscientist, Herculano-Houzel, became interested in the source of this number of neurons. She searched the literature but could not find an original source. Talking with other neuroscientists, she could not find anyone who knew the source. Her conclusion was that no one had ever measured the number of neurons in the human brain. She decided to measure the actual number of neurons in the human brain. The method she developed was to dissolve brains, or parts of brains, in a detergent that destroys the cell membranes but not the nuclei of the cells. Agitating this solution resulted in a homogeneous distribution of nuclei. Putting a small sample under a microscope, the number of nuclei in the sample could be counted. Using neuronal nuclear protein, which only binds to the nuclei from neurons, she could distinguish the neurons and glial cells in her samples. It is then a simple calculation to determine the number of nuclei of neurons and glial cells in the starting sample, which was a whole brain or a part of the brain. She determined for the human brain the average number of neurons is 86 billion and the average number of glial cells is 85 billion [2]. If you think 100 billion is a nice number to quote and is close enough to 86 billion, consider that a baboon's brain contains about 11 billion neurons, less than the difference between 100 and 86 billion! Fourteen billion neurons represent considerable cognitive power. Of the 86 billion neurons in the human brain, about 16 billion are in the cerebral cortex, where cognition occurs. The cerebral cortex only contains 19% of the human brain's neurons, but it is about 80% of the brain's volume. The cerebellum—which is involved in movement, posture, and balance—contains 69 billion neurons, or about 80% of the neurons in your brain. There are a little less than 1 billion neurons in the brainstem.

Even though some animals have larger brains than humans, the human cerebral cortex has more neurons than the cerebral cortex of any other animal. (The chimpanzee's cerebral cortex contains 6 billion neurons.) Often, we will encounter something associated with the brain or learning that has been believed to be true, such as the human brain containing 100 billion neurons and 10 times as many glial cells as neurons, and it was a long time before anyone questioned, and determined, that it wasn't true.

A neuron consists of a cell body, dendrites, dendrite spines, a single axon, and terminal boutons at the ends of the axon terminals as seen in figure 1.1. The axon carries electrical signals from the cell body to other neurons, or to muscles and glands. The dendrites carry signals from other neurons to the cell body. The electric signal in the axon is referred to as an action potential. The dendrite's reach is limited to the region around the cell body. Most axons are of length 1 mm but can range in length from a few hundred microns to 1 m such as those that travel from the base of your spine to your feet. Axons have diameters of 1–25 microns while dendrites are thin compared to axons. A large axon can be 95% of the volume of the neuron.

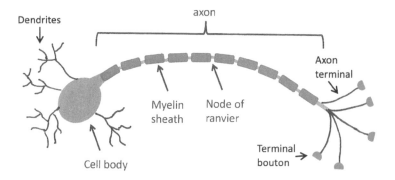

Figure 1.1 A neuron

An axon will develop collaterals, as illustrated in figure 1.2, which are side branches allowing an axon to reach different brain regions to make connections. The axon terminals allow for connection to dendrite spines of many different neurons in each of these regions. Axons can typically send signals to more than 1,000 other neurons, in some cases as many as 10,000 other neurons. Similarly, a neuron can receive signals from thousands of other neurons through the dendrites. (On the dendrites of a type of neuron called a Purkinje cell in the cerebellum there can be about 200,000 dendrite spines for making connections to axons.) The connections between an axon from one neuron to a dendrite on anther neuron is called a synapse. The number of synapses in the human brain is estimated to be in the range of 100-200 trillion. A synapse is not a direct connection, it is a gap, referred to as the synaptic cleft. The synaptic cleft is less than 40 nm wide. The part of the synapse on a dendrite are protrusions called spines. The part of the synapse on the axon are at the end of the terminals and called boutons, although there can also be synapses along the length of the axon. These synapses along the length of an axon are referred to as en passant synapses. The synaptic gap is small enough that a chemical signal can be sent across it to facilitate communication. The neuron initiating the signal is called the presynaptic neuron and the neuron receiving the signal is called the postsynaptic neuron.

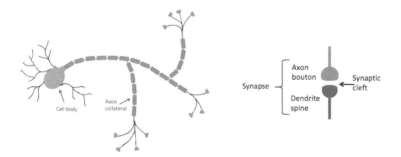

Figure 1.2 Collaterals and a synapse.

In the presynaptic neuron are sacs called vesicles that contain thousands of neurotransmitters. When an electrical signal is sent down the axon of the presynaptic neuron, neurotransmitters are released into the synaptic cleft. The neurotransmitters diffuse across the synaptic cleft, where they attach to receptors on the postsynaptic neuron dendrite spine, resulting in an electric signal that transmits up the dendrite to the cell body. After the signal has been transmitted, the remaining neurotransmitters must be cleared from the synaptic cleft. Some return to the presynaptic neuron bouton, this is called reuptake. Some will diffuse out of the synaptic cleft.

When you are learning, there are physical changes occurring in your brain. You are adjusting the connection strength between existing neurons. With increased activation synapses strengthen, a process referred to as long-term potentiation (LTP). This frequent activation results in more neurotransmitters released from the axon with each subsequent activation and in the formation of more receptors on the dendrite side of the synaptic cleft. Just the opposite happens if you have a synapse between neurons that does not get used. There is a reduction in the neurotransmitter receptors on the dendrites and a weakening of the connection, a process called long-term depression (LTD). LTP and LTD result in the electrical signals flowing differently through your neural networks. With learning you can also form new synapses (synaptogenesis), or even pruning of synapses, between neurons. Formation of new synapses have been observed in less than one hour in the motor cortex of mice learning new motor tasks [3]. There are over 100 different types of neurotransmitters. With sustained long-term stimulus, there can also be a change in the neurotransmitter a presynaptic neuron emits and a comparable change in the receptor of the post-synaptic neuron. [4]. The creation of new synapses, synaptogenesis, occurs all through life but decreases with age. **Learning results in adjusting of the connection strength between existing synapses, formation of new synapses and changes in neurotransmitters—physical changes in your brain.**

Myelin is the electrical insulation found around axons. With increased myelin, signals travel faster down the axon, as much as 50 times faster, which results in you being able to think faster! (How electrical signals travel down an axon, and the role myelin plays, is complicated and involves understanding chemistry and electrical circuits including transmission lines. This understanding is not necessary for the purposes of this book.) The process of myelination begins shortly before birth in the brain stem and is very rapid during the first two years of life. But myelination continues to occur, albeit at a slower rate into early adulthood. Beginning in the brain stem before birth, myelinization proceeds upward along the back of the brain and then towards the front of the brain. The final area of the brain where myelination occurs is the prefrontal cortex, which begins after puberty and isn't completed until early adulthood.

The many ways in which your brain can change structure is referred to as neuroplasticity. The root of the English word plastic is the Greek word plastos, which means to mold by using clay, wax, etc. The brain is constantly molding itself as you encounter new experiences, i.e., learning. We can't tell what changes will occur with learning, or how those changes results in a mental model. (Mental models will be discussed in the next chapter.) Unlike a computer, where we know how two numbers are added, we don't know how a mental model for addition works. But we do know some of the things that will enhance the formation of these mental models in the brain, the subject of this book.

Especially when you are young, dendrites and axon collaterals are sprouting and growing to facilitate synaptic formation between neurons. The younger you are the more neuroplasticity you will have. There are certain skills that are best, and sometimes must, be acquired during windows when you have maximum neuroplasticity. The vision window begins at birth. Signals from your eyes, which act like two cameras, result in firing of neurons that develop the vision system. You must receive these signals shortly after birth or you vision will be impaired or even blindness can result. To acquire a native-like language ability with no accent requires learning the language before the age of about 10. To have perfect pitch, the ability to hear a tone all by itself and know what note it is, requires music training before the age of 6. Although your axons will have myelin when you are young, full myelination starts at the back of the brain after birth, the area involved with vision processing, and moves forward to the prefrontal cortex, the last area for full myelination. As far as maturity, which comes from your prefrontal cortex, the myelination doesn't fully finish until about age 25 or slightly later.

The concept of neuroplastic windows is illustrated in figure 1.3. Although certain skills are best acquired while neuroplasticity is high, you maintain neuroplasticity all your life as indicated by the windows not going to zero in figure 1.3.

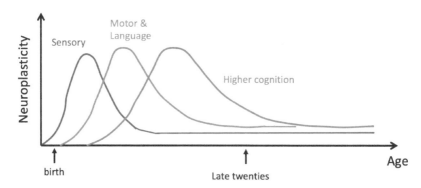

Figure 1.3 Windows of Neuroplasticity

You can continue to learn, change your brain, all through life. You can still learn a language even if you start at age 70. You just won't be able to speak without an accent because necessary neurons, for certain pronunciations, would have been lost when you were still a young child and not using them.

At birth the volume of the human brain is 370 cubic cm and by age 2 it is 1,100 cubic cm, which is about 85% of its adult size. The number of neurons does not change appreciably. This increase in size is because of a huge increase in number of synaptic connections. By age 2-3 there are twice as many synaptic connections as you will have as an adult. Then through experiences (learning) the vast and varied capabilities of humans develop. As you learn, the neurons used will make connections and strengthen. The synapses you use less will weaken and some will be pruned away. This overproduction is fortunate in that it leads to the vast array of different abilities humans can develop and why each of us is unique. Like how a statue is formed by removing stone, who you become is sculpted by removal of some neural connections and strengthening of others.

It was thought the human genome would have on the order of 100,000 genes to build our complex body and brain. When the human genome project was completed, there were on the order of only 20,000 genes! The reason complex humans can result from this small genome is because our gene code sets up a brain that can continuously learn and we have a long childhood. Our brain is equipped to learn languages, to ride a bike, to play a violin, to understand quantum physics, to be a surgeon, etc. When we are born our brains can do very little. From experience, from learning, we continually are building neural circuits to accomplish these tasks. That is why humans need a long childhood, to develop (learn) the necessary neural circuits. This also accounts for the huge diversity in human abilities. It all depends on what we are exposed to and the directions we take with our lives. Even as adults, we can continue to develop new neural circuits; that is what learning is all about.

After you are born, your senses—sight, sound, smell, touch, taste, and proprioception (awareness of one's body position)—are sending electrical senses to your brain, which is responding by building connections and the ability to process these inputs, such as to discern shapes, distance, and colors in the case of vision. The region of your brain for vision processing matures first. This is followed by the motor and language regions and then the higher cognitive regions. This development follows a backward C pattern in the brain beginning with the lower back region of the brain (occipital lobe that contains the visual area) moving upwards and then forwards.

In this early stage of brain wiring, every input is resulting in changes, wiring, of your brain. Your brain is building the capability to understand the inputs and respond accordingly. The infant is learning. Slowly the brain starts to be able to control when something will result in brain changes. This selectivity to sensory inputs becomes necessary to focus and master skills. As you go from infancy through early childhood, you go from where most sensory inputs are causing changes in your brain to where most are not; you are controlling what does, or does not, change your brain. At this point changes in your brain occur when you are interested in something, so you pay attention and focus on it; when you are rewarded or punished for something; or when you are surprised by something. As we will discuss later, developing a passion for what you are studying will greatly improve your learning. You enjoy the subject, so you want to learn, and your brain is primed for doing the necessary wiring. A student who is engaged and motivated will learn in a classroom. A student who is disengaged and inattentive will not.

A newborn is somewhat of a blank slate. The person they become, and the skills they will have, depends on the experiences and opportunities they encounter growing up. The same child can become an engineer, medical doctor, musician, teacher, etc. depending on these experiences growing up.

You still have neuroplasticity when you become an adult, otherwise you could not learn anything new. If before reading the above you did not know about neuroplasticity, learning about neuroplasticity resulted in changes in neuron connections in your brain so that you now know! (There are further changes caused by this learning in your brain during your subsequent sleep, which we will discuss in chapter 11.)

As mentioned earlier, there is an explosion in creation of synaptic connections between neurons after birth. As we learn in childhood some of these get strengthened and flourish, the ones used, and others weaken and even pruned away, the ones not used. But you do not completely lose all the unused, weakened connections. They remain and can start to be used at a later age. In someone who becomes blind, there are still some weakened neuron connections that take auditory and touch signals to the visual cortex. After going blind, a person can gain an increased sense of touch, for reading Braille, and hearing, for echolocation. This is because those weakened connections start to strengthen with use. Over a longer timescale, axons will grow into the visual cortex followed by new synapses forming to further improve the sense of touch and hearing by utilizing your visual cortex.

Your learning begins as passive when you are born and then can be passive or active. By sometime around your mid-twenties, you can only learn actively. By passive is meant learning occurs by just exposure to information or experiences. An infant takes in all these visual inputs from the eyes. The infant's neurons are rewiring in response to these visual inputs so that the images from these two cameras, your eyes, is a single image. But the blood vessels in your eyes cast a shadow and your optic nerve is a blind spot. The neurons arrange in the infant's brain to fill in these areas, so an unobstructed image is seen. This is all done passively, and it must occur at the beginning, when we are infants, as seen in figure 1.3 for the sensory window. The discovery of this early window for developing normal vision that closes [5] led to the Nobel prize for David H. Hubel and Torsten N. Wiesel. But it also perpetuated the incorrect perception that after the brain matures it cannot change. Even though normal vision requires early development, you still have some neuroplasticity in your occipital lobe, the visual processing region of your brain, even as an adult.

An example of this is what occurs with monovision. As we age, many of us require vision correction (bifocals) for seeing both near and far.

Monovision is where one eye is corrected to see far, and the other eye is corrected to see near. This correction can be with contact lenses or through corrective surgery. After a period, the brain adjusts. The superposition of the blurred and clear vision from the two eyes is not noticed, even as one looks at far and near objects and the in-focus and out-of-focus switches between eyes.

A child learns a language passively, just by being exposed to it. As an adult you can only learn a language actively. We subscribe to a channel of foreign language television shows. My wife and I became enamored with French TV series and have watched all the episodes of shows like Candice Renoir, The Art of Crime, Cherif, Murder In, Alice Nevers, and Tandem. Since we do not speak French, we utilize subtitles. I have not gained any understanding of the French language from hundreds of hours of this passive watching. I could learn French at my age, but I would have to engage in active learning.

For active learning to occur, you must be alert and focused on what you are doing. That is why an interest in the subject you are trying to learn is helpful, so that you will pay attention. Learning is effortful as you engage in a purposeful practice. (A large part of this book is the introduction of purposeful practices and Chapter 8 is a discussion of the concept of purposeful practice.) It is effortful because your brain, which is 2% of your body by weight, uses >20% of the oxygen and fuel being pumped by your circulatory system. **Your brain prefers to do things reflexively and not put the energy into active learning.** That is why the subject must be of interest; there is a reward or punishment; or you are surprised by something for learning to occur.

Repeating a task over and over will not result in learning; your neural circuits will not change. Learning will only result in learning if it is accompanied by the release of acetylcholine. The acetylcholine release occurs because you are interested in something; you are rewarded or punished for something; or you are surprised by something. When you are attentive and motivated, the nucleus basalis in the base of your brain releases the neurotransmitter acetylcholine. There is also an increase in the neurotransmitter dopamine, which is associated with anticipation of a reward. Acetylcholine and dopamine have been found to be necessary for neuroplasticity to occur.

It was once thought that neurogenesis, the creation of new neurons, did not occur in the adult mammal brain. In the 1960s, Joseph Altman observed neurogenesis in the adult brains of Guinea pigs [6]. Altman's discovery of neurogenesis in an adult mammal's brain was either ignored, or ridiculed, and Altman did not receive tenure at MIT. In the 1990s, Altman was vindicated when neurogenesis in the hippocampus region of adult mammal brains, of mice [7] and humans [8], was rediscovered. In chapter 3 we will learn the important role the hippocampus plays in memory. One important thing to do to insure these new hippocampal neurons survive is to use them. **So, we should be learning every day!**

Although we can grow new neurons in our hippocampus, most other regions of the brain do not grow new neurons. But we can still rewire and grow these other regions of our brain. The new hippocampal neurons are only about 0.004% of your total neuron population. But increases in brain regions have been observed with MRI because of learning, exercise, and meditation. A study of learning affecting the brain structure was performed by Dragganski et al. [9] with medical students in Germany. After two years of preclinical study, there are three months of extensive study before medical students in Germany take exams in biology, biochemistry, chemistry, human anatomy, physiology, and physics. MRI scans were taken just before the start of the three months of studying, and the first or second day after the exams. Increases in volume in areas of the brain were clearly visible in the students who studied for the exams; no such increases were observed in control subjects. Control subjects had no exams in the last six months and were not in the process of studying for any exams, but they were like the medical students in education status and scanned at the same times. We will look at other observations of increases in brain regions from learning, exercise, and meditation in subsequent chapters.

Another thing you can change in your brain is the circulatory system that delivers the oxygen and fuel for cognitive processing. That is partly why you will encounter chapters on nutrition and exercise.

Neuroplasticity was first suggested back in 1890 by William James in his book *The Principles of Psychology* where he wrote, "Plasticity, then, in the wide sense of the word, means the possession of a structure weak enough to yield to an influence, but strong enough not to yield all at once. Each relatively stable phase of equilibrium in such a structure is marked by what we may call a new set of habits. Organic matter, especially nervous tissue, seems endowed with a very extraordinary degree of plasticity of this sort; so that we may without hesitation lay down as our first proposition the following, that the phenomena of habit in living beings are due to the plasticity of the organic materials of which their bodies are composed" [10]. Unfortunately, in the early 20th century the plasticity concept was ignored, and it became dogma that the adult brain was fixed and didn't change. I find this thinking, that the adult brain does not change, extremely surprising. Maybe it is because I am an electrical engineer who used to design microcomputers. How can there be no change if there is learning? An adult can learn a new language. This not only means remembering all the vocabulary words, but the grammar; in the case of a language like French the gender of words; in the case of a language like Mandarin the tones; in some cases, a different alphabet; and the ability to recognize the very different sounding speech of different people. This takes an enormous amount of computing capability so there must be much change in brain structure to provide this language function. Of course, an adult's brain is not as good as a child's brain at doing this. We see this because, as mentioned, if one does not learn a language by about age 10 you will not have native-like language ability such as no accent. So, an adult's brain is not as plastic as a child's brain, but nevertheless there must still be enormous plasticity for the adult brain to learn something as complex as a new language.

In the 1800s, there were two views regarding the brain and nervous system. One view was that the brain was composed of cells like all other parts of the body. The other view was that the brain was made of continuous tissue, like our blood circulatory system. In the 1890s, neuroanatomist Santiago Ramón y Cajal was able to identify individual cells, which today are called neurons, in brain tissue. He is known as the father of modern neuroscience and received the Nobel Prize in Physiology or Medicine in 1906 for his work. In his 1913 textbook, *Regeneration and Degeneration of the Nervous System*, Ramón y Cajal wrote, "Once development was ended, founts of growth of the axons and dendrites dried up irrevocable." Ramón y Cajal was a giant in this field and is probably why his thoughts, that the adult brain does not change, became dogma for decades, for most of the 20th century. I am amazed how this concept was accepted and not questioned for decades, as it obviously could not be correct. In figure 1.4a is a blank piece of paper, which contains no information. In figure 1.4b there has been written "The capital of Uzbekistan is Tashkent." There is now information contained on the paper, which required the addition of ink. You probably did not know the capital of Uzbekistan until you just read it. But now you know and if you walk away, at least for the next few minutes, if someone asked you "what is the capital of Uzbekistan" you could tell them it is "Tashkent." You must have stored this information, which would have required some physical change in your brain just like adding ink to the paper is a physical change.

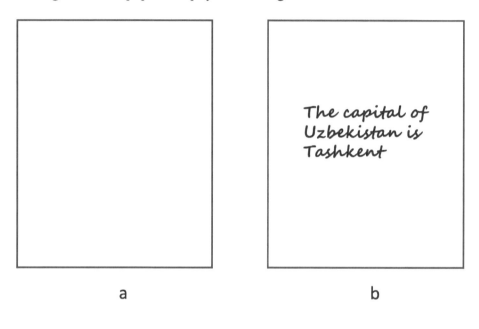

a   b

Figure 1.4 Illustration of the concept of storing information.

Somehow all these wiring changes in the brain result in coding of memories; processing of vision, sound, smell, and taste; our being able to use mental models; our ability to solve problems; and our ability to create new things. How this structure accomplishes this is not known. But much is known about how best to make these processes happen, which is the major topic of this book. While it is not known how the brain performs thinking tasks, what functions different parts of the brain play in this complex process are known. The function of different parts of the brain has been determined because of studying patients who have had injuries to certain regions of the brain, the result of brain surgeries, and more recent the ability to view brain activity using functional magnetic resonance imaging (fMRI). fMRI tracks the flow of blood in the brain and detects where the blood is providing oxygen to neurons, which is where activity is taking place. In chapter 3 we will look at the role the hippocampus plays in memory, discovered because of surgery on a patient referred to as patient H.M. in the literature.

Extending from your brain, down your spinal column, and throughout your body are nerves, extensions of your brain. This is how your brain controls your movement and gets feedback on what is happening with your body. Your brain has a mental model of your body. You can close your eyes and tell where every part is. This is called proprioception. This model developed from your movements. With rich variety in your movements, brain plasticity results in a better mental model. If you start to limit your movements brain plasticity will cause a reduction in this mental model. That's why when old people start to walk by shuffling their feet, because they are afraid of falling, they will make their ability to balance and not fall worse. They are not exercising those neural circuits anymore.

The brain consists of the cerebrum, which has two hemispheres referred to as the right hemisphere and the left hemisphere, the cerebellum, and the brainstem. It is the cerebrum that is of interest to us. The cerebrum is where higher functions such as interpreting sensory inputs, speech, reasoning, emotions, learning and control of movement occur. The two hemispheres of the cerebrum are connected by a thick grouping of nerve fibers called the corpus callosum. Some of the nerve fibers in the corpus callosum originate in the right hemisphere, and some in the left hemisphere, so that there can be communication between the two halves of our brain. Each hemisphere controls, and receives input, from the opposite side of the body. For instance, the left hemisphere controls your right hand and signals from your right visual field go to your left hemisphere. The hemispheres are referred to as the cerebrum and are segmented into regions that are referred to as lobes. The cerebrum is 80% of the volume of your brain and contains 16 billion neurons, 19% of the neurons in your brain.

The frontal lobes, called that because they are in the front of the brain directly behind your forehead, are where conscious thoughts are. It is where our personalities originate, where we solve problems, plan, and concentrate. The frontal lobes also control movement and speech.

The parietal lobes are in the upper middle of the hemispheres. This region controls your sense of touch and pressure, your sense of taste, and your awareness of your body.

The temporal lobes are in the lower middle of each hemisphere. The temporal lobes are where auditory signals are received and processed. The temporal lobes are involved in the encoding of memories, especially the region called the hippocampus. Your ability to recognize others occurs in the temporal lobes.

The occipital lobes are on the backside of the brain. It is in the occipital region where visual input is sent and processed to give us the sense of sight.

There is a distinct region, referred to as the cerebral cortex that covers the surface of the cerebrum. It is 2-4 mm in thickness. The cerebral cortex has folding (gyrification), which results in ridges (gyri) and furrows (sulci) that produces a surface area of up to 2000 square cm. The cerebral cortex is the most recent part of the brain to evolve. The cerebral cortex interprets sensory inputs; produces speech, reasoning, and emotions; controls movement; and is where learning occurs.

The cerebral cortex consists of the neocortex and the allocortex. The neocortex has 6 main layers while the allocortex three or four main layers. In humans most of the cerebral cortex, about 90%, is neocortex.

The hippocampi are two seahorse shaped regions, each called a hippocampus, in the temporal lobes. Hippocampus is the Latin word for seahorse and hence the name for these regions. As we study, information is initially stored in the hippocampi. We will learn that when we sleep, this information is transferred from the hippocampi to long-term storage in the neocortex, which frees up the hippocampus to take in new information the next day. The amygdala are two almond shaped regions in the temporal lobes. Since the amygdala is almond shaped, the name comes from the Latin word for almond, amygdala. The amygdala is involved in emotional responses, especially fear and aggressive behavior. The amygdala is involved in the initiation of our fight or flight response, which will be discussed in detail in chapter 16.

Earlier we mentioned that almost 50% of the cells in our brains are a different type of cell than nerve cells and these are the glial cells. There are different types of glial cells (astrocytes, oligodendrocytes, microglial, ependymal, and radial) that perform different functions in the brain. Glial cells do not have axons or dendrites. The largest number of glial cells are called astrocytes. The astrocytes are star shaped cells that are involved in regulating neural transmitters and synaptic connections.

Oligodendrocytes are glial cells that form the myelin sheath that surrounds the axons of neurons. Myelin functions as an electrical insulator, which increases the speed of transmission of an electric signal down an axon. Myelin is white. When you hear a reference to white matter associated with the brain it comes from the white of the myelin sheath.

Microglial cells are immune cells. When there is an injury or toxin, the microglial cells move to this location and clear away dead cells or remove the toxin.

Ependymal cells line the ventricle system, cavities containing protective fluids, in the brain. The ependymal cells produce the cerebrospinal fluid (CSF) and have cilia that beat to circulate the CSF. The CSF is continuously produced and is replaced every 6-8 hours. The brain essentially floats in the CSF, which protects it during impacts.

The final type of glial cell is the radial glial, which are essentially stems cells that can become new neurons, which even happens in the hippocampi of adults. Radial cells can also become other types of glial cells.

The most important takeaway from this chapter is the concept of neuroplasticity. Your brain is constantly changing. You can actively improve your brain and adjust it to achieve goals. If you are not actively improving your brain the opposite will be happening, you brain will lose neural circuits and capabilities.

Chapter 2: What is Learning? Mental Models, Creativity and Solving Complex Problems

The initial part of learning is placing in long-term memory a mental model. A mental model is a mental representation, a neural circuit, of some external reality. It is something stored in your brain. It allows you to recall facts, to recognize patterns, to solve a problem, to design something, to apply an algorithm, to perform a skill like surgery, to play a sport or musical instrument. As you learn, everything new is understood through your existing mental models. This process of learning involves changes in your brain, as discussed in chapter 1. As you are reading this paragraph, your brain is rewiring itself.

The reality you perceive is mainly the mental models inside your brain created from the small amount of information you receive from your senses. After you are born, your brain takes the inputs from your senses and uses neuroplasticity to create mental models of reality. The receptors in your eyes detect the frequencies of a thin sliver of the electromagnetic spectrum and your brain turns that into color. That color is just inside your head. Your nose detects molecules and sends electrical signals to your brain that interprets smells. Again, these smells only exist in the mental model inside your brain. The sounds you hear are just mental models interpreting the compressions and expansions of air within frequencies of 20 Hz to 20 kHz. There are only these air vibrations, not the sounds you hear in your head.

Factual knowledge is when you can recall or recognize something such as, what is the mascot of Purdue University? (It is a train engine, the Boilermaker Special.) Conceptual knowledge is when you understand principles and relationships and can apply them to situations, such as the fraction problem I will discuss below. A good mental model gives you a conceptual understanding. What most students do is look for a procedure or algorithm to solve a problem—essentially just factual knowledge. I often have students come to my office for help with a problem. Rather than showing them how to do the problem, I start to explain the concept behind the problem. Some will interrupt me and say all they want to know is how to work the problem! Initially just learning an algorithm is easier than the harder work to understand a concept and why it is the approach of most students. But the extra effort to learn something deeper will pay dividends. Without that conceptual understanding, you won't recognize a problem that is similar, which you could solve if you understood the concept. Understanding a concept forms a much stronger ability to retrieve that memory, which is a goal of learning—to be able to recall something later and apply it to a situation you encounter. Having a mental model that includes a conceptual understanding is far superior to just having a mental model that is a procedure in your head, with no understanding of why the procedure works.

Without a conceptual understanding you cannot connect different mental models to solve more complex problems or create something new. Having that conceptual understanding will help you in future courses, which build on material you are currently learning.

Our brains contain two separate memory systems, which you will learn about in Chapter 3. We have a conscious explicit, and a sub-conscious implicit, memory system. In conscious memory we store facts, such as the capital of a country, the multiplication tables, verb conjugations, or events, such as a concert or wedding we attended. In our subconscious memory we store procedures such as the motor skills necessary for riding a bike, catching a ball, performing a surgical procedure, playing the piano, or typing on a keyboard.

When you first started to learn to ride a bike, you were wobbly and would often have to put a foot down. Over time, you developed models in your brain about how to maintain your balance, brake, turn, and to get off without falling. These are things you do when you ride a bike without consciously thinking, but your brain is subconsciously accessing a mental model to perform the act of riding a bike.

Another example is typing. When you are learning to type, you place which fingers touch which keys in conscious memory. Eventually you get to where you do not think of hitting the "U" with your right index finger. Typing gets placed in your procedural, sub-conscious memory. You get to a point where if you try to think of which finger you use to hit the "B" you might have difficulty, but you do it correctly when typing and not consciously thinking of what you are doing! You will also perform the task much faster when you are using unconscious procedural memory than when you have to think about each action.

Some mental models are developed by the process of evolution and our called instincts. An example is a bird being able to build a nest.

In this book we will be dealing with the development of conscious and subconscious mental models, improving our ability to apply these mental models, and to interconnect mental models to solve complex problems, to think critically, or to create something new.

Let's look at an example of a conscious mental model. You have been taught a mental model for fractions and proportions. Let's say the model you have is the algorithm that to find the fraction of something you multiply that something by the fraction. For instance, if you were asked to find half of 16 you would perform the following calculation,

$$\frac{1}{2} \times 16 = \frac{1}{2} \times \frac{16}{1} = \frac{16}{2} = 8$$

This is a very simple model. You can have very little understanding of the concept of fractions and still perform the calculation asked for, what is half of 16, or a quarter of 16, or three-quarters of 16.

Let's look at a slightly more complex problem that will require a deeper understanding, a more complex mental model. Ann and Betty jointly own a farm—Ann owns ½ and Betty owns ½. Ann has two offspring who will inherit her half and Betty has six offspring who will inherit her half. What fraction of the farm will the children own? If your mental model did not go beyond "to find the fraction of something you multiply that something by the fraction," you could not figure out the difference in fractional ownership for Ann's and Betty's children.

Let's develop your mental model to better understand the concept of fractions, so you could do the fractional farm ownership problem with the following image.

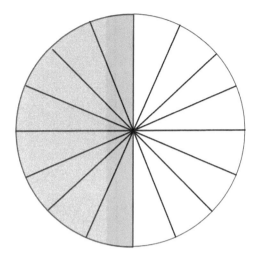

Fig. 2.1 Mental image of ½ of 16.

The circle represents some whole. We will divide this whole into 16 parts to represent the first problem. You can think of this as a pizza with 16 slices. Shading half the circle we visually observe that 8 slices is half of the circle agreeing with our algorithm,

$$\frac{1}{2} \times 16 = 8$$

With this additional mental model imagery, we can now proceed with solving the problem of the offspring's fractional ownership of the farm. We can represent the farm with a circle where half the circle is blue to represent Ann's half and half the circle is green to represent Betty's half.

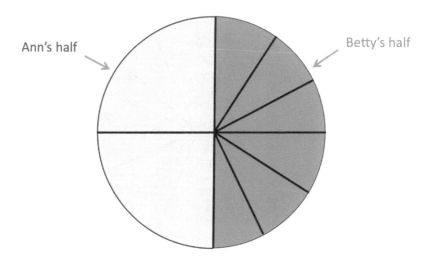

Fig. 2.2 Mental image for solving offspring's fractional ownership.

We have divided Ann's half in half to represent the ownership of her two offspring. Ann's children will each inherit ¼ of the farm as seen in the image or with our algorithm,

$$\frac{1}{2} \times \frac{1}{2} = \frac{1}{4}$$

We have divided Betty's half into sixths to represent the ownership of her six offspring. Betty's children will each inherit 1/12 of the farm as seen in the image or with our algorithm,

$$\frac{1}{6} \times \frac{1}{2} = \frac{1}{12}$$

Most students approach their classes by remembering algorithms so they can solve the problems they will encounter on a test. With this approach you will not be able to connect this simple memorized algorithm to more complex problems you will encounter outside of your classroom. After your class is over, you will soon not be able to retrieve this algorithm from memory because it will have little meaning. You will not have learned it deeply. Just memorizing the algorithm is faster and easier than learning the actual concept. If you learn the actual concept, the mental model will be more durable. You will recognize when you encounter a problem where this mental model will be useful. Therefore, your approach should be to understand the concept, not to blindly memorize a procedure to solve a problem.

As problems become more complex, you may have to draw on two or more mental models. Your mental models cannot be isolated, you need to have a connection between them. Then you can combine the ones you need for each problem. This takes a conceptual understanding of these models, not just some algorithm you have memorized. This is captured in a piece of advice I give students. **Do not focus on the grade, focus on the understanding and you will get better grades.**

An example, with mental models and remembering strings of digits, is the work that Anders Ericsson, a post-doctoral student, and Steve Faloon, an undergraduate student, did at Carnegie Mellon University [11]. Anders hired Steve to investigate working memory and if it could be improved. Most people can hold about 6-7 digits in working memory. You can remember a 7-digit phone number long enough to dial it. The limit of working memory is why the length of two-factor identification codes is typically 6 digits long.

Steve and Anders would work together for an hour three to five times a week. Anders would read a string of random digits and Steve would repeat them. If Steve got them correct, Anders would read a string one digit longer. When Steve got them incorrect, Anders would reduce the number of digits by two in the next string and start again.

After a few sessions, Steve could still only recall 7 digits, confirming what is known about the limit of working memory. Steve was getting frustrated and not sure if it was worth continuing. But he eventually got to where he could remember 79 digits! Steve did this not by improving his working memory but developing mental models to represent the digits.

If Steve just kept repeating the digits from his working memory, he never would have gotten beyond 7 digits. The time spent this way with Anders would be naïve practice. Instead, Steve discovered how to spend the time doing purposeful practice. The purposeful practice was much harder, but without purposeful practice Steve would have never made any progress.

Steve was an avid runner. He started grouping sequences of numbers as running times he had in long-term memory, either his best times, or world, or Olympic records for certain distances. I don't know how he discovered this concept, but it was probably serendipitously. He probably heard an eight-digit sequence such as 90534218. He had never gotten an eight-digit sequence correct, but this time he did because a group of the digits meant something to him. For instance, maybe 421 was his best time running the mile, 4 minutes, and 21 seconds. Remembering 421 did not take up 3 places in his working memory, just one. This association of 3 digits with a running time allowed him to recall the 8 digits. By forming associations of 3-4 digits with something familiar, something he already had a mental representation of, would result in 6-7 things in working memory allowing recall of about 20 digits. This association is also referred to as chunking. To increase his recall, Steve then developed more sophisticated mental models, introducing organization in his retrieval structure eventually getting to where he could recall about 79 digits.

Steve was not recalling more digits because of improvement in his working memory, but because of the mental models he was building. Asked to repeat a random sequence of letters and Steve could only recall 6-7, despite being able to recall 79 digits. Steve did not have mental models for recalling letters, just for recalling digits. It was not a change in Steve's working memory, but in mental models, leading to his improved performance in recalling digits.

What was happening with Steve Faloon being able to remember more digits illustrates what happens as you become more expert at something. There is a limit to what you can hold in working memory. As someone acquires more and more sophisticated mental models, they can handle more information and they are not limited by their working memory. A doctor trying to diagnose a patient may be presented with many symptoms, some relevant and some not. As a doctor becomes a better diagnostic it is because, like Steve Faloon with remembering large strings of digits, they can observe a pattern emerging from all the symptoms they can handle at once using their more sophisticated mental models. The symptoms are not isolated pieces of information, the doctor can look at them all at once to find a pattern, the likely cause of the patient's illness. **The more sophisticated the mental model becomes the more organized and accessible the knowledge is.**

Subconscious mental models have been illustrated with chess players. The study involved three groups, national-level, mid-range, and novice chess players. They were shown a board at some point in a game for several seconds. They were then asked to recall the pieces and their positions. They were then shown pieces that were just randomly placed on the chess board for several seconds. They were then asked to recall the pieces and their positions. The results are shown in table 2.1.

Table 2.1 Comparison of recall of chess pieces for players of different levels

	Game	Random
national	most	2
mid	half	2
novice	4	2

National-level players had developed an ability to recall where all the pieces were if they were looking at placement of pieces at a point in an actual game of chess. It is a pattern they have seen before as they have studied hundreds of thousands of actual games. However, when the pieces were placed randomly, they could recall no better than a novice.

When national-level players were looking at a board during a game they were not seeing individual pieces. They were not putting the pieces and positions in working memory. They were seeing a pattern that would come about only during an actual game, an ability developed through years of study. These patterns are held in long term memory; Chase and Simon named them chunks [12]. This is exactly what Steve Faloon was doing to remember digits; he was chunking them together.

We will later encounter that the type of study matters to reach such peaks of ability. Just playing games of chess will not make someone a grand master. Grand masters had to study games by masters; try to figure out the next move. If they got it wrong, they then figured out what they missed and why the actual move made by the grand master was a better move. They analyze games they played to figure out where they made a move that resulted in a loss and what might have been a better move. They studied end games and opening traps. They did purposeful practice.

Let me illustrate a subconscious mental model that you have. Look at the following list of words for five seconds and try to memorize them. Also try to remember how many times a word occurs if it occurs more than once,

was age worst it was the times it the of times wisdom it the age of it was the of foolishness best was of

It is an impossible task to do in 5 seconds. Now look at the same set of words in a different arrangement for five seconds and try to remember them.

It was the best of times, it was the worst of times, it was the age of wisdom, it was the age of foolishness

The second time you could recall most, if not all, of the words because you have a mental model for sentences and meanings. You may also recognize it, have a mental model of it, as part of the first sentence of the Charles Dickens' novel, *A Tale of Two Cities*. Consider how you developed your reading skills. You built your ability to read with purposeful practice. You first had to learn the alphabet. Then the sounds that go with each letter. You progressed to syllables, words, and then phrases. You learned the concept of sentences. In the second arrangement you are not seeing individual words, just like the chess masters were not seeing individual pieces. You no longer are aware of all those intermediate steps it took to get to where you can read. You can look at a sentence and it stays in your brain because there is meaning. In the second arrangement of the words, you also memorized a sequence of 82 letters in just a few seconds!

The national-level chess players did not practice being able to recall where the chess pieces were, but to be good at playing chess. This is also why chess grand masters can play blind chess. They never see the board, but are just told their opponent's move, sometimes playing dozens of other players. They never worked at developing blind chess playing abilities. They have developed subconscious mental models for the game of chess that allow them to play blind chess.

As you develop mental models, you also want to form connections between these mental models. Charlie Munger refers to this as developing a latticework of mental models. The more mental models you have, and from different disciplines, the better the thinker and problem solver you will be. Being able to draw on multiple mental models allows you to solve more complex problems, or to create something entirely new. Let me illustrate this with an example.

When he was an undergraduate, Claude Shannon double majored in mathematics and electric engineering [13]. One of the courses he took was a philosophy course. In that course they discussed Boolean logic.

George Boole was a 19th century philosopher, logician, and mathematician, who was a professor of mathematics at Queen's College, Cork, Ireland. Boole showed that logic problems could be solved using a simple algebra using the operations of And, Or, and Not [14]. The variables in Boolean logic are statements that are true or false. Boolean algebra is then a way to manipulate these variables to obtain the simplest function that will tell you if a starting set of values for these variables will result in a true or false conclusion.

Seventy years after Boole passes away, while a graduate student studying for a master's degree at MIT, Shannon had a summer internship at AT&T Bell Laboratories. To Shannon, the relays (electrically operated switches) in the circuits he saw at Bell Labs were like the true/false variables in Boolean algebra. At that time, these circuits were mainly designed using intuition. Being an electrical engineer and understanding how circuits operate, and being familiar with Boolean logic, Shannon connected these two mental models to create something new—digital circuit design. Shannon applied Boolean algebra to design these circuits, which would result in much simpler circuits that accomplished the same operation as the ones being built at Bell Laboratories. This was the creation of the field of digital circuit design that has led to digital computers, which are ubiquitous in our lives. At that time, Shannon was the only person in the world who had those two mental models, which he could connect. In Shannon's time these switches were electrical relays. Later they would be vacuum tubes and eventually transistors and the basis for modern digital computers.

If you are interested and have a mathematical inclination, Boolean algebra, and implementation with switches, is described further in Appendix A.

Steve Jobs very simply stated what creativity was when he said, "Creativity is just connecting things." These things are the mental models you have in your head. This is illustrated in the following quote from Job's commencement address at Stanford University on June 12, 2005. "Reed College at that time offered perhaps the best calligraphy instruction in the country... I decided to take a calligraphy class to learn how to do this. I learned about serif and san serif typefaces, about varying the amount of space between different letter combinations, about what makes great typography great. It was beautiful, historical, artistically subtle in a way that science can't capture, and I found it fascinating. None of this had even a hope of any practical application in my life. But ten years later, when we were designing the first Macintosh computer, it all came back to me."

As has been mentioned, until the last few decades it was believed that the human brain was fixed. But in the last few decades, scientists have found that the brain is remarkably adaptive. When you develop a mental model, your brain is changing. A dramatic illustration of how plastic the human brain can be is seen in what happens to adults who lose their eyesight. It is well known that people who become blind develop an enhanced sense of hearing and touch. This is because regions of the brain that had been used for vision have been acquired for use in hearing and touch [15]. As blind people learn braille, their sense of touch is enhanced by incorporating other regions of the brain in the processing of touch. The mental model for touch becomes more sensitive and uses more of the brain. This repurposing of regions of the brain has been observed using MRI [16]. It has also been found that for violinists and cellists, the brain region controlling the left fingers is expanded compared to non-musicians. There is an increase in control of the left fingers with part of the brain region typically associated with the left palm now involved with the left fingers [17]. It is true that the brains of young children are more adaptable than the brains of adults. To acquire absolute pitch requires training before age 6 and learning a language is much easier for a child, but the brain remains adaptable throughout life. You can learn, develop new or improved mental models, at any age.

A theme in this book is that there is no telling how much you can learn, or how good you can get at something. Only with putting in sustained effort, over years or sometimes decades, to develop mental models can you see how good of a musician, writer, teacher, surgeon, engineer, scientist, athlete, etc. you can become. We are born with different innate talents, but the work one puts in plays a much larger role in what we become than differences in innate abilities.

We will also look at what is known about how best to learn—to develop these mental models. Some practices have been known for well over a hundred years and some have been discovered just over the past few years or decade. Unfortunately, these practices that enhance learning are seldom presented to students. I hope to rectify that.

With learning you not only have to put in the time, but you also must use the right practices. Anders Ericsson refers to these right practices as purposeful practices. Techniques that seem more effortful and slower. A recurring theme we will encounter is the learning is better if there is some degree of difficulty, which occurs with the right type of practice. You get better, learn, when you must put in some effort. Many of you may have played a sport and it is common knowledge you don't get better if you practice with someone you are much better than, or someone who is much better than you. Someone you are much better than takes no effort to play. Someone who is much better than you and whatever you do yields no results. It is when someone is a little better than you that you can make the most progress. With effort you discover ways to earn a point, what you need to do be able to score against a little higher level of competition. Getting better at playing a sport is learning just like an academic subject. It should not be surprising that to learn, whether a sport, academic subject, a skill like carpentry or playing a violin, means making mistakes. When you go back, figure out the mistake, and correct the mistake it will lead to the greatest learning.

You need to study at a level that is demanding, but where you can still make steady progress. If what you are working on is too easy, not much will be changing in your brain. If what you are working on is too hard, you do not understand anything, no positive changes will occur in your brain, i.e., no learning. It is when you are working/studying at the edge of your ability/knowledge that you will make the most progress (learning).

Part of learning is developing mental models, representation of some external reality in your memory. Let's look at what is known about how memory works and our first purposeful practice, spacing.

Chapter 3: Memory and Spaced Study

Humans have two memory systems, a conscious or explicit memory and a subconscious or implicit memory, as mentioned in Chapter 1. These two separate memory systems were discovered by Brenda Milner [18] [19] working with Henry Molaison, who was referred to as patient H.M. in the literature to protect his privacy, until his death in 2008.

Henry had severe epilepsy, which was not responding to medication. In 1953, Henry had surgery that included removing portions of his hippocampi, two seahorse shaped regions in the brain. The singular of hippocampi is hippocampus, which I will use. The good news for Henry is that his epilepsy was greatly improved. The bad news for Henry, and good news for researchers, was the effect it had on his memory.

Henry retained his pre-surgery long-term explicit memories such as where he was born, the names of family members and friends, his address and phone number, etc. Post-surgery, Henry could not form any new long-term explicit memories [20]. Every day that Brenda went to see Henry, for Henry he was meeting Brenda for the first time. Even after three decades! So, the hippocampus is not where long-term memories are stored since Henry kept his pre-surgery long-term memories. But since Henry could not form any new long-term explicit memories post-surgery, the hippocampus plays an important function in creating new long-term memories. The role the hippocampus plays in the formation of long-term memories will be discussed below and in depth in chapter 10 on sleep.

Prof. Milner discovered that the removal of Henry's hippocampus did not affect his ability to learn, and retain, new implicit memories such as new motor skills. For instance, if Henry did not know how to type pre-surgery, he could learn how to type post-surgery. (The skill task Milner used involved drawing a star when he could only see the star and his hand in a mirror. I just think it is clearer to imagine learning to type.) Of course, even after Henry had learned to type, if you asked Henry if he knew how to type, he would say no, but then he could type effortlessly!

He had a skill memory without any conscious awareness. Skills and procedures are stored unconsciously. Different parts of the brain are involved in explicit and implicit memories.

When I was first learning of Brenda Milner's research, while searching for one of her publications, I came across a picture of Brenda lecturing in 2014. It had been over 60 years since she had begun working with Henry and she was still an active researcher. Every year I present seminars on learning. I always check to make sure that Brenda is still with us. As I write this in September of 2022, Brenda is 104 years old and still active in the Department of Neurology and Neurosurgery at McGill University!

The first scientific study on learning, an early investigation into memory, was performed by Hermann Ebbinghaus in 1885 [21]. Ebbinghaus created three-letter nonsense syllables where the first and third letters were consonants, and the middle letter a vowel, such as MOT, BAF, or NID. He did this so what he was trying to memorize would be new to him; it was not something with which he might already have familiarity. Ebbinghaus then took a subset of these syllables and memorized them. He then checked how many he remembered after one-day, then after two-days, then after three-days, etc. He found that he was remembering fewer words each day. There was an exponential decay in the number of words he remembered with a time constant of τ,

$$\text{number of words remembered} = (\text{initial number of words})e^{-t/\tau}$$

where t is the time. Shown in figure 3.1 curve a is an illustration, not the actual data, of what Ebbinghaus observed showing an exponential decay in the number of words remembered—the forgetting curve. In 1914 Edward Thorndike would name it the "Law of Disuse."

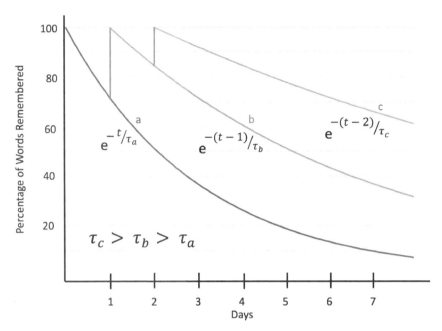

Figure 3.1 Ebbinghaus' forgetting curve.

Suppose it took Ebbinghaus 20 minutes to memorize the list. If he spent an additional 40 minutes working on the list, he would do no additional learning. When he came back the next day and the day after that he would have forgotten the same number of words as when he only spent 20 minutes memorizing them. He would still be on curve a.

When you initially study, the information goes into your hippocampus. Once it is there you don't strengthen the storage by additional studying. We'll learn in chapter 10 on sleep that during sleep the information in your hippocampus is transferred to long-term storage in your cerebral cortex. If Ebbinghaus had spent an additional 40-minutes studying, there would be no difference in what was in his hippocampus so there would be no difference in what gets transferred to long-term storage with sleep. But there is another way Ebbinghaus could use this additional time to strengthen memory storage; just not on that first day.

Ebbinghaus took a new subset of syllables from his list and memorized them. After one-day he found the same decrease in the number of words he remembered as he did with his first trial. But this time he studied the list again until he remembered all the words. He then came back one-day, two-days, three-days, etc. later to see how many words he could remember. He found he was still remembering fewer words each day, but the forgetting was slower than in his first trial. His forgetting had a longer time constant τ_b. This is illustrated in figure 3.1 curve b.

Ebbinghaus now took a third subset of words and memorized them. He came back the next day to determine how many words he had forgotten and studied the list a second time until he remembered all the words. He came back the next day to determine how many words he had forgotten and studied the list a third time until he remembered all the words. He then came back one-day, two-days, three-days, etc. later to see how many words he could remember. He found he was still remembering fewer words each day, but the forgetting was slower than in his second trial. His forgetting had a longer time constant τ_c. This is illustrated in figure 3.1 curve c.

Ebbinghaus had discovered a very important learning concept based on how our memory works. **The concept is that to put something in permanent memory you want to use spacing**. Every time you relearn something, such as the list of words in Ebbinghaus' case, it makes it harder to forget. But that additional effort of studying must come after the previous studied material has been transferred to long-term storage with sleep.

If Ebbinghaus had 60 minutes to learn his list of words, he shouldn't spend all that time massed on the first day studying if he could remember the list after 20 minutes. With 20 minutes, or 60 minutes, of studying he would have still found that same initial rapid loss of the number of words remembered. Instead of spending 60 minutes with mass study, he should space his studying and spend 20 minutes each day for three days if his goal was to remember his list of words.

What should the spacing interval be? One day, two days, more? You don't want the interval to be so long you are starting from the beginning. But you want some forgetting to have occurred. This means some effort must be put in to relearn what was forgotten. You want the spacing to be at least one day because of what happens with our memory when we sleep.

To recap, with study the information is going into the hippocampus. It is when we subsequently sleep that the information is transferred from the hippocampus to long term memory locations in the cortex regions of our brains. This act of transferring is probably not perfect and accounts for some of the decrease Ebbinghaus observed in the words he remembered the next day. After he studied enough to learn the list of words, additional studying would not change what was in his hippocampus, and subsequently how many words were lost during sleep when the information was being transferred. **That is one thing spacing your studying does. It allows for more episodes of information transfer between the hippocampus and long-term storage locations in your brain.**

Each night when you are sleeping and transferring the same information, you are firing the same set of neurons. This results in strengthening the synapses, the connections between neurons, for this memory. This process is termed long-term potentiation (LTP) and is another factor in the strengthened memory Ebbinghaus observed when he spaced his learning.

Usually when students study, they do it wrong using massed, instead of spaced, studying. They wait until right before an exam to study. They might do well on the exam pulling an all-nighter, but if the point was to learn the material, they did not do that because they will have a rapid loss of the material.

If you have a test coming up and you plan on studying 7 hours for it, you are much better studying for a week for one hour a day than a continuous 7 hours just before going in to take your exam. As we will learn later in chapter 5 on incubation and chapter 10 on sleep, there are additional learning benefits from spacing your study besides the memorization effect discovered by Ebbinghaus.

You can think of your memory like your muscles. If you want to get stronger, you don't go into the gym and lift weights for 8 hours. You go into the gym and lift weights for an hour and come back every few days to lift weights for an hour again. Think of putting material in permanent memory the same way you would exercise to get stronger!

The fact that spaced, rather than massed, studying is much better was discovered well over 100 years ago, but this better method of studying is rarely conveyed to students. In 1901, in his book *Talks to Teachers on Psychology and to Students on Some of Life's Ideals*, William James stated, "Cramming seems to stamp things in by intense application before the ordeal. But a thing thus learned can form few associations. On the other hand, the same thing recurring on different days in different contexts, read, recited, referred to again and again, related to other things and reviewed, gets well wrought into the mental structure" [22]. Cramming is the term students usually use to describe blocked study; a typical way students use to prepare for an exam. This quote by James is about the benefit of spaced studying. But it also foreshadows the idea of "latticework of mental models" and another important tactic to incorporate into your studying that we will look at in chapter 5: Interleaving.

There are two reasons you forget something, either the memory has disappeared, or you are not able to retrieve the memory. When you are studying, there are two things you are working on, storage strength and retrieval strength. The LTP that occurs when you are sleeping results in the increase in storage and retrieval strength. Therefore, you need to do spaced studying. When you do massed study, such as "pull an all-nighter" to cram for an exam, you don't have much storage or retrieval strength for the material. You have not learned it even though you might do ok on an exam.

Your cerebral cortex contains about 16 billion neurons and each neuron links with 1,000 to 10,000 other neurons through synapses. This means as many as 100 trillion connections. Estimates are that your brain can store at least a million gigabytes. It is believed that the human brain has a storage capacity greater than what we can learn in a lifetime. Once information is really learned, forgetting must be the retrieval that fades with time [23]. This is an evolutionary development because we needed current information to be most accessible to survive. We needed to know where the predators were yesterday, not a year ago. We needed to know where we were finding food recently, not a year ago. You need to know where you parked your car today not last week! William James also recognized the need for forgetting over 100 years ago when he said, "If we remembered everything, we should on most occasions be as ill off as if we remembered nothing."

Even though we may not currently need something we learned, this information may be useful to us in the future. That is why our brains evolved so that when we learn something new, it is not at the expense of something we already learned. As you learn something new you are not overwriting something you have already learned. Mental models you are currently using are the ones easy to retrieve, but if you must start using an older mental model you will regain retrieval strength for this mental model.

An example is something I experienced with driving. I had only driven in the US where we drive on the right-hand side of the road. I was going to the UK and would be driving in Scotland where they drive on the left-hand side of the road. I was a little nervous as I was also going to be shifting with my left hand instead of my right hand. The first thing I encountered pulling out of the Edinburgh airport was a roundabout with multiple lanes. Although we now have many roundabouts in my town, back then we did not have any, and I had never encountered a roundabout. There was much honking, and I was glad I had purchased the extra rental car insurance! I did survive that first day without an accident. But I was relying on consciously thinking about what I was doing to drive. I don't remember exactly, but within a day or two I was completely driving with procedural memory, I did not have to think about what I was doing. In chapter 10 on sleep, we will see the important role that sleep plays in not only storing memories but improving how well we perform physical, procedural, tasks. When I returned to the US, I was able to quickly shift back to using my older mental models for driving on the right-hand side of the road. I have not been back to Scotland, or another country where they drive on the left-hand side of the road. But when I do, I suspect I will quickly adapt to driving on the left-hand side of the road as the mental model should still be in my head.

I have encountered a situation where you would think it would be much simpler to change the mental model you use than which side of the road you drive on. At least for some of my students it is not. In the junior-level course I teach on electromagnetics, we use three coordinate systems, Cartesian, cylindrical, and spherical. My students probably have seen these in high-school math, but they are also covered in a sophomore college calculus class they have had. You may not be familiar with all three of these coordinate systems, but probably have encountered the Cartesian system where the coordinates of a point are (x, y, z). Shown in figure 3.2 are the Cartesian coordinates (x, y, z) and spherical coordinates (r, θ, ϕ) for point P. In spherical coordinates r is the distance from the origin, O, to point P; θ and ϕ are angles as defined in figure 3.2. The difficulty for my students is that American mathematicians have a different convention than most of the rest of the world [24]. American mathematicians, and the way my students first learned, interchange the role of φ and Θ. In their calculus text my students encountered (r, φ, Θ), while in my course, and forever after, they will encounter (r, Θ, φ) when dealing with spherical coordinates. I do not know why, but this causes great difficulty for some of my students, which is much greater than I encountered switching from driving on the left-hand side of the road instead of the right-hand side of the road. Maybe it is because it is such a subtle difference, but someday I hope to figure out why so that I can help my students with this relearning.

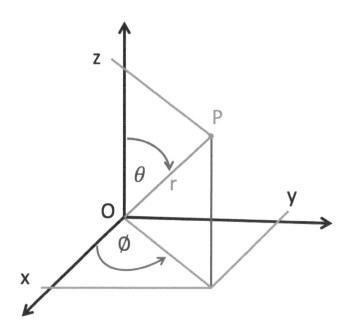

Figure 3.2 Cartesian and spherical coordinates of point P.

With 16 billion neurons in the cerebral cortex and 1,000 to 10,000 connections between neurons, there is more than enough capacity to store a lifetime of learning, but that doesn't mean memories are like photographs. They can change with time. We are constantly altering those memories as we think about them, or in the case of knowledge, as we are adjusting them as we learn more about a subject and build more sophisticated mental models.

I don't recall having the difficulty mentioned on the change in convention with spherical coordinates. It could be that I did not learn spherical coordinates well enough in calculus for it to be an issue for me when I encountered the more typical convention. Alternatively, it could be the **curse of knowledge**. The curse of knowledge is that instructors know the material they are teaching so well they do not recall the difficulties they encountered when learning this material. Instructors don't recall their initial more primitive mental models and what it took to build more sophisticated mental models. Where this impacts a student is that instructors do not provide the small little details in the teaching process that would help the students with understanding what is being presented. The instructors don't recall where they had difficulties and what it was that helped them get a grasp of the material.

Something we do in our department, which I really like and helps with the curse of knowledge students encounter from professors, is that we do much utilization of undergraduate teaching assistants (UTAs). The UTAs in my course mainly hold office hours; times when students in the class can go for help with understanding material and homework issues. The UTAs often have just had the course the semester before, and if not, certainly very recently. The UTAs remember the issues they had with understanding the material, and what helped them, so they can better help students coming to office hours. The UTAs do not suffer from the curse of knowledge like I probably do when explaining concepts to students. Although I do put much effort in trying to figure out how best to explain from a point of view that my students can follow. Even after teaching for 39 years, I still tweak things every semester to improve on how I teach.

The UTAs probably benefit as much as the students they are helping. These are **spaced retrieval exercises** for the UTAs. In addition, to teach something you really must understand it. It cannot just be a procedure you have memorized. Teaching forces you to develop a conceptual understanding of the material, a much more sophisticated mental model. Everyone who has had to teach something knows that to really learn something you should teach it. Richard Feynman said, "If you want to master something, teach it. The more you teach, the better you learn. Teaching is a powerful tool to learning."

If it is a mental model that you need ready access to, you also need **retrieval strength**. That strength will depend on how recently you accessed that mental model and how many cues you have for retrieving it. Techniques we will discuss that increase the number of cues and increase retrieval strength are varying where you study (chapter 4) and involve as many senses—auditory, visual, and kinesthetic—as possible (chapter 10).

To convince yourself that it is the retrieval that fades, imagine you were trying to remember the name of your third-grade teacher. If you were shown a list of four names, three you never heard before but the fourth being the name of your third-grade teacher, you would have no trouble now remembering your third-grade teacher's name. You just needed an aide to help with the retrieval of the memory. You probably have had that experience where you cannot remember something, but you know that you have it in memory. Often it will come back to you later, when you are not trying to retrieve the memory. This effect is related to another important part of studying called incubation, which we will discuss in chapter 6.

Let us look at a couple of studies that illustrate the advantage of spaced studying compared to blocked studying. The first one is from the work of Rohrer and Taylor [25]. In this study, undergraduate students were taught how to determine the number of permutations of a sequence. A permutation is the number of different ways you could list the members of the sequence. For instance, the sequence of abbbcc has 60 permutations—abbcbc, abcbcb, bbacbc, etc.

The students were split into two groups referred to as the spacers and massers, see table 3.1. (Massers is another name for blockers.) The spacers were taught how to find the number of permutations and given 5 problems to solve. They had 45 seconds to find the number of permutations and then they were shown the solution for 15 seconds. One week later they were given 5 more problems. The massers, all in one session, were taught how to find the number of permutations followed by the same 10 problems the spacers were given. The massers were using block studying and the spacers only one spacing. One week after, and four weeks after, they were tested. (That would be one week, and four weeks, after session two for the spacers.)

Table 3.1 Practice schedule, there was one week between session one
and session two.

	Session 1	**Session 2**
Spacers	5 problems	5 problems
Massers		10 problems

After one week the spacers solved 70% of the problems correctly and
the massers 75%. But after four weeks the spacers solved 64% of the
problems correctly and the massers only 32% correctly. With just
spacing the studying between two sessions instead of one session, the
power of spaced learning over block learning is dramatic. Much greater
retention was observed by incorporating just one spacing compared to
the massed studying. Spacing is important to incorporate into your
studying if you need to retain the material for a test later in the semester,
if you need to know this material in a future class, or for this material to
be available to you to use later in life. We will learn later, spacing does
not just help with memory retention, it also benefits understanding and
the connection of the newly learned mental model with other material
you have previously learned.

The next study involved surgical residents learning microsurgery, a
procedural memory [26]. Thirty-eight surgical residents were randomly
divided into two groups. Each group would have 4 short lessons in
microsurgery. The first group completed all four lessons in one day,
which was the common practice for training in microsurgery at this
hospital. The first group used blocked learning. The second group had a
spacing of one-week between each lesson. The second group used
spaced learning. A test a month after the last lesson involved reattaching
the severed aorta of a rat. Group one, which used blocked learning,
scored lower on all measures compared to group two, which used spaced
learning. The blocked group took longer, used more hand movements,
and had lower surgical success including 16% of the blocked learners
damaging the aortas beyond repair resulting in the death of their rats.
All the rats who were operated on by residents who used spaced learning
survived!

The blocked learning of microsurgery had been the standard practice
at this hospital. They immediately switched to using spaced learning for

teaching microsurgery. If you ever must have surgery, ask your surgeon if they were taught with blocked or spaced techniques!

What is the ideal spacing interval to use? One study investigated the spacing interval with the learning of English-foreign language word pairs. This was a long-term study and required intense participation. So, the four subjects were a family of professional psychologists—a father, a mother, and their two daughters—who would share authorship of the study. This has become known as the "Four Bahrick Study!" [27]. Each member would study 50 different English-foreign language word pairs under six different study conditions, 300 words in total. The languages chosen were ones each member had no familiarity. Three studied French, and one studied German, vocabulary. Shown in Table 3.2 is the matrix of the study conditions. Two different number of spaced study sessions, 13 and 26, and three different intervals, 14, 28, and 56 days, were used. The 13 sessions with 14 day spacing lasted 182 days, about 0.5 years. The 26 sessions with 56 day spacing lasted 1,456 days, just slightly short of 4 years! In each session flash cards were used with the word in English on one side and in the foreign language on the other side. In each session they studied until they knew all 50 words. After the last study session for each of the 6 conditions, the subjects tested their vocabulary after 1, 2, 3, and 5 years. The 13 sessions with 14-day spacing tests were at years 1.5, 2.5, 3.5 and 5.5 after the study started. The 26 sessions with 56-day spacing tests were at years 5, 6, 7, and 9 after the study started.

Table 3.2 Matrix of experiment conditions for the Four Bahrick study.

Number of study sessions	Spacing between study sessions (days)
13	14
13	28
13	56
26	14
26	28
26	56

There is a graph in the Bahrick paper of percentage of words recalled versus year and spacing interval. It is some combination of the 13 and 26 sessions for each spacing interval. As best as possible, I have created Table 3.3 from the data in this figure.

Table 3.3 Words recalled based on spacing and time to testing.

Years to test	14-day spacing	28-day spacing	56-day spacing
1	62%	65%	78%
2	55%	60%	65%
3	45%	62%	65%
5	35%	45%	58%

Not surprisingly, the longer the time to the test, the retention interval, the less words recalled. At least for this study of learning foreign vocabulary and the three spacing lengths chosen, the longer the duration between study sessions the better the learning [27]. With two months, instead of two weeks, there is more forgetting that will make the next study session more difficult. But this seems to be a common theme, that increased difficulty, at least up to a point, results in better learning.

Let's look at another study of how the length of the spacing effects how long you will retain the information. The retention interval is the time between the last study session and the test. This study of spacing intervals and retention intervals was performed by Cepeda et al. [28]. There were 1,354 subjects and 26 different conditions. The conditions were spacings of 0, 1, 7, 14, 21 and 105 days between the two study sessions and retention intervals of 7, 35, 70, and 350 days after the second study session. The material was learning 32 obscure facts such as "Who invented snow golf?" (It was Rudyard Kipling.) The subjects were tested for both recall and recognition (pick the correct answer from five equally likely answers). Initially there is an increase in recall and recognition with increased spacing and then a slow decrease. The optimum interval for the spacing depends on the length of the retention interval as shown in table 3.4. A limitation of this study is that only two study sessions were used, and it is likely improved recall and recognition would occur with an increased number of study sessions.

Table 3.4 The effect of spacing on retention interval of recall and recognition.

Retention interval (days)	Optimum Spacing for recall	Optimum spacing for Recognition
7	1	1
35	11	7
70	21	7
350	21	21

What spacing should we use when we study? The type of material being learned—mathematics, surgical techniques, English-foreign word pairs, obscure facts, etc.—could require different spacings and different number of study sessions. What is clear from all the research is that any spacing is better than no spacing.

If you are in school, courses are a semester in length, about four months. You have two goals with your learning. You want to retain the material after the course, so that you can use it in life, and of course you want to achieve a good grade. The course has a finite period for you to do your learning. Of course, you can revisit the material later after the course is over to enhance your retention. This will happen when you encounter situations where you must utilize the material from your courses. Grades are critical, so a student also has the concern of retention for the next upcoming assessment, usually an exam. Unlike some of these research experiments where the same material was studied in each session, in a course the material is continually building. What I tell my class is to take whatever time they intended to study for an exam and spread that out for the full week before their exam, preferably an equal amount each day. Some of the material for the exam will be introduced during the week before your exam. You will have fewer spaced sessions for the newer material. For a course with a cumulative final, you should be able to have enough spacing sessions for all but the very last material of the semester. (Of course, you should be revisiting material after the course to solidify your learning and understanding to have it available to use in future courses and life!)

At Purdue University, where I teach, most courses are three credit hours. These are scheduled as 50-minute sessions on Monday, Wednesday, and Friday or 75-minute sessions on Tuesdays and Thursdays. Our semesters are 15 weeks of class and one week of finals. When I have a choice, I always ask for a section that meets three times a week for 50-minutes, because they represent a 50% increase in number of spacings, over the sections that meet twice a week for 75-minutes. There is new material presented each class, but there is always review of older class material inherent in each class. I feel my students can retain, and learn, more because of the increased spacing with three 50-minute class sessions, instead of two 75-minute class sessions, per week. (Of course, students should also be studying the course material between classes.) Whenever there are two sections, one that meets three times a week and one that meets two times a week, I never have competition for the three times a week sections. Most faculty prefer to be interrupted "from research" only twice a week to teach. I don't know which format the students prefer. But now that you know the spacing effect, if you have the choice pick a section that meets more often for shorter times.

When I was an undergraduate at Purdue, 1971-1975, we did not have the Tuesday and Thursday 75-minute lecture sections. We had Tuesday, Thursday, and Saturday 50-minute lecture sections. I know I would never be able to convince faculty, nor students, we should go back to Tuesday, Thursday, and Saturday 50-minute lecture sections because they are better for learning!

We also offer courses during the summer, which by necessity must fit into an eight-week window. A course during the summer meets for 60 minutes every day of the week for 7.5 weeks to have the same number of class minutes as a course during a regular semester. This means half the time for students to utilize spacing in their studies during the summer session. There cannot be as much, or as durable of, learning during these summer sessions. If there is a course with material you feel is going to be very critical for you to learn, try to take it during a regular semester, not during an intensive session, such as a shorter summer session or one of these intensive two-week boot camps that have become popular.

Chapter 4: Your Study Environment

If you search for advice on where you should study, you'll probably find what my students tell me they have been advised over the years by teachers, school websites, counselors, etc. Here is what I found at one university website, "The first step to creating your study space is to choose a comfortable location. This can be a personal office, a desk in your bedroom, or a chair at the kitchen table. The important part is to choose an area with minimal interruptions—a quiet, relaxing space where you can focus and get work done. By dedicating a particular area to your schoolwork, you can train your brain to focus exclusively on studying, and not your list of to-dos or other distractions."

It is very common for us to study in one place. This is often a desk in our room where you can control your environment such as to minimize sound, or play the music of your choosing, access to all materials—books, notes, internet, etc. But is this the best environment for studying?

Studies show that it is beneficial to vary where you study, including the background sounds. The improvement found in learning with varied study locations and background sounds is probably related to our mention of the retrieval fading, not the actual memory fading. Studying the same thing in different locations may make the retrieval less dependent on some location cue, or you increase the number of cues available to retrieve the memory by studying in different locations. Exactly why is not known. But this is contrary to that typical advice given to students to have a set place that is quiet and free of distractions to go to study. Let's look at some studies of the effect of environment on learning.

The first study involved memorization of a list 36 of words [29]. This study involved a very unusual environment. Eighteen scuba divers studied these 36 words submerged at 20 feet. One hour later, they were split into two groups of nine and tested. Group 1 took the test on land and group 2 took the test submerged at 20 feet, the same place they studied the list of words. The underwater group remembered 30% more of the words! Taking an exam in the same location you studied improves performance. But you don't usually take your exams in the room where you usually do all your studying. This is where studying in various locations might help, as seen in the next study, probably because your retrieval becomes less dependent on cues from your study environment.

This next study involved more typical environments, a neat brightly lit room, and a dark cluttered basement [30]. The subjects memorized forty, four-letter words. They were split into three groups and each group had two 10-minute study sessions spaced a few hours apart. Group 1 had both study sessions in the brightly lit room. Group 2 had both study sessions in the dark cluttered basement. Group 3 had one study session in the brightly lit room and one study session in the cluttered basement.

Three hours after the last session all three groups were tested in a third room, a normal classroom. Group 1 and group 2, which had both their study sessions in the same room, recalled an average of 16 words. Group 3, which had a study session in each room recalled an average of 24 words, 50% better than groups 1 and 2! It is not known why studying in different locations improves learning, but you might as well take advantage. The improvement in learning, with studying in different locations, is probably because your retrieval depends less on cues from your study environment.

Another study by Steven Smith involved the effect of background sound on studying [31]. The participants were not aware of the purpose of the study and maybe didn't even notice the background sound, or if it had changed. Fifty-four students in a PSYC 101 class were recruited to learn 40 words. These students were divided into three groups. Group 1 studied in silence, group 2 studied while listening to jazz, and group 3 studied while listening to Mozart.

They would be tested 5 minutes after studying and again two days after studying. For the tests each group was split into three, so that part of each initial group could be tested under the sound conditions experienced during their study and under the sound conditions experienced by the other two groups while studying—9 total test groups.

A very interesting observation is the role background sound plays with recall. The group that took the test while listening to the same music they were listening to while studying recalled significantly more words than when tested under different sound conditions. The sense of hearing somehow aided in the recall when the same music was playing during the testing as during the studying. If there was no music playing, or if the music was different, the sense of hearing could not aid in the recall. We will see later in chapter 10 that the more senses involved in the learning process the better the learning.

This is probably like the experience you have when you hear a certain song play and it brings up a memory of something that occurred in your life. The sense of smell can also play a role in recall. You have probably had memories evoked when you smell something, such as a fragrance, that reminds you of a person, or the smell of a baked good that reminds you of a holiday.

The results for those who studied in silence is a little less clear as to what was happening. Recall was still better for those who studied with music playing and taking the final recall test with the same music playing than studying in silence and taking the final recall test under any background sound conditions. But those who studied in silence recalled more words with background music playing than with a silent background. The studying in silence, and the resulting lower recall score when taking the test in silence can be explained by no auditory cues for recall. But what was happening when the study in silence group took the recall test with Mozart or Jazz playing? This was not directly addressed by Smith, but I have a few thoughts.

Mehta et al. [32] found that a moderate level of ambient noise (70 dB, about what you would experience in a coffee shop) enhanced performance on creative tasks. This is what might have happened for those who had studied in silence but had Mozart or Jazz playing during the initial and final tests resulting in better recall.

As we will learn in chapter 6 on testing, a very good study method is testing. The initial test for the group that studied in silence was a study event under Jazz or Mozart conditions. This led to the group that studied in silence to perform better when they had Jazz or Mozart playing during the final test than the silent study group who took the tests in silent conditions.

It is not clear from Smith's study exactly how you could use sound to improve your learning. I have a suggestion. You now know to space your studying. During each spacing have the background sound different. Sometimes quiet; sometimes music, but different music each session; and sometimes noise like the background sound in a coffee shop. This will either make your recall less dependent on the background sound or increase the number of potential recall cues from sound.

Although these studies involved memorization, it probably holds for learning, and subsequent testing, of more complex subjects. The implications are that you should study in various locations—your room, the coffee shop, outside on a park bench, in a library, etc. Also, since you recall material better in the location where you have studied, if possible, go to the room where you are going to have your exam to do some of your studying!

Chapter 5: Interleaving

Another powerful learning technique is interleaving, which almost comes automatically if you are using spaced learning and studying multiple subjects, as is typical for a full-time student taking classes. But we will see that you should also use interleaving within the study of each subject. Instead of spending a long study session, or multiple study sessions, on one topic, interleaving involves shorter sessions on a given topic and then switching to other topics. This sounds, and indeed feels, like a less efficient form of learning, but many studies have confirmed the benefit of interleaving.

The first experimental demonstration of the benefits of interleaving, performed by Kerr and Booth, involved a skill, tossing of a bean bag at a target [33]. The subjects were 38, eight-year-olds, who were attending a Saturday morning physical education class. The subjects were to kneel with a blindfold and throw a golf-ball size bean bag at a target on the floor. After each throw, they pulled up their blindfold to see how well they did at landing the bean bag on the target. The 38 children were split into two groups. Group 1 practiced at throwing at just a target three feet away. Group 2 practiced by alternating throws at a target two feet and a target four feet away, interleaving their throws, but never throwing to a target three feet away.

A competition was held between the two groups throwing at a target three feet away. Group 2 that had practiced their throws by interleaving, but never having practiced at throwing to a target three feet away, handily won the competition. Interleaving resulted in better mental motor skills for this task. This is opposite to our intuition. It seems like practicing with the target that was going to be used in the competition would be better than practicing at different targets. The science shows otherwise.

Kerr and Booth repeated this experiment with twelve-year old children and a target four feet away. This time the interleavers practiced throwing at a target three-feet and five-feet away. The other group practiced at throwing only to a target four feet away. In the competition between the two groups throwing to a target four feet away, the interleavers again won the competition, and the results were even more dramatic.

Subsequently, there have been other studies to illustrate the benefit of interleaving to develop physical skills. The use of interleaving with hitting a baseball was investigated with the California Polytechnic State University baseball team [34]. These players would already be considered experts compared to the general population, but as we will see interleaving works even for experts trying to get better. Thirty players were randomly assigned to one of three groups, a control group of 10 players who received no additional batting practice, 10 players in a blocked group, and 10 players in an interleaved group. The blocked and interleaved groups each received two additional batting practice sessions per week for 6 weeks of 45 pitches. The pitches were 15 fast balls, 15 curve balls, and 15 change-ups. The blocked group would receive 15 pitches of one type, such as fast balls, then 15 pitches of the next type, such as curve balls, and finally 15 pitches of the last type, such as change-ups. The interleave group received 15 fast balls, 15 curve balls, and 15 change-ups in a random order. For instance, two fast balls, a change-up, a fast ball, three curve balls, a change up, etc. The pre-analysis showed no difference in hitting between the three groups. The post-analysis indicated the interleaved group's hitting improvement was twice the improvement that the blocked group showed from the control group.

Another study, which looked at the use of interleaving to learn how to identify artists, was performed by Kornell and Bjork [35]. The subjects were undergraduates at the University of California at Los Angeles. They were to learn how to look at a painting from one of 12 different artists and determine the artist. They would study 6 paintings by each of the artists. They would be shown a painting on a computer screen for 3 seconds along with the name of the artist. During the test, they would be shown paintings by the artists that were not part of the paintings studied and then asked to identify the artist.

Kornell and Bjork conducted several different experiments but let us look at just one. Each student was presented artist's paintings in either a massed, or spaced, format. The sequence for the 12 artists was MSSMMSSMMSSM, where M stands for massed and S for spaced. Each M represents one of six artists whose six paintings were all shown in sequence. Each S represents six paintings, one from each of the other six artist, shown to the students randomly. Six artists were presented in a blocked manner and six were presented in a spaced manner. For each student, the artists whose paintings were presented as massed were randomized.

On the initial test after studying, the students were shown an unfamiliar painting by one of the 12 artists. They were given 13 answers to select from, the names of the 12 artists and "I don't know." After submitting an answer, the students were told if they were correct. If they were incorrect, they were given the name of the artist. For artists the students studied in a spaced manner, the students identified about 65% of them correctly. For artists the students studied in a massed manner, the students identified about 35% of them correctly. The students were given three similar subsequent tests. The gap between the percentage identified correctly between the artists they studied spaced and massed narrowed to about 10 percentage points by the fourth exam. By giving the correct answer during the test, the students were learning. Tests are considered assessment vehicles. As we will learn later in chapter 7, and demonstrated in this Kornell and Bjork study, **testing is also a powerful learning tool**.

After the test, Kornell and Bjork explained what spaced and massed learning are to the participants, and that there was a 30-percentage point better performance (65% correct instead of 35% correct) identifying artist that were learned with spaced study compared to artists that were learned with massed study. They then asked the students "Which do you think helped you learn more, the massed or the spaced method?" Despite knowing the obvious better performance with artists they studied with a spaced method, 78% of the students responded that massed learning was better, or just as good, as spaced learning! The rapid initial learning with blocked learning, as opposed to spaced-interleaved learning, are obvious but the plateau reached with blocked learning is not. This is illustrated in figure 5.1. You need to trust the experimental observations and replace massed studying with spaced, and interleaved, studying. With massed studying you are quickly building initial mental models, but then the development of the mental models plateau. With interleaved learning, more complex mental models are developed that includes differences between the artists. With interleaved learning the retrieval strength is building slower, but there will be more cues. This makes the interleaved learning more effortful, and doesn't feel as effective, but leads to deeper learning.

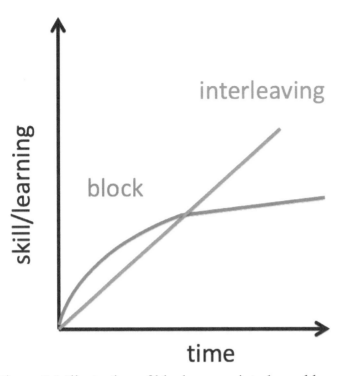

Figure 5.1 Illustration of block versus interleaved learning.

A study that will be more relevant to STEM students was performed by Rohrer and Taylor [36]. The participants were 18 undergraduate students at the University of South Florida. They were taught how to find the volume of a wedge, a spheroid, a spherical cone, and a half cone. The students were divided into two groups, the interleavers and the blockers. There were two practice sessions and a test session, each spaced one-week apart. Both practice sessions consisted of four tutorials and 16 problems. There was a tutorial on finding the volume of each of the four solids, which was repeated in each practice session. The students were then given 40 seconds for each problem, and then were shown the solution for 10 seconds. The 16 problems consisted of finding the volumes of four wedges, four spheroids, four spherical cones, and four half cones. The interleavers read the four tutorials and then did the practice problems, which were randomized. The blockers would read one tutorial and then do the four problems pertaining to that tutorial, move on to the next tutorial and the four problems pertaining to that tutorial, until they had done all four solids.

The performance on the problems during the two learning sessions was superior for the blockers (89% correct) compared to the interleavers (60%). This is not surprising as the blockers knew what structure each question pertained to but the interleavers did not. The blockers were also shown the tutorial immediately before the subsequent four problems pertaining to that tutorial.

The performance on the actual test a week after the second practice session was very different.

The test consisted of 8 new problems, 2 on each solid, which were randomly presented. The test was the same, including the ordering of the problems, for each student. This time the interleavers performed significantly better than the blockers. The interleavers correctly found the volumes for 63% of the test questions while the blockers correctly found the volumes for only 20% of the test questions! This is over a factor of three difference in performance!

You can certainly see why it would seem that blocked learning is better than interleaved learning from the difference in performance solving problems during the learning sessions between the blockers and interleavers. But during the learning sessions, the students using blocked learning were essentially told which mental model to use to solve the problems. During an exam, and certainly when you need to figure something out in real life, you are not going to be told which mental model to use. You must identify what is being asked, so that you can retrieve the appropriate mental model to solve the problem. The interleavers performed better on the test because their learning involved determining which was the correct mental model to use. Besides identifying a type of problem on an exam, so that you know which mental model to use, interleaving improves transfer of knowledge. This is when you encounter a problem that does not look like any problems you have encountered so far, but you recognize that you have a mental model that will work in solving it.

I often have students, who performed poorly on an exam, tell me they really knew the material. There are many reasons a student might feel they knew the material. One of them could be the way they studied, using blocked studying. They then may have had difficulty during the exam recognizing each type of problem and the approach to take. This is like what you hear regarding athletic performance. We have all heard of someone being referred to as great in practice but not in a game and vice versa. This could be because practices are more controlled than what is encountered in an actual competition. In practice, players are often working on a specific move, whereas in a game it is a continuous flow of moves, with the opponent trying to surprise you with what is coming. It is similar when you take an exam. For a problem on a physics test will I have to utilize the conservation of momentum? Or will conservation of energy need to be employed? Or is it a more complex problem that will require the use of both conservation of momentum and energy? When you study you want to introduce such difficulties in your studying by interleaving. The interleaving will develop that ability to recognize which mental models are needed when you see a problem. That is when you really know the material for the exam.

In another study, Taylor and Rohrer demonstrated the benefits of interleaving with a group of 24 fourth grade children of ages 10 and 11 [37]. There were 12 boys and 12 girls. The children were to learn how to determine the number of faces, corners, edges, or angles given the number of sides of a prism's base. (Rohrer had been a high school math teacher.) The students attended a session where they learned how to do these calculations, and then they would take a test the next day. The students were randomly assigned to a group that learned using a block technique or an interleaved technique. Both groups saw the same tutorials, examples, practice problems, and test problems. As a check that the participants did not know how to do the calculations, they all took a pre-test to find the number of faces, corners, edges, and angles of a prism. No student provided a correct answer. They all then watched a tutorial on prisms. The tutorial defined faces, edges, corners, and angles of a prism; and how to find the number of faces, corners, edges, and angles of a prism knowing the number of sides of the base.

There were then two problem phases. The partial-problem phase was a gentle start so as not to overwhelm the students where only the first step of the solution was required, indicate the correct formula to use. An upper-case F, C, E, or A represents a full solution shown to the students. A lower-case f represents a student being asked to find the number of faces, c the number of corners, e the number of edges, and a the angle.

Partial-Problem Phase

Blocked: Fffffff Ccccccc Eeeeeee Aaaaaaa

Interleaved: FCEA fcea efac aecf cafe aecf efac fcea

In the full problem phase the students would have to indicate the correct formula, insert the number, and perform the calculation.

Full-Problem Phase

Blocked: Fffff Ccccc Eeeee Aaaaa

Interleaved: FCEA fcea cafe fcea

The results of the subsequent test the next day are astonishing. The blocked study group scored a 38% while the interleaved study group scored a 77%. This study, the others mentioned in this chapter, and many more in the literature indicate there is no contest. Interleaving is greatly superior to blocked study. It doesn't matter what you are trying to learn. A skill such as hitting a baseball, badminton serves, playing a musical instrument, or even tossing a bean bag! Or an academic subject such as math, chemistry, identifying artists, learning foreign-language words, or history.

It certainly feels like we are learning better when we are doing massed/blocked learning than when we are doing spaced and interleaved learning. This is an illusion. We must force ourselves to use spaced, and interleaved, learning because the data clearly indicates spacing and interleaving are far superior methods of studying.

When people try to get better at something they eventually encounter a plateau. To get past your plateau you need to challenge yourself in a new way. A common example is in weightlifting. It is known that with weightlifting, to increase the weight you can lift you have to change your routine, not just trying to add weight, which works initially. In fact, weightlifters do not wait to reach a plateau, they proactively change up their routines. It is no different with any other endeavor, and probably why interleaving has proven an effective learning technique. It is like cross-training for your brain.

Fortunately, the typical semester at a university, or in high school, is well set up for spaced and interleaved learning. In my university the semesters are 15 weeks of class and 1 week of finals. A typical load would consist of about 5 classes. Going to class, keeping up with homework assignments, and starting early on projects ensure that you will be using spaced and interleaved learning. I say fortunate because the perception is that massed is better for learning. The perception that massed learning is better is why you see programs like coding bootcamps and short intense training, such as during a weekend, for professionals. In my department, about 15 years ago there was a push by some faculty members to restructure our courses to 8-week modules. Students would take the same number of courses in a semester, but they would be more massed. Instead of taking four courses over the whole 16 weeks of a semester, they would take two courses the first eight weeks and two other courses the last 8 weeks. This 8-week format was proposed and piloted because of this perception that massed concentrated effort would lead to better learning. This was thought of as a first step to going to three-week courses that students would take one at a time during the semester. Fortunately, even though this was piloted in a couple of classes, it did not become practice. At the time I had not started my research into learning, so I did not know this was not a better way of offering our courses. No one in my department knew as no one was opposed to this plan.

Chapter 6: Incubation

Another reason spaced learning is so effective is because of something called incubation that happens between your spaced learning sessions. The value of incubation has been known for well over 100 years, yet it is rarely utilized because spaced learning is rarely utilized. When you block (cram) study for an exam, your learning will not benefit from incubation. Incubation is not only important for learning, but for solving difficult problems, and creating something new.

During incubation you are not consciously thinking about what you have been studying, a problem you have been trying to solve, or trying to create something new. You are doing other things—taking a walk, playing a pick-up game of basketball, having coffee, taking a shower, and even sleeping.

Hermann von Helmholtz, a 19th century German physicist and physician, observed, and utilized, the operation of incubation, which he described in this quote, "Happy ideas come unexpectedly, without effort, like an inspiration. So far as I am concerned, they never come to me when my mind was fatigued, or when I was at my working table…they came particularly readily during the slow ascent of wooded hills on a sunny day."

There are many other anecdotal examples such as the above from Hermann von Helmholtz. Dimitri Mendeleev was struggling to find a pattern for the elements. It was while sleeping, and during a dream, that the concept of the periodic table came to Mendeleev.

The concept for the novel Frankenstein came to Mary Shelley in a dream. Well, it was probably more like a nightmare!

Leo Szilard was a nuclear physicist who was a good friend of Albert Einstein's and worked with Enrico Fermi on the first nuclear reactor. The morning of September 12, 1933, Szilard was walking in London and waiting at a traffic light to cross the street at the intersection of Russell Square and Southampton Row. He was irritated by a comment he read in the morning newspaper, which Earnest Rutherford made during a lecture. Rutherford was talking about the energy in atomic nuclei and made the flippant proclamation that there would be no practical way to access this energy, something Szilard was trying to figure out how to do. Szilard was on the walk because he was irritated by the Rutherford comment. He wasn't trying to think of how to practically release the energy, he was just walking to calm himself. The light changed and Szilard, still fuming, started to step off the curb. An idea just popped into his head; if an atom could be found that when struck with a neutron and split resulted in two neutrons that could then split additional atoms, you could realize a nuclear chain reaction. Szilard was not thinking purposely to create the concept of the nuclear chain reaction, which is utilized in the operation of a nuclear reactor or atomic bomb [38]. He had gone for a walk to get his mind off Rutherford's comments about nuclear energy; not to discover the idea of a nuclear chain reaction.

In his publication Mathematical Creation [39], Henri Poincaré discusses some of his mathematical creations and how they occurred. Poincaré states that "Among chosen combinations the most fertile will often be formed of elements drawn from domains which are far apart," reminiscent of our discussion of latticework of mental models and Shannon's discovery of digital circuit design. They were usually a sudden illumination because of long unconscious prior work. To quote Poincaré, "There is another remark to be made about the conditions of this unconscious work: it is possible, and of a certainty it is only fruitful, if it is on the one hand preceded and on the other hand followed by a period of conscious work." One example was when Poincaré was on travel for a geological excursion and not thinking of his previous mathematical work. He was stepping onto an omnibus when the illumination came to him. Another example was when Poincaré was on military service and occupied with things other than mathematics. He was walking down the street and the solution to a mathematical difficulty just suddenly appeared to him. Poincaré was recognizing the role incubation played in his discoveries: the need for conscious preparation, a period when his mind was not consciously thinking of his mathematical problem, and post conscious follow up work.

In 1926, Graham Wallas coined the term incubation for this unconscious processing and presented the stages of the creative process [40]. There is the initial preparation. The time you spend at your desk studying, such as doing homework problems. There may be a problem that you cannot figure out how to solve. Then there is the incubation stage, when you have put this homework problem aside, and you are doing something else, where your mind is not consciously thinking of the problem. You may be taking a stroll, a nap, playing a sport, or cooking. Then at some point there is the illumination stage. When an idea comes to you as to how to solve the problem, or at least how to make some progress. It may just pop into your head. Or it might become apparent when you sit down to look at that homework problem again. Verification is the final stage when you sit down at your desk and solve your problem. Wallas speculated, "Some kind of internal mental process is operating that associates new information with past information. A type of internal reorganization of the information seems to be going on without the individual being directly aware of it."

If you are skeptical, I can provide an example of incubation you might have experienced. You take an exam and there is a problem that stumps you. You have no idea how to even start it. Then sometime after the exam, when you are no longer thinking about that problem or even the exam, how to do the problem pops into your head! I know that happened to me when I was a student! As I will discuss in the next chapter on using testing to learn, you want these incubation events to happen as part of your studying routine, not after an exam!

As we will learn in Chapter 10 on sleep, one of the things that happens during sleep is incubation. John Steinbeck said, "It is a common experience that a problem difficult at night is resolved in the morning after the committee of sleep has worked on it." This is often expressed by "sleep on it."

Paul McCartney claims he wrote the song Yesterday in his sleep, "I woke up with a lovely tune in my head. I thought, that's great, I wonder what that is? There was an upright piano next to me, to the right of the bed by the window. I got out of bed, sat at the piano, found G, found F sharp minor seventh – and that leads you through then to B to E minor, and finally back to G."

Keith Richards of the Rolling Stones would wake up with a tune in his head, go back to sleep, and then could not remember it in the morning. Richards began keeping a guitar and cassette recorder by his bed so that when he would wake up with a tune in his head, he could record it. On the morning of May 7, 1965, Richards awoke and noticed the tape was at the end, but he did not remember waking up to record anything. He rewound the tape and played it. There was about 30 seconds of what was to become the song (I Can't Get No) Satisfaction, followed by the sound of the guitar hitting the floor, and then 45 minutes of snoring! This would become one of the Rolling Stones' greatest hits and is always ranked as one of the top Rock and Roll songs of all time.

If you are doing spaced and interleaved studying, you are already providing periods for incubation to occur. Since I learned about incubation, I now notice it happening all the time. As I was writing this book, I would often wake up with thoughts about how to present something. I used the voice message app on my iPhone when this would happen to record these thoughts a la Keith Richards!

When you have a project with a deadline, it is important to start it early and to continually come back to your project. It doesn't matter what the project is. It could be a paper you have to write, a computer program you have to code, a demonstration you must put together, or a capstone project. By starting early and coming back to the project, you allow for incubation periods, which lead to improvements in your project that would not occur if you waited until near the due date to get started.

On several occasions I have committed to major projects that I was not sure how well they would turn out. I usually could only make a little progress each day. But each new day I had something more to add that I didn't have the day before. Eventually I completed the project, and I was amazed at how well it turned out. I now realize that what must have been happening was incubation. I hope this book is another example!

I have created about 50 demonstrations of electromagnetic concepts for a class I teach. Some were straightforward, but often they would not work at first. I didn't immediately figure out why they were not working. But I would often have an idea pop into my head when I was doing something else. Sometimes this idea would work. Sometimes it would not. But eventually the incubation would result in leading me to get the demonstration to work. Sometimes it has taken a couple of months to get a working demonstration. I learned more about electromagnetics, thanks to spacing and the subsequent incubation, getting these demonstrations to work.

It is difficult to perform studies on Incubation because it depends on task type, the incubation period, and what is done during the incubation period. It is a much different activity finding alternative uses for an object like a brick, a typical type of task for studying incubation, than coming up with a mathematical proof. It is not surprising some studies have concluded the benefit of an incubation period and some have not. Sio and Ormerod did a meta-analysis of empirical studies of incubation in the literature [41]. They found that there is an incubation effect. Incubation was more useful for divergent thinking tasks than for linguistic and visual insight tasks. (A divergent thinking task would be coming up with how many other uses you can find for a brick or given a photo coming up with a caption.) The longer the incubation period the greater the effect. If the incubation period was filled with cognitive demanding tasks the result was a smaller incubation effect. So, take some time to do something fun or relaxing between study sessions.

When you use spaced learning, the time between studying sessions allows for incubation to occur. This results in your mind forming a deeper understanding of the material you studied, and making connections with other mental models you have. I am convinced that incubation has worked for me.

As examples, try to solve the following three problems. It might require incubation. I'll post the solutions in Appendix B.

Problem 1
You are given 9 dots as shown; Without lifting your pencil, draw four straight continuous lines that go through all the dots.

Problem 2

You are given the following six equal length sticks. Arrange them to form four equilateral triangles.

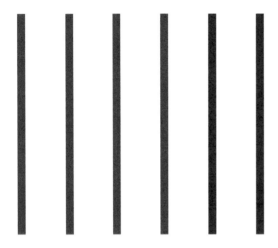

Problem 3

Before Mt. Everest was discovered, what was the highest mountain in the world?

Chapter 7: Testing

A very powerful way of studying, a purposeful practice, is testing. Students and instructors typically view testing as an assessment tool. But we will see testing is a very good learning tool, so much so it should be your number one study method. Testing is a recall exercise, so it aids retention. Testing provides feedback, which greatly aids in the learning process. From this feedback students discover gaps in their knowledge so they can go back and learn the missing concepts. (From talking with students, I have learned that they rarely do this, especially if they did poorly on an exam. It is too painful for them to look back at their poor performance. This is one benefit of Concept Point Recovery (CPR), which is the topic of chapter 17. With CPR students realize the learning benefit of looking back to understand what they missed on an exam.) Frequent testing keeps students on task and is a spaced learning exercise. When you are studying a subject, new material builds on previous material. A test helps prepare you for the next material.

The benefit of using testing to learn was demonstrated by Roediger and Karpicke [42]. One hundred twenty undergraduates at Washington University participated in their study. The subjects studied two scientific passages, one on the sun and one on sea otters. They were split into two groups of 60. The first group studied each passage twice for 7 minutes, the study-study group. In between each study session they spent 2 minutes solving multiplication problems so that they would not be thinking about what they had just read. The second group studied the two passages once for 7 minutes, had a 2-minute session where they solved multiplication problems, and then in the next 7-minute segment wrote down as much as they could recall from the passage, the study-test group. The act of recall by the students is a testing of what they learned from the passages. Each of the two groups was split into three groups, so 20 students in each. One group was tested 5 minutes, one group was tested 2 days, and one group was tested 1 week after their last session.

The results of this experiment are shown in figure 7.1. Immediately after the last session, the study-study group did about 5 percentage points better than the study-test group. At retention intervals of 2 days and 1 week, the study-test group did significantly better than the study-study group. A recall test was a much better form of studying, than a rereading of the passage, for retention of the material.

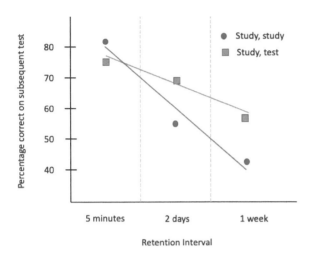

Figure 7.1 Demonstration of the learning benefit of testing.

The use of retrieval, instead of a second study, of the passages is harder. It takes more effort to recall what you have just read than to reread it. If the study activity is a little harder, then the learning is stronger as Roediger and Karpicke observed. Using a different study technique, recall instead of rereading, should build additional retrieval cues making the memory stronger.

In his 1890 text, *The Principles of Psychology* [10], William James said, "A curious peculiarity of our memory is that things are impressed better by active than by passive repetition. I mean that in learning by heart (for example), when we almost know the piece, it pays better to wait and recollect by an effort from within, than to look at the book again. If we recover the words in the former way, we shall probably know them the next time; if in the latter way, we shall very likely need the book once more." James was probably writing from personal experience. But the benefit of this active recall was scientifically established by Abbott [43] and Gates [44]. When you are studying by reading, you should periodically look away, or close your eyes, and recall what you have been reading. Gates found that the ideal percentage of such self-testing you should do as you read is 60%.

In 1939 Spitzer published a study of 3,605 Iowa sixth-grade pupils and the effect of spaced testing on learning of an article of 577 words in length on bamboo [45]. This article was content new to the children, factual, of proper difficulty, and like their regular schoolwork. The children were told they were to read the material to learn it. A twenty-five-question test was used to determine retention of the article. The children were divided into 8 groups. In Table 7.1 are the students' scores by group and the day the test was administered. 0 days represents taking the quiz the same day the article was studied, 1 day represents taking the quiz the next day, and so on. Some groups took the test three times some groups only one time.

Table 7.1 Spitzer study of testing to improve learning.

	0 days	1 day	7 days	14 days	21 days	28 days	63 days
I	13.23	13.07			12.18		
II	13.20		11.84				10.74
III		9.56		8.93			
IV			7.87		8.15		
V				6.97		7.10	
VI					6.49		7.07
VII						6.80	
VIII							6.38

There are several interesting things to discern from the table. First the longer before the first quiz is taken the lower the score. This is essentially Ebbinghaus' forgetting curve. Since this was a multiple-choice test, scores seen from taking the first test at 14 days, or later, are what you would expect from guessing. Taking the quiz the same day as studying, and again days after that, was an effective study technique. This was essentially combining spacing with the testing effect. For group I, taking the quiz on days 0 and 1 essentially led to them remembering 92% of what they knew on day 0 when they took the quiz on day 21. Whereas group IV, which took the test on day 7 for the first time, scored 67% of the score of group I on day 21. Spitzer concluded,

"Immediate recall in the form of a test is an effective method of aiding the retention of learning and should be employed more frequently. Achievement tests or examinations are learning devices and should not be considered only as tools for measuring achievement of pupils."

Another study that looked at the effectiveness of low-stake quizzes as learning activities was performed by McDaniel et al. [46]. This study utilized multiple-choice quizzes, followed by feedback, in an eighth-grade science class. There were three quizzes spaced across the unit on some of the topics to be later assessed on a summative test. Performance on the summative test was 13-25% higher on topics which were quizzed compared to topics that were not quizzed. The quizzes therefore were a very efficient learning activity.

The more effortful the retrieval during the test, the more effective the test will be for learning. A closed book test will result in more learning than an open book test [47]. A test where the student must supply the answers (short-answer or essay), versus a multiple-choice test where the students just recognize the correct answer, will result in more learning [48]. As is often seen, the more effort the greater the learning. Of course, the student must be provided, and take advantage of, feedback after the quiz or exam so they can learn what they did not know.

You should make it a habit to self-test by doing recall. In the evening, you should spend some time recalling what was talked about in class that day. The recall activity is even more effective if you involve your hand and the sense of touch by pulling out paper and pencil, and writing down what you are recalling. We will see in chapter 10 that the more senses you bring to bear the better the learning and that includes the sense of touch. When you are walking to class you can recall what was discussed in the previous class. At the end of the week, you should sit down and list the things you learned that week. When you recall what was discussed in class, or what you have read, you are firing the neurons and synapses of that memory, which strengthens them. This process is referred to as long-term potentiation (LTP). Expressing what you have learned in your own words greatly aids your understanding and recall of the material. You can also use this recall to connect the material you are learning with material you already know, to build that latticework of mental models. This process of constantly using recall as a self-test will greatly improve your learning. It is a much better, a much deeper learning, than just rereading your textbook or your notes. It can especially help if you write down what you are recalling. This makes it more active and involves the sense of touch. You should not only be recalling material, but also reflecting on it. Try to understand concepts, figure out what are the important take aways, and how this material connects to other things you have learned. **Never stop working on building that latticework of mental models.**

When you practice recall on what you have been studying, it is also a reflection activity where you realize what you understood and what you still don't understand. You'll then clearly know what you need to work on, and you can spend less time on what you already know. You still want to spend some time revisiting what you understood to solidify your memory and connect it with other concepts.

Lyle and Crawford tested this concept of recall after each class in a statistics of psychology class at the University of Louisville [49]. There were two sections of the course, one that functioned as control and one that was PUREMEM (Practicing Unassisted Retrieval to Enhance Memory for Essential Material). There were 77 students in the PUREMEM section and 78 in the control section. Lyle taught both sections. The course met twice per week for 75-minute lectures. In both sections there were four non-cumulative exams that were similar. The questions on the exams were multiple choice and consisted of computational, noncomputational, and application problems. In the PUREMEM section, during the last 5-10 minutes of class students put away their notes and answered 2-6 questions that were projected on essential material from that day's lecture. The answers would consist of one or two words, a number, or a figure, which the students turned in and accounted for 8% of their grade to ensure students took them seriously. So, each PUREMEM only accounted for 0.38% of the grade, and students did well on the PUREMEMS with an average of 86% correct. The four exam scores for the PUREMEM section had a significantly higher average and a lower standard deviation (average = 86% SD = 0.09) than the control section (average = 78% SD = 0.14). In the PUREMEMS section only 5.4% of students scored below 70% while 27.1% in the control section scored below 70%. An anonymous survey at the end of the semester of the PUREMEM section showed a very positive attitude to the concept of the PUREMEMS and the students felt it helped their learning.

As you progress up the educational system there are fewer tests. In college, it is not unusual to only have two exams—a mid-term and a final. This is probably a consequence of the effort (time) to construct, and grade, an exam at the university level, especially for a large class. (At a research university most faculty want to minimize time spent teaching as the reward system is set up for research production.) It becomes even more important for you to incorporate self-testing into your study program as you move up in the education system since you will encounter a reduced frequency of testing. I have seen students have difficulty because they wait until just before an exam to try to learn the course material that will be on the exam. In a course with just a mid-term and a final that is a prescription for failure.

Fewer high-stakes tests will also raise students' test anxiety directly impacting their test performance. In the courses I teach, because of the benefit of frequent testing, I have three one-hour 100-point exams during the semester and a two-hour 150-point final. The first exam is given during week 4 and thereafter a test occurs every three weeks. I have some colleagues who go to the effort of having 6 exams during the semester and a final, about one exam for every two weeks of the semester, but this is the exception. Another advantage of having a high frequency of testing is that it lowers the stakes of each test thereby reducing student anxiety. Students often have the illusions they are learning, which frequent testing would also reveal before it is too late. Because your courses will often not be constructed with frequent testing, you must take initiative and frequently incorporate recall into your routine—after class, while reading, at the end of the day and at the end of the week.

In the STEM field, working problems is a very effective form of purposeful practice, a way of testing what you have learned. The practice of struggling to solve a problem, rather than being shown or looking up the solutions, is referred to as **generation**. In many courses past exams are available. I provide students in my class blank copies of my previous exams in addition to the solutions. I advise students to approach these "practice" tests as if they were taking them. Use the same time limit and other restrictions (closed book, closed notes, no calculator, etc.). When finished with the test do not immediately look at the solutions to problems with which you were having difficulty. Go away and do something else, even wait until the next day so that you have had a sleep session. This allows incubation to occur. When you go back to the practice test the next day, if you have figured out how to work any of the problems you had difficulty with, because of the incubation that has occurred, you will have learned the material much deeper than if you had just looked at the solutions. The learning is stronger if it is self-generated, rather than someone telling you the answer, or from looking up the solution. **By stronger I mean you have a more sophisticated mental model that is developing connections to other mental models in your brain.** Even if you don't get the solution, but have made an effortful attempt, when you are shown the solution, it will result in more LTP; more likely when you encounter this problem again, or a similar problem, you'll be able to solve it.

I am sure most of you have had that experience when taking an exam that you encounter a problem you have no idea how to approach. Then sometime after the exam, when you are no longer thinking about the exam, how to do the problem pops into your head. You want that to happen when you are studying, not when you are taking the test! (I know I keep repeating things, but I am helping you with spaced study as you read!)

Do not start this process of using testing to study starting the day before the exam. If you have an exam coming up, and you plan to study for 7 hours, do not spend that time in one large block just before the exam. Ideally spread it out over a week with one hour each day. This will give you plenty of time to use testing and incubation to learn the material. I always provide my class with four previous exams. They have plenty of testing material for a week of spaced studying utilizing the testing effect to prepare for an upcoming exam. If you do not have enough, or any, practice exams another good activity is to come up with your own test questions. If you can get to where you can generate the type of questions that would be on an exam you have really learned the material!

For teachers reading this, I want to make some comments about pretesting. I don't do a pretest for my course, but I will hand out the final exam from the previous semester. I tell the students to sit down for a little while and look it over as if they were trying to take it. I say a little while, because it is unlikely they will be able to do any of the problems. But I always felt this was beneficial. It primed them for the material we would be covering, and they would have some idea of the test structure they would encounter. There has been some research on the effects of pretesting. But the research has been on multiple choice tests while my tests are problems that must be worked out.

One issue found with a multiple-choice pre-test is that it exposes students to incorrect answers that may look attractive resulting in difficulty learning the correct information later [50]. This can be alleviated if right after the pre-test the students read the relevant course material and learn the correct responses [51]. One study by Little et al. [52] illustrated the benefit of a multiple-choice pretest on a subsequent post-study test. Experiment 1 in Little et al. involved 25 undergraduates at UCLA. The material involved two passages, one on Yellowstone National Park and one on Saturn. Ten pairs of multiple-choice questions on the same topic were developed for each passage. Each pair involved different questions but the same responses; the correct answer was different for each question.

For instance, here is one such pair of questions from Little et al. [52] with the correct response in bold,

What is the tallest Geyser in Yellowstone National Park?
    a)   Old Faithful
    b)   Steamboat Geyser
    c)   Castle Geyser
    d)   Daisy Geyser

What is the oldest Geyser in Yellowstone National Park?
    e)   Old Faithful
    f)   Steamboat Geyser
    g)   Castle Geyser
    h)   Daisy Geyser

The questions were randomly divided such that 10 questions, one from each pair, would be on the pretest. Each participant studied both passages in the following way: The students would take a 4-minute pretest on one passage and then study that passage for 10 minutes. The students would study the other passage for 14 minutes. Five minutes after the students were done studying a passage, they were given a 40-question multiple-choice test on that passage. 20 of the questions were the 10 paired questions plus 20 questions on other facts in the passage.

Taking the 4-minute pretest proved more effective for learning than an additional 4 minutes of study. For pretest questions, the average correct response was 63%. For the other paired questions that were not on the pretest, the average correct response was 43%. A multiple-choice pretest immediately before studying material proved beneficial. Occasionally book chapters have review questions at the end of the chapters. This result suggests trying to work the review questions immediately before reading the chapter might be beneficial. (I know I did not provide review questions at the end of the chapters. Maybe in the second edition!)

I don't know exactly when, but in college at some point, I started to utilize recall to learn. I would take out scrap paper and recreate the main course concepts. When I would first start this process, there would be many concepts I could not recall, or recreate. I would then have to look at the text or my course notes. Eventually I got to where I knew the course concepts, they had become a part of me.

When I teach, I do not use prepared slides (PowerPoint). I have an iPad connected to the overhead projector and I write and talk. As I teach, I am practicing recall. I learn the material better every time I teach it!

Chapter 8: Purposeful Practice

I have liberally used the term purposeful practice. In this chapter, I am going to discuss the difference more fully between purposeful practice and naïve practice. With purposeful practice you get better. With naïve practice you do not get better, or nowhere near as quickly as with purposeful practice. With purposeful practice you reach levels that are unobtainable with naïve practice. You want to spend your study time doing purposeful practice.

To understand the concepts of purposeful and naïve practice, let's engage in a thought experiment. Consider two groups with equal athletic abilities who have never played any basketball. Each group is going to practice one hour three times each week for 16 weeks. About the equivalent of class time for a three-credit hour university course. One group will only engage in purposeful practice, and the other group will only engage in naïve practice. The naïve practice group will divide up into two teams and play a game of basketball for one hour each practice session. During their practice sessions the purposeful practice group will do drills practicing dribbling, passing, shooting jump shots, shooting free throws, blocking out to grab rebounds, defensive stances and positioning, running set plays such as pick and rolls, etc. The purposeful practice group will never divide into teams and play a practice game. At the end of the 48 practice sessions, the two groups will meet and play a game. Do you have any doubt which group will win, and do so soundly? The group that has never played an actual game or the group that only played games? Hopefully it makes sense to you the purposeful practice group would completely dominate the naïve practice group.

Most students spend their study efforts finding, and memorizing, procedures with which to solve problems that will appear on a test. This is naïve practice. I had earned all As, except for one B, in high school. When I took my first test in college, a calculus test, I received a C. This turned out to be very fortunate because of how I reacted. I concluded that unlike high school, in the college population I was just an average student. I don't know why, but I distinctly remember that I decided I had to really understand what I was learning to obtain a job when I graduated because my grades were not going to make me stand out. On my next calculus test I received an A, and I ended up with an A in that course, and all my future math courses. I stumbled on the fact that if I studied to learn the material the grades would come. Studying to learn the material takes purposeful practice. Purposeful practice is more effortful than naïve practice, but it results in much better retention, and understanding, of the material. **The spaced and interleaved practice we have talked about is more effortful and purposeful practice. Using self-testing and incubation to learn are purposeful practices. Changing where you study is purposeful practice.** All these things take a little extra effort. When you study to learn, you have a concept in your memory, which is easier to remember and recall, but more difficult to initially obtain, than a procedure that you follow blindly. **You have a more sophisticated mental model.** When you encounter problems that are different than the ones you have been practicing, it is much more likely you will see the connection and be able to apply what you have learned if you understand the concept, and not just a procedure. **Learning is not a grade you obtain on an exam. It is the mental models you have developed that will enable you to undertake even more complex tasks than you would encounter on an exam**.

I have had several graduate students who exhibit this lack of having a deeper conceptual understanding. In the admission process to our graduate program, the grades a student obtained, and where they went to school, get weighted heavily. I have taken on graduate student who looked good on paper, that is they obtained A's in all their courses and went to highly ranked universities. But working with them I often found they didn't have a strong understanding. It was difficult for them to do research because research was not a fixed algorithm to be followed. It is research because you must create, or discover, something new. One of my best graduate students was someone I met in an undergraduate course I taught. From interacting with him during the semester it was clear that he acquired concepts and understood how those concepts fit in with what he learned in his other courses, yet he was only a B student as an undergraduate! He probably only got into our graduate program because of my recommendation, and the fact I was willing to support him with a research assistantship. The takeaway is that you don't want to spend your study time memorizing the steps of solving a problem. You should take a purposeful approach; you want to understand concepts. Then if the problem is different from the ones you encountered during your studies, you will have less difficulty recognizing the concept that it will take to solve the problem.

I like to invert problems on tests that students have seen in class, on homework, or on previous tests. In other words, the answer is given. The student needs to find one of the inputs. If they just memorize an algorithm, the steps, for solving the problem, they will have difficulty. They will not be able to work in reverse because they won't even recognize the problem was something they studied. If they have a mental model of the concept, the problem should be no more difficult. Let's look at an example.

This may be a problem encountered on a homework assignment:

Tickets for a school play cost $10 for adults and $5 for children. Diane sold five adult tickets and 8 child tickets. How much money did Diane make?

$$(5 \text{ adults}) \times \left(10\, \frac{\text{dollars}}{\text{adult}}\right) + (8 \text{ children}) \times \left(5\, \frac{\text{dollars}}{\text{child}}\right) = y = \text{money made}$$

$$50 \text{ dollars} + 40 \text{ dollars} = y = \text{money made}$$

$$\$90 = y = \text{money made}$$

If a student just memorizes the steps to get the answer for the above problem, an algorithm, but didn't develop a mental model of the concept, they could have difficulty encountering this version of the problem testing the identical concept.

Tickets for a school play cost $10 for adults and $5 for children. Diane sold five adult tickets and made $90. How many children tickets did Diane sell?

$$(5 \text{ adults}) \times \left(10 \frac{\text{dollars}}{\text{adult}}\right) + (x \text{ children}) \times \left(5 \frac{\text{dollers}}{\text{child}}\right) = 90 \text{ dollars} = \text{money made}$$

$$(50 \text{ dollars}) + (x \text{ children}) \times \left(5 \frac{\text{dollers}}{\text{child}}\right) = 90 \text{ dollars}$$

$$(x \text{ children}) \times \left(5 \frac{\text{dollers}}{\text{child}}\right) = 40 \text{ dollars}$$

$$x \text{ children} = \frac{40 \text{ dollars}}{(5 \frac{\text{dollars}}{\text{child}})} = 8 \text{ children}$$

The above problem is a simple example, which you might look at and think the two versions of the problem are not that different. As you move up to more advanced topics, two statements of the same problem could look much more different than the above example. Let me show you an actual example from the course I teach on electromagnetics. I know the statement of what I am asking will not mean anything to you. But I think you will see from the two statements of the problem they look totally different even though they are the same problem, just asked in reverse.

When you encounter Gauss' Law in electromagnetics this is the typical why a problem would be asked.

At z = 2 m and z = -2 m are infinite planes of surface charge density $\rho_S = 6 \frac{C}{m^2}$.

At z = 0 is an infinite plane of surface charge density $\rho_S = -8 \frac{C}{m^2}$.

Find the electric flux density field everywhere.

On a test I have asked it in this way. Given the following electric flux density field,

$$\mathbf{D} = 2\,\hat{\mathbf{a}}_z\ \frac{C}{m^2} \quad \text{for } x > 3 \text{ m}$$

$$= -4\,\hat{\mathbf{a}}_x\ \frac{C}{m^2} \quad \text{for } 0 < x < 3 \text{ m}$$

$$= 4\,\hat{\mathbf{a}}_x\ \frac{C}{m^2} \quad \text{for } -3 \text{ m} < x < 0$$

$$= -2\,\hat{\mathbf{a}}_z\ \frac{C}{m^2} \quad \text{for } x < -3 \text{ m}$$

What are the surface charge densities that are producing this electric flux density field?

The above questions are regarding the exact same structure and charges, and Gauss' Law is needed to solve both. Even for many students in my class, after studying Gauss' Law, the second version can cause difficulty if they are just trying to memorize a procedure for solving Gauss' Law problems.

As another example, consider being asked to find 8% of 50. If you understand the concept, you can invert the problem and easily have the answer. It is the same as finding 50% of 8, which is 4.

There are some endeavors where it has been shown that the amount of purposeful practice you put in correlates with how good you become at that endeavor. Examples are playing chess, a musical instrument, or golf. The same is true for academic endeavors. Memorizing facts and algorithms is naïve practice resulting in mental models that can be applied to only very similar problems. When presented with different types of problems you will have difficulty recognizing which algorithm to use. Purposeful practice will result in more sophisticated mental models. When you encounter a problem stated very differently, but you have this more sophisticated mental model of understanding the concept, you will recognize how to approach the problem to solve.

Learning the violin is an endeavor where the techniques, and the purposeful practices to get better at the techniques, are well-known. It takes instructors who know the practice process, and a student who wants to put in the required effort. A study of violin students at the

Berlin University of the Arts was conducted by Anders Ericsson and colleagues [53]. They had the professors group the students who were in the performance program in one of two tiers. The first tier (Best) consisted of students that were exhibiting the ability to be international soloist. The second tier (Good) consisted of students who were very good, just not in the same category as the Best tier students. The third tier (Teachers) consisted of students who had not been admitted into the performance program but to the music education program. The students in this third tier would not be able to earn a living performing but would be violin teachers for the next generation.

All the students were then asked to estimate how many hours they had practiced violin since they first picked up the instrument. These students had a set practice schedule since they started playing, which increased as they got older, so they were able to provide a relatively accurate estimate of their practice time. These students did not spend their practice time just playing music. These students had music teachers who evaluated the students each week and assigned deliberate practice techniques that have been developed over decades.

At any given age, the Best students had significantly more accumulated practice hours than the Good students, and the Good students had considerably more accumulated practice hours than the students who would go on to careers as music teachers. By age 18, the Best students had accumulated an average of 7,410 hours, the Good students an average of 5,301 hours, and the students in the music education program an average of 3,420 hours of practice time. At least in this population of students, the differences were not innate talent, but the accumulated amount of purposeful practice.

Also recruited was a group of professional violinists from two orchestras with international reputations, the Berlin Philharmonic Orchestra, and the Radio-Symphonie Orchestra Berlin. By age 18, this group of professionals had accumulated an average of 7,336 hours of practice time, essentially the same as the Best students.

Ericsson also surveyed the students regarding their sleep and found clear differences in the sleep patterns between the three tiers. Essentially the Best Students got more sleep on average each night than the Good students, and the Good students got more sleep each night than the teachers. The Best students also took more naps than the Good students, who napped more than the teachers. We will discuss the role of sleep to learning in chapter 11.

In school you are always taking a course on a new topic, or a course that is an advancement on some subject. School always has you at the edge of your understanding. It is a perfect opportunity for getting better because school is always putting you at the edge of your comfort zone. To get better you must be challenged, not just repeating something you can already do or already know. To be successful you must put in purposeful practice.

Ericsson named the practice these violin students did as deliberate practice. Deliberate practice is purposeful practice following a system that has been developed for improvement. For fields such as musical performance, chess, sports, and especially individual sports such as gymnastics, figure skating, and golf, training techniques have been developed over decades, or even centuries in the case for violin. Feedback is immediate. What needs to be worked on for improvement is obvious. Coaches and teachers can be employed to guide what needs to be improved and how. That is why world records are constantly being bettered, because of continuous improvement in training techniques, in how to do purposeful practice.

For other fields such as becoming a teacher, pilot, doctor, engineer, or businessperson, superior performance is harder to judge. It is not always obvious what needs to be worked on to improve. Ander's strict definition of deliberate practice does not apply. But it is obvious that the amount of the right type of practice, purposeful practice, will lead to improvement.

After an exam, a student who has done poorly will come to see me and mention that they had spent a lot of time studying and knew the material. I have no doubt they spent a lot of time studying, but I suspect they were doing naïve practice, not purposeful practice. When I ask them how they studied, they will tell me things like how they would read and reread their textbooks and notes. They got to where they were very familiar with the material and mistook familiarity with understanding the material. They were doing the same thing over and over expecting that to improve their understanding. Instead, they had to do things that are more effortful to improve their understanding. **They had to do things that provide feedback so they can monitor their progress and identify where they should emphasize their efforts rather than mindless repetition**. One reason some forms of testing are good learning activities is that you get this feedback as to what you do, and do not, know.

Another thing I would glean from talking to students about how they studied is that they spend time trying to learn techniques for solving problems, rather than understanding the concepts behind the problem. The goal of your studying should be to understand the concepts. It is more important to understand the why than the how. The how will come from the why. I have had students come to my office for help with a homework problem. I start to explain the concept behind the problem; they will stop me and say they just want to know how to solve this type of problem! The whole point of going to school is to learn and understand the material, after which you will be able to solve problems you encounter, not just blindly following a procedure you memorize to solve a problem to pass an exam, which you will forget after the course is over. You must give the task of learning your full attention. Once you put in the hard purposeful practice to understand the material, the taking of exams will be the easy part! If you understand something, and build a mental model, you will get good grades and have something to use in your next courses and in life.

To get better at anything, as Anders Ericsson has found, the practice must be deliberate, purposeful, effective. **Purposeful practice is hard. Rereading your textbooks and notes is not hard. Looking at solutions to a problem is not hard. Purposeful practice is effortful because it is working on something that is slightly beyond your skill or knowledge level; you work to figure it out on your own, not asking someone or looking up a solution—at least not before you put in some effort.**

When you study, you are trying to acquire new knowledge, techniques, and skills. To do that, much of your study must be solo purposeful practice. Musicians improve more rapidly with solo practice than practicing with others. Another example to illustrate this was a study done by Angela Duckworth and colleagues at the Scripps National Spelling Bee. Spelling contestants have two basic practice techniques, being quizzed and solo studying of words from lists and dictionaries. Duckworth et al. [54] had contestants fill out detailed questionnaires. Their performance correlated with two things. One was how much time they spent studying, their grit, a topic we will discuss in chapter 11. The other was spending more time doing solo study, which is a more purposeful form of study.

Purposeful practice makes you better but is less enjoyable because it is hard work. When you are engaged in purposeful practice you are extending your capabilities or understanding, which is difficult. That means it is hard to put in more than an hour of purposeful practice at one time without taking a break. Probably 3-5 hours of purposeful practice is a limit for one day. But with purposeful practice comes rewards, meaningful positive feedback. Seeing the rewards from purposeful practice will make it a little easier, and more enjoyable, to return to hard work. You will get to a point where you feel awesome not just from the reward but from putting in hard work. You associate completing hard work with feeling good. Since purposeful practice is hard work, getting adequate sleep and being healthy are important. That is one reason sleep, exercise, and nutrition are topics of future chapters.

We have encountered forms of purposeful practice. When you are spacing your learning sessions you are allowing some forgetting to occur so when you go back to restudy the material it is a little harder. Interleaving is a purposeful practice. When you interleave solving different types of problems it feels, and is, harder than just working on one type of problem until you can do it before moving on to the next type of problem. The interleaving of subjects and topics is harder but teaches you to recognize the problem you are encountering. On tests, and in life, the problems are mixed. You must recognize the problem you are encountering. Interleaving with different subjects naturally occurs in school and this is a perfect opportunity for interleaving. In school you are studying four or five different subjects every semester. Do not spend two days just studying calculus, the two days before the calculus test. Spend an equivalent of two days of studying for the calculus test but spread it out over a week interspersing with study sessions of your other classes.

Testing is an excellent form of purposeful practice. **When you are reading something, you should spend as much time pausing and trying to recollect what you had been reading as time you spend reading. This is harder than just reading and is a form of testing**. You are self-testing, and you will not only remember the material better, but you will understand it better. When you are working a homework problem and get stuck, do not immediately ask for help. Give the problem time to incubate and see if when you come back to it you can make more progress. This is harder than just asking someone how to solve the problem, but if you figure out how to work the problem on your own, you will have learned the material much deeper.

When I teach a class, I give my students at least four previous exams. I tell them to start a week before our actual test. I tell them to take one of the exams; sit down with no text, notes, or solutions for the exam and spend one hour working it as they are going to have to for our actual exam. After that hour, do not look at the solutions. Take a break from it and do something else to allow incubation to occur. Then study one of your other subjects to allow for some interleaving. Come back to the exam the next day and see if you can solve any of the problems you could not solve the first time. If you still cannot figure out how to solve a problem, look at your notes and text and see if you can figure it out. If not, only then look at the solutions. Now take the second previous exam and do the same procedure. This is hard, but by the time you have finished that fourth exam, you will probably have a good grasp of the material. Along the way, you will expose the concepts that you do not understand, and you can work on those.

Another way you should be constantly self-testing yourself is taking out a pencil and blank paper. Then try to recall and write down everything that you covered in a class earlier in the day. This is hard, you won't recall everything, but what you do recall you will remember better and connect it to other parts of the course. Writing is important. When you write you bring in another sense, the sense of touch, which helps the learning process. I will talk more about this in chapter 10. If you have been continuously self-testing with paper and pencil, by the time the test is approaching, you should be able to recreate most of the material to be covered on the exam.

Purposeful practice is a form of success that begins with failure. You are practicing something at the limits of your ability. You will make mistakes, you will get stuck, you will fail. But with each practice session you get better, and eventually successful at learning that new skill, or turning a weakness into a strength.

At Washington University 177 undergraduates were surveyed [55]. They were asked to list the strategies they used when studying. This was an open-ended question except they were specifically asked if they reread their notes or textbook (item 1 in the table 1) and they were specifically asked if they practiced recall after studying a textbook chapter (item 9 in the table 1).

The most often mentioned study strategy, mentioned by 83.6% of the students, was rereading their notes or textbook, what we know is a naïve practice strategy! Studies have shown that rereading something like a section in a textbook, or a Scientific American article, does not improve performance on a subsequent summative assessment [56]. The 9th most often mentioned strategy, by only 10.7% of the students, was practice recall, what we know is a very effective, purposeful practice strategy. In addition, 54.8% of the students ranked the naïve practice of rereading their text or notes as their #1 strategy, while only 1.1% of the students ranked the purposeful practice of self-testing as their #1 strategy. I am confident that 99% of you reading this book can greatly improve your learning by following the advice of incorporating recall self-testing into your study sessions.

If you are studying a subject such as math, you want to use techniques as you will encounter them on the exam or later in life. If the exam is going to be problems, you don't want to spend time rereading your text or looking over solutions to problems. You want to spend time encountering new problems like the ones you will encounter on the test and trying to solve them. You not only want to learn from your studying how to solve a particular problem, you want to be able to identify the problem so that you know which approach, which of your mental models, to utilize in solving the problem. So, these problems should be interleaved, each successive problem requiring a different mental model.

Another strategy was highlighting, which 6.2% of students used and 1.6% of students listed as their #1 strategy. The believed benefits of highlighting are the act of selecting what is important is elaborative thinking, plus it is easier to go back and find important information [57]. Several studies have shown that highlighting is beneficial [58] [59] [60]. It improves the recall of the material that has been highlighted [61] [62]. However, many students are not good at identifying important information, and often mark too little or too much [63]. For most students, training is required for highlighting to be effective [64] [65] [58] [59] and no study has found that highlighting is effective for pre-college students without training [66]. Interestingly, for students who have acquired the skills for highlighting, it is the act of highlighting, and not the going back and review of the highlighted material, that provides benefit [67] [68] [69].

I have never highlighted my texts. I just feel that is marring a book. But I do something similar that is a more active participation than highlighting. I take notes as I read; I put the points in my own words. This is an act of recall and elaboration. Taking notes as you read also gets the sense of touch more involved in the learning process than highlighting, which we will see in chapter 10 is important to help the learning. Because the literature indicates most students do not highlight effectively without training, I suggest my method of taking notes, instead of highlighting, as you read.

Elizabeth and Robert Bjork coined the term **desirable difficulties** for such learning techniques as spaced practice, interleaved practice, recall, generation, and testing [23]. It has been consistently observed that if the learning is made mildly more difficult, the learning is stronger and there is a deeper understanding. What is learned can be better utilized for inference, reaching a logical conclusion from the facts, rather than just being able to recall facts.

Another example of the effect of adding a little difficulty to the study resulting in a deeper understanding involved students studying a text where they were first shown an outline to study. The outline was either consistent or inconsistent with the text. The students who studied the consistent outline did better on cue-recall and recognition tasks and were able to write summaries more closely following the actual text. But for tasks that required a deeper understanding and application of the material, inferring from the material they studied, the students who studied the inconsistent outline did better [70]. The only explanation seems that the inconsistent outline added some difficulty to the learning. Additionally it has been observed that the learning is better if it is made a little more effortful by removing 30% of the letters from the text and leaving blanks [71], or using a font that was more challenging to read [72].

Another way to think of desirable difficulties is that you must be more active, less passive, with your learning. Instead of looking up a solution you are generating the solution. Instead of picking an answer from multiple choices you are supplying the answer, or better yet you are supplying a short essay.

Chapter 9: Specialize or Build a Latticework of Mental Models?

The studies of learning to play a musical instrument or chess are cited to imply one must specialize, the earlier in life the better, and one must put in 10,000 hours of purposeful practice to become an expert. This was popularized by Malcom Gladwell in his book *Outliers* [73]. He chose the accumulated practice for the best violinist at age 20 from Ericsson's study, which was 10,000 hours. This became a meme. If Gladwell had picked any other age, he would have gotten a different number, but 10,000 hours was a nice number to start a rule around. Yet Ericsson's Best violinists, after 10,000 hours of practice, were nowhere near international orchestra level. They would have to start as a member of an orchestra for a smaller city and need many more years of purposeful practice to work their way up to an orchestra like the Berlin Philharmonic. Someone does not stop improving or learning because they reach an innate limit to their ability. They stop improving or learning because they stop doing purposeful practice. With continued purposeful practice, you can always get better. It also depends on the field how many hours it will take to be among the best in the world. Steve Faloon became the best in the world at remembering digits after about 200 hours. Today it probably takes a lot more time to be among the best at remembering digits, but nowhere near 10,000 hours. Also don't let 10,000 hours look daunting and prevent you from undertaking something. With whatever amount of purposeful practice you do, you will get better. You don't have to become the world's best at something. The writing skills you need to publish a blog are nowhere near, and doesn't take anywhere near the time to obtain, the skills you need to write a novel.

Hogarth has termed environments as kind or wicked [74]. A kind environment to learn in is where the procedures for acquiring the knowledge are well known, and as you learn there is instant feedback to allow you to correct your understanding or what you are doing. Learning to play a musical instrument, play chess, a sport like golf, or multiplication tables involve kind learning environments. Learning to play the violin is not easy, but it is a kind learning environment. The techniques to get great sound out of a violin are known, the purposeful practice needed to learn the techniques are known, and there is instant feedback when you are doing something wrong. You can get very good, become world class, spending your time just on learning this one activity since it involves a kind learning environment. Even so, you still might improve more, or faster if you are interleaving with other activities, such as studying dance or other musical instruments. In fact, a meta-analysis of 51 studies showed that when they were young, world-class athletes participated in a variety of different sport activities, and started their main sport later, than national-class athletes [75]. This is reminiscent, and probably related to, interleaving being a better approach to learning.

Most of life is a wicked environment. In a wicked environment you may not get feedback, at least not immediately, or the feedback can lead you in the wrong direction. You are constantly encountering different scenarios. You may have to call on knowledge from many different fields to solve a real-world problem or create a new approach. This is why Charlie Munger encourages building a latticework of mental models. Munger is talking about building a generalized knowledge base.

About 90% of hi-tech startup companies fail. Everyone who starts such a business is convinced they have an idea that will lead to a successful business. The venture capitalists who invest in a hi-tech startup do so because they believe it will be a success. But the environment is wicked. The information the founders and investors of the company are analyzing is misleading, incomplete, or they don't envision how the world will change during the startup phase. That is why they are wrong 90% of the time!

Learning environments are often set up to be kind. Students approach their studies by taking kind approaches. We have learned that the learning is better if it is effortful. It is better if the environment is more wicked. That is why interleaving helps. You are constantly changing the type of problem, or the topic, you are studying. If you encounter a problem in a more realistic setting, you will be better able to identify what is being asked and which mental models to draw from. Even on a test, the problem types will probably be a random set of mixed types that you will have to identify to be able to solve.

Since life is wicked, the more mental models to draw from, and the more interconnected they are, the better. In life a mental model can become obsolete, and why you need to be constantly developing new mental models. If you were learning programming in the 1970s, chances are you were learning the programming language FORTRAN; in your first job all you did was program in FORTRAN. Today if you were looking for a coding job, you would be much better served knowing Python than FORTRAN.

You also may have to change the mental model you are using as your environment changes. If you live in the US and are crossing the street, you must look left for approaching cars. If you then move to the UK, where they drive on the left side of the road, you must now look right for approaching cars, or you will not be living long in the UK. Of course, my mental model is to always look both ways in case a car, or much more likely a bike, is coming from the wrong direction!

Malamud has found data that supports it is beneficial to postpone specialization in career pursuits [76], which means developing a more diverse set of mental models is a more purposeful practice. The data looked at was from 1972 to 1993. In Britain, there is a difference when students in Scotland and students in England choose their majors, but their labor markets are well integrated, and Scotland and England are commonly governed. Students in England choose their specialization early. In England students apply to specific university programs when they are still in secondary school. In fact, English students often specialize in the last two years of high school studying just 3-4 subjects in what's call Advanced level (A-level). These 3-4 subjects can all be in the same broad field such as all science, all humanities, or all arts. The degree in England is a single subject honors degree. If a student in England switches their major in college, they essentially must almost start all over and it is another four years to a degree. In Scotland the choice of specialization comes much later for students, and they spend more time exploring different disciplines. Students in Scotland applying to university are not admitted to a specific discipline. During their first two university years they are required to explore different fields before choosing a specific discipline; they usually are on track to make a choice between 2-3 different specialties at the start of their third year in university.

In England, a college graduate will have more skills for a particular field, such as electrical engineering. But in Scotland, a college graduate will have more information before selecting a particular field and more likely to have a match quality—a given specialization fitting their interests. Not surprisingly, occupational switching, switching to an occupation that is unrelated to one's field of study, is 10 to 20 percentage points lower in Scotland than in England. In Scotland students had more time and more knowledge before embarking on a specific major.

Initially, the English graduates have higher wages than the Scottish graduates, but by six years after graduation they are the same and then become higher for the Scottish graduates [77]. The early higher wage for the English graduates is due to having more skills because they specialized earlier. Since the Scottish graduates have better match quality, because they chose specializations after having more information and exploration, they have more grit for their occupation, and they don't end up completely switching occupations and going to a lower starter wage. In chapter 10, I will discuss grit and its role in career success. In addition, the Scottish graduates have more diverse mental models to draw on.

I speculate the Scottish graduates probably continue to explore diverse interests. If you look at Nobel prize winners, they are 22 times more likely to be musicians, painters, writers, woodworkers, etc. than other scientists [78]. To think critically, to solve complex problems, to create something new requires being able to bring to bear conceptual understanding of diverse disciplines. You may have one area where you are an expert. To be a critical thinker you need to be able to apply that expertise to other areas. You get that by studying, developing mental models of other areas, and forming connections between these different models in your head. If Claude Shannon did not have mental models for electric circuits and Boolean algebra, and did not connect them, he would not have invented digital circuit design.

In the department where I teach, we offer two degrees. A Bachelor of Science in Electrical Engineering (BSEE) and a Bachelor of Science in Computer Engineering (BSCompE). I think this was a mistake. Faculty are eager to channel students in their narrow field of study, and the common core of these two programs is less each year as these degrees specialize. A single degree, Bachelor of Science in Electrical & Computer Engineering, would force a little more breadth in our students. A student graduating with a BSCompE will be a great programmer and the Googles, Microsofts and Facebooks of the world will be very happy with them. Elon Musk taught himself to code beginning at age 10 [79]. At age 12 he sold his first computer game,

Blastar, for $500. When he went on to college, he studied physics and economics instead of continuing with a narrow focus and specializing in computer engineering. Would there be a SpaceX Corporation and a Tesla Corporation if Elon Musk had not used his undergraduate education to broaden his mental models?

The world is constantly changing, and the skills needed today may not serve you in the future. You must continually work on expanding your matrix of mental models. In this way you might even bring to bear knowledge and skills from an unrelated field to a new area you are encountering. There is no doubt it takes a lot of time and purposeful practice to get good at something. But you may get better, be more creative, and able to undertake more complex tasks if you interleave with learning other seemingly unrelated subjects. Explore all your interests, don't feel you have to specialize, especially too soon.

Chapter 10: Engage All Your Senses

There is a myth that each of us has a learning style, such as visual, auditory, read/write, or kinesthetic. Unfortunately, it has become dogma. I often have students tell be they are a visual learner, or an auditory learner. There is no scientific evidence that we have a learning style. We might have a style preference, but there is no proof we learn better that way.

There have been many studies that indicate such learning styles exist. But four prominent researchers in the field of learning reviewed these studies to see if the research methods were rigorous enough to support the conclusions [80]. Their criteria necessary to prove learning styles exist are the following. Students would be divided into groups based on their learning styles. Students from each group would be randomly assigned to receive one of different instruction methods (visual, auditory, reading/writing, or kinesthetic). All students would take the same test on the material they were taught. If learning styles did exist, then the visual students who were taught visually should perform better than visual students who were taught audially. This should hold true for all learning styles. Pashler et al. concluded, "the learning-styles literature has revealed only a few fragmentary and unconvincing pieces of evidence that meet this standard, and we therefore conclude that the literature fails to provide adequate support for applying learning-style assessments in school settings." Furthermore, they found studies with appropriate structured research showed no evidence of learning styles [81] [82].

Labeling yourself as learning with a certain style could be a detriment to your learning because it will limit you from trying other techniques. If your teacher is explaining something verbally, and you believe your learning style is visual, you might stop listening. As an example, let's say you consider yourself an auditory learner and you are going to take a class on painting styles; one thing you will be tested on is looking at a painting you have never seen and asked to identify the artist. Do you think someone verbally describing an artist's style will be better, or looking at paintings by that artist, to learn to identify that artist's paintings? The presentation style of the material should match the subject matter. All students will learn artists' styles better with visual being the dominant method of instruction. Being labeled with a learning style may even prevent you from taking a course, or entering a field of study, in which you have interest. Do not let the misguided concept of learning styles affect your learning.

There is evidence that the more senses we bring to bear the better we will learn [83] [84]. You have probably had that experience where you hear a song, and it brings back a memory. Or you catch a scent of a perfume, and it invokes the memory of someone. Or you see someone you don't know, but they bring back a memory of someone because they have some similar features. Your senses can all play a role in providing clues to memory retrieval, even your sense of touch. The more senses sending signals to your brain as you are studying probably results in more neuron wiring occurring, leading to stronger learning.

I always tell my students to start a problem by drawing a picture. Drawing a picture engages your sense of touch. Having drawn a picture, you are now engaging your visual sense to help understand what is being asked. I remember a fellow student, when I was an undergraduate, who used to call it "thinking with a pencil." In addition, you can be verbalizing what you are drawing to bring in your auditory sense.

On occasion I have had a student come for help during office hours. During the act of explaining to me their issue, they suddenly understand the concept. I don't know if it is because of incubation, or the active verbalization, which resulted in the illumination. There have been some studies that indicate "thinking aloud" while doing math problems leads to solving the problems faster, and more likely to obtain the correct answers [85].

When in class, you should not be a passive listener. You should be active, taking notes and asking questions. By taking notes you are bringing your sense of touch to bear in the learning process. To assess the effect of different student classroom behaviors on learning, Perry Sampson developed an active learning platform. On this platform the students could view Sampson's PowerPoint slides. Sampson could pose questions to which the students could respond on the platform. On the platform the students could also ask questions, take notes, and indicate confusion, with each action linked to the spot in the lecture where the action was taken [86]. There were several student behaviors that were compared to exam scores.

A student was counted as in attendance if they logged onto the learning platform and performed one task—taking notes, answering a posed question, posting a question, or indicating confusion. If a student did not, it was assumed they were not there. (Though they could have been there asleep, or not paying attention, which should still count as the student not being in attendance.) Attendance did not influence the student's exam performance.

Answering questions in class had a small, but direct relationship to exam performance. Answering questions posed in class correctly had a somewhat larger direct relationship to exam performance.

Interestingly, the two factors that had the largest, and very significant, relationship to exam performance was volume of notes taken and noting confusion during the lecture. Students scoring >90% on the exams took almost 70% more notes than the class average while students scoring <70% took almost 25% fewer notes than the class average. Similarly, students scoring >90% on the exams indicated confusion almost 70% more times than the class average while students scoring < 70% indicated confusion almost 25% fewer times than the class average. The greater the volume of notes, or the noting of confusion, the more engaged the student, which you would expect would increase learning. Taking notes probably also brings the sense of touch into the learning process. But typing on the keyboard, as the students in Sampson's study, does not as actively engage the sense of touch as writing on a piece of paper. It has been shown that writing is superior to typing in the learning process when one is taking notes [87].

Sampson also compared the incoming GPAs of students in his class to their behavior in his class. He grouped the students as those with an incoming GPA of >3.5, between 3.0 – 3.5, and <3.0. There was no significant variation in incoming GPA with attendance. Attendance was not the factor that accounted for the difference in incoming GPA. There was a slight decrease in percentage of students that answered questions in class as incoming GPA decreased. The highest GPA group answered 1.7 times as many questions correctly in class as the lowest GPA group. Of course, this is what you would expect.

A significant factor was that the highest incoming GPA group (>3.5) was three times as likely to note confusion in class than the lowest incoming GPA group (<3.0). This indicates that the highest incoming

GPA group was much more engaged; they were obviously less confused in general than the lowest GPA group, but they were more active in noting when they were confused. The other most significant factor was that the highest incoming GPA group (>3.5) took **four times** the volume of notes as the lowest incoming GPA group (<3.0)! This again indicates more engagement for the highest GPA group, but also the addition of the sense of touch in the learning process.

Sampson's results are not the only ones that show students need to be active in the classroom to enhance their learning. I believe PowerPoint has had a very negative effect on education because it turns students into passive listeners. At least at the college level, most classes are taught with a PowerPoint. When my daughter was in college she said to me, "Dad, I go to all my classes. But there is no point. They provide their PowerPoint slides and in class all they do is read them to us!" There is a big push to put active learning into the classroom, such as breaking the class up into groups that work "actively" together on problems. If you want to make students active in class, return to instructors using "chalk and talk" so the students must be actively taking notes. Involve their sense of touch in their learning. Make them reword what is going on in class in their own words as they take notes.

Another problem with PowerPoint presentations is that the material is presented rapidly. Students cannot absorb it at that rate. Plus, a passive learner's attention is going to drift from what is being presented. This is the same as what happens when one tries to meditate, as will be discussed in chapter 16. In meditation you are paying attention to your breath. At some point you realize you are thinking of something else and not paying attention to your breathing. When this happens in a class with a PowerPoint presentation you miss so much that you might be lost for the rest of the lecture, even if you start paying attention again!

Even though getting adequate sleep is essential for learning for many reasons, as will be discussed in chapter 11, students don't get enough sleep. In a passive PowerPoint presentation they fall asleep, or experience microsleeps, and miss what is being presented. If a student is actively taking notes, it will help keep them awake, although this is no substitute for getting adequate sleep, which is so critical to the learning process.

My position as Associate Head for Education in our department involved making teaching assignments. When I assigned someone to a course they had not taught before, which is the situation with new faculty, I often was asked who they should talk with to get the PowerPoint for the course! I could not teach from someone else's PowerPoint. It would mainly be reading to the class what they were seeing on the screen. In one case I had several students in a class come to me to complain that the instructor was just reading the PowerPoints to them. They then told me the PowerPoints even had another university's letterhead! This instructor found an available PowerPoint online for a similar course at another university! Not teaching from PowerPoint would greatly enhance learning in classes without the need to invent new ways to incorporate active learning in classrooms.

Something related to our discussion of better learning by engaging more senses is the condition of synesthesia. An example is grapheme-color synesthesia where with every digit, or letter, a specific color is perceived. Someone with grapheme-color synesthesia would not perceive the following digits as black, but each would have a color

012345789

Synesthesia is probably caused by crosstalk between different sensory areas of the brain. The additional perceptions resulting from synesthesia can result in a greatly increased ability to remember.

There are many other types of synesthesia, of which I will mention a few. Chromesthesia is a type of synesthesia where sounds trigger a perception of color. For instance, when a musical note is played, a color is also perceived. Someone with spatial sequence synesthesia will associate points in space with ordinal sequences. Auditory-tactile synesthesia occurs when sounds cause sensations in parts of the body. Lexical-gustatory synesthesia occurs when hearing words will result in certain tastes.

An extreme example of someone with synesthesia was Soloman Shereshevsky. Shereshevsy was a newspaper reporter for a Moscow newspaper. During their daily assignment meetings, all the other reporters would take notes while Shereshevksy would just sit there. One day the editor confronted Shereshevksy about being lackadaisical. Shereshevksy explained he could remember everything, and proceeded to repeat everything that had been said, word for word. The editor then sent Shereshevsy to see Alexander Luria, a memory specialist he knew.

Alexander Luria was a neuropsychologist who performed behavior studies on Shereshevsky for 30 years and referred to him as S when he published to protect Shereshevsky's privacy. Luria determined that Shereshevsky had five-fold synesthesia [88]. When one of his senses was stimulated there was a resulting reaction in all his other senses. The result was Shereshevky's phenomenal memory. When Luria and Shereshevksy first met, Luria rattled off a list of random numbers and words that Shereshevksy repeated. Even 15 years later, when Luria asked Shereshevksy to repeat that initial list he could do it.

Synesthesia is not something we can develop; it is something we are born with. Only 2-4% of the population have synesthesia, and a much smaller percentage have multiple synesthesia, let alone five-fold as Shereshevksy. I think the reason learning improves when you involve more senses is because it is a way to produce an effect like synesthesia, which was the source of Shereshevksy's phenomenal memory.

Chapter 11: Sleep

This chapter on sleep, and chapters 14 on nutrition and chapter 15 on exercise, are on topics you might not expect to find in a book on learning. Sleep, nutrition, and exercise play important roles in the body's health. These activities are just as important, or even more so, for the health of the brain. The brain is only 2% of the body's weight yet utilizes 20-25% of the body's oxygen and energy supplies. Not only will our brains function better during our lifetimes with adequate sleep, nutrition, and exercise, these three will go a long way in preventing the age-related deterioration that results in diseases like Alzheimer's.

The Center for Disease Control stipulates a minimum of 7 hours of sleep each night. It is known that the day after going on daylight savings time (DST), when most people lose an hour of sleep, there is a 24% increase in heart attacks, whereas there is a 21% decrease in heart attacks in the Fall the day after going off DST, when most people get an extra hour of sleep. After going on DST there is an 8% increase in strokes the following two day, spikes in medical errors, workplace injuries, and suicides; there is a 6% increase in fatal car crashes the following week. There is also an increase in harshness of sentences handed down by judges right after going on DST.

Besides its role for the health of the brain and body, sleep plays many roles in the learning process. Sleep is often sacrificed for last-minute cramming for an exam. If the goal is to learn, we will see the loss of sleep is very detrimental to many aspects of learning. The percent of the population that can survive on less than 6 hours of sleep per night without showing any impairment is zero!

Some consequences of too little sleep are familiar. The crankiness that results from lack of sleep. With normal sleep, MRI scans show modest activity for the amygdala, a brain region involved in emotional responses especially fear and aggressive behavior, and a nice strong communication between the prefrontal cortex and the amygdala. The prefrontal cortex is where we exercise control over our responses and emotions, and hence control of the amygdala. With reduced sleep, MRI scans show a 60% increased activity in the amygdala and essentially a severing of communication between the prefrontal cortex and the amygdala.

When we are tired, there is an inability to function on mental tasks at a high level, or to adequately access our memories. It is not unusual for a student who has performed poorly on an exam to tell me they knew the material, but they just could not function when taking the exam because they had been up all-night studying.

When we are tired, we experience an impaired ability to learn. With Patient H.M. in chapter 3 we saw the hippocampus plays a necessary role in forming new long-term memories. MRI scans of those who have been sleep deprived show no significant activity in the hippocampus. For those who have had normal sleep the hippocampus is active. Lack of sleep shuts down our ability to form long-term memories, which is critical to the learning process.

David Dinges has studied how sleep deprivation affects concentration [89]. He measured the concentration of his subjects by having them press a button when a light appeared on a screen. Whether or not a response occurred, and how long after the light the response occurred, were recorded. The light occurred randomly, and the subject's performance was measured for ten minutes. The experiment started with all subjects getting eight hours of sleep the night before, and then their baseline responses were measured. The subjects were divided into four groups. The control group continued to get a full eight hours of sleep each night. The second group was kept up for 72 hours. The third group slept for four hours each night, and the fourth group slept for six hours each night, during the two-week study.

The control group maintained their initial baseline response performance during the two weeks of the study. The three sleep-deprived groups all showed slower response rates. But the sleep-deprived groups also occasionally failed to respond to a light. What was happening was a brief complete loss of concentration, something that is referred to as a microsleep. (Imagine driving a car on a highway and a microsleep occurring, a couple of seconds of complete loss of concentration, while driving 60 mph or more.)

The group without-sleep showed an escalation of these moments of lost concentration with each night of no sleep, which would probably have continued to increase each day if the study had not been stopped after 72 hours for these participants. For the group that was receiving four hours of sleep each night, after six nights their performance was comparable to those who had not slept for twenty-four hours. (Being awake for 22 hours you will be as cognitively impaired as someone who is legally drunk.) After eleven days of four hours a night of sleep, their performance was comparable to someone who had been awake for 48 hours! For the group receiving six hours a night of sleep, after eleven days their performance was comparable to someone who had stayed up all night.

After several days of less than eight hours of sleep your concentration, and obviously your ability to study, will be impaired. Dinges' study only lasted two weeks. The concentration impairment continued to worsen during the duration of this two-week study, and probably would have continued to deteriorate with continued reduction in sleep.

You may have had to go with reduced sleep because of your workload and feel that you have not experienced any impairment. That is exactly what Dinges found with his subjects. He had clear proof of the concentration impairment from lack of sleep, but when interviewing the subjects afterwards they were unaware of the extent of their impairment! Your suboptimum sleep each night to gain an extra hour or two of wake time is impairing your learning while awake. (We will soon see that there is much more you are losing with respect to your learning from reduced sleep.) While we are awake a chemical called adenosine continually increases in our brains. It is only during sleep when adenosine is removed. Getting reduced sleep each night results in starting with a higher and higher adenosine level each day. The higher concentrations of adenosine each day may be one reason continual lack of sleep results in greater and greater impairment. You cannot be efficient studying, let alone taking an exam, when you have had lack of adequate sleep.

There are two things that influence when we sleep, an internal rhythm and the chemical we just mentioned, adenosine, whose concentration builds in our brains while we are awake. Your circadian rhythm and the adenosine in your brain are independent influencers on when you sleep.

All living things, including plants have a circadian rhythm. Such rhythms were first discovered in a plant by Jean-Jacques d'Ortous de Mairan in 1729. Circadian rhythms in humans were discovered by Nathaniel Kleitman, and his graduate student Bruce Richardson, with an experiment requiring amazing fortitude in 1938 [90]. They descended deep into Mammoth cave, where they would be completely in the dark for 32 days. During this time, they monitored a host of functions such as their body temperature and naturally occurring sleep and wake periods. They found that humans have a natural rhythm, just like de Mairan's plant. Surprisingly, the rhythm was greater than 24 hours. For the younger Richardson the cycle was 26 hours, which was greater than for the older Kleitman whose cycle was a little more than 24 hours. Why our biological cycle is longer than 24 hours is unknown. The suprachiasmatic nucleus sits just above where the optic nerves cross in the brain so that it can sample the signals coming from your eyes. This sampling of light is a prime factor in resetting our slightly longer than 24-hour circadian rhythm so that it doesn't drift from the 24 hours of the day.

I know the length of my circadian rhythm has shortened as I have aged. In college I always found it difficult to get to sleep. I remember thinking I would function better with a 26-hour day! I always stayed up too late and then did not get adequate sleep. I was unaware of the Kleitman and Richardson study until a few years ago, but my younger circadian rhythm was in line with Richardson's and my older circadian rhythm is in line with Kleitman's!

This internal circadian rhythm originates in your brain in the suprachiasmatic nucleus. The suprachiasmatic nucleus communicates to the rest of the body with the chemical melatonin. After dusk, the suprachiasmatic nucleus instructs the pineal gland to release melatonin into your bloodstream signaling throughout your body that darkness has occurred. Melatonin does not generate sleep, but it signals to other brain regions it is time to initiate sleep. During sleep the concentration of melatonin falls and with light the suprachiasmatic nucleus signals the pineal gland to stop the release of melatonin.

Things that vary during the day with the circadian rhythm include blood pressure, body temperature, muscle strength, bowel movements, and when we sleep. This is illustrated in figure 11.1. A disproportionate number of Olympic records are set in the late afternoon, when muscle and cardiovascular strength are greatest caused by the circadian rhythm [91].

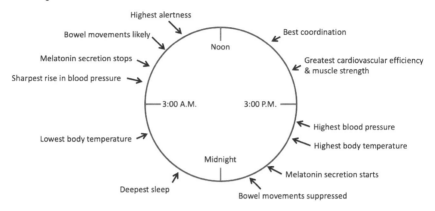

Figure 11.1 Circadian rhythm.

Everyone does not have exactly the circadian rhythm pictured in figure 11.1. Genetics play a role. About 40% of the population are morning types who prefer to wake at dawn and function optimally in the morning, morning larks. About 30% of the population are evening types who prefer to go to bed late and wake up later in the morning, night owls. The rest of the population is somewhere between morning and evening types. Because of the way society has set work and school schedules, morning types are at a distinct advantage. Since night types can't help that they cannot go to bed until later, and must get up earlier to match society's schedule, night types tend to obtain less sleep than morning types.

Chronotypes probably evolved as a survival technique. Humans are vulnerable when asleep. Hunter gatherers sleep as a collective. That means there is a decrease in hours of vulnerability from 8 down to 4 hours for hunter-gatherer societies, the type of society in which humans evolved.

As young children age into their teenage years, their chronotype shifts from morning to evening types. The result is less than 15% of teenagers get the sleep they need. Into late teens and early twenties, most want to go to bed between 11:00 p.m.–1:00 a.m. As we further age into adulthood are chronotype begins to shift back. Later, in our senior years our chronotype shifts back even more. (Why there are early bird specials!) I was an evening type when in college but have become a morning type as I have aged.

While you are awake, the concentration of a chemical called adenosine continuously builds up in your brain. This is the second influence, along with your circadian rhythm, that determines when you sleep. The concentration of adenosine in your brain is a measure of how long you have been awake. Adenosine causes that sleep pressure you feel that tired feeling. During sleep, adenosine is removed from your brain. Without adequate sleep, you cannot clear all the adenosine from your brain. If you are continually getting inadequate sleep, there is an increased concentration of adenosine in your brain each day resulting in chronic fatigue and subsequent health issues.

The way caffeine works to make you feel more awake is by outcompeting adenosine for the adenosine receptors in your brain. Caffeine does not change the amount of adenosine in your brain, nor does it stop the continual buildup of adenosine while you are awake.

During sleep you go through various stages. These stages can be identified by the frequencies of the electrical activity in the brain. In addition, there is one stage where there is rapid movement of the eyes behind the closed eyelids. This stage is referred to as REM for rapid eye movement. The various other stages are referred to as NREM, non-rapid eye movement, stages 1 through 3. There is eye movement during NREM stage 1, but it is at 1/10 the speed that occurs during REM sleep. It becomes increasingly more difficult to wake someone as they progress from REM to the various stages of NREM sleep. It is hardest to wake someone from NREM stage 3. Figure 11.2 shows typical electric activity, an electroencephalogram (EEG), versus time for the various stages of sleep. The various stages are characterized by the range of frequency components of their electrical activity. The frequency components of REM sleep are very similar to the frequency components when we are awake; it is difficult to distinguish an awake from a REM EEG scan. In a sleep clinic, besides an EEG, subjects eye movements, an electrooculogram (EOG), and their muscle tone, an electromyogram (EMG), are monitored to be sure the subject is in REM sleep and not awake. (You may see mentioned NREM sleep sages 1-4. In 2007 the American Academy of Sleep Medicine reclassified NREM stages 3 and 4 as a single stage. So, the current classification of sleep has four stages, NREM stages 1-3 and REM, the fourth stage.)

During NREM sleep neurons are firing in synch, on and off together, with low frequency. Also seen in figure 11.2 are sleep spindles, which are bursts of slightly higher frequency activity that occur during both light and deep NREM sleep. People with more frequent and stronger sleep spindles are sounder sleepers.

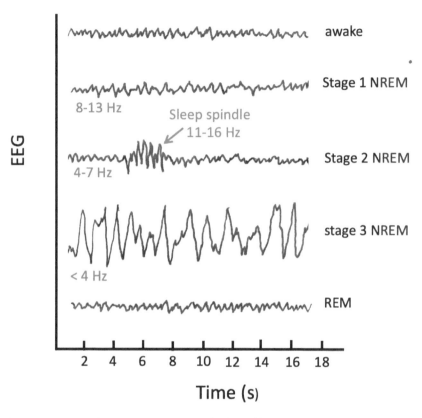

Figure 11.2 Brain wave patterns during different stages of sleep.

Shown in figure 11.3 are the stages that occur during a night's sleep. Figure 11.3 is known as a hypnogram, named after Hypnos the god of sleep in Greek mythology. When we sleep, we cycle with a cycle length of about 90 minutes, between stages of deep sleep and REM sleep. During the first four hours more time is spent in deep sleep than REM sleep and during the last four hours more time is spent in REM sleep than deep sleep. This means if you sleep for 6 hours, instead of 8 hours, you are reducing your sleep by 25%, but you will be reducing your REM sleep by 60% or more. If you wake someone during REM sleep, 95% of the time they will tell you that they had been dreaming. We also dream during non-REM sleep but not as vividly and it is difficult to recall any details.

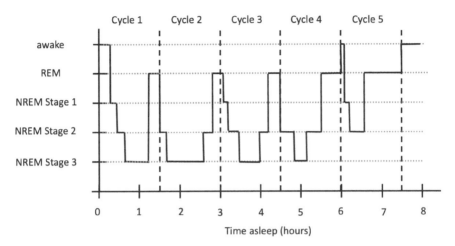

Figure 11.3 Typical sleep pattern.

REM sleep, and the cycle nature of sleep between REM and NREM, was discovered by Eugene Aserinsky and Nathaniel Kleitman [92]. Aserinsky wrote an interesting account of these discoveries [93]. Aserinky originally observed REM sleep with his eight-year-old son. He subsequently conducted experiments on 20 adults observing REM sleep and the brain wave electrical activity that occurred during REM sleep. By waking individuals at various stages of sleep, Aserinsky found that dreaming was occurring during REM sleep.

Kleitman's next graduate student, William Dement, further investigated when we are dreaming. By waking individuals at various stages of sleep, Dement discovered that during NREM sleep we are dreaming 7% of the time and during REM sleep we are dreaming 80% of the time [94]. More than 90% of our dreaming occurs during REM sleep.

There is no accepted definition of what is dreaming. In studies, the definition of dreaming varies from the vivid imagery we usually think of when we think of dreaming to recall of any mental activity when we are awakened. If the definition of dreaming is recall of any mental activity than the estimates of dreaming during NREM sleep is much higher [95] than the Dement study. About 10% of adults will claim that they do not dream. If they are brought into a sleep clinic, and awakened during REM sleep, they will be surprised to tell you that they were dreaming! Those 10% dream, they just don't remember that they dream. We don't remember most of our dreams, and probably only remember the most recent dream when we awaken. Even this most recent dream will be forgotten, unless the dream is unusually remarkable, or we actively think about it.

Dreaming is different during REM and NREM sleep. During REM sleep the release of the neurotransmitter serotonin is completely blocked. The way the drug lysergic acid diethylamide (LSD) works is by blocking the release of serotonin. It may be this blocking of serotonin release during REM sleep that results in the vivid, sometimes strange and bizarre, dreams we have that do not occur during NREM sleep. (There is a reduction in serotonin release during NREM sleep but not the total cessation as there is during REM sleep.)

Another difference between REM and NREM dreaming is that during REM sleep our bodies are completely paralyzed. This prevents us from acting out our REM dreams. There is no such paralysis during NREM sleep. Since we do not act out our NREM dreams, the motor cortex in our brains is not activated during NREM dreaming as it is during REM dreaming.

We will see that much learning occurs during sleep. Different types of learning occur during different sleep stages; sleep stages probably evolved to facilitate these different types of learning. Putting facts into long-term memory; consolidating procedures when we are learning to type or ride a bike; categorizing; deeper understanding; connecting between different mental models; solving difficult problems; and creating are some of the things that occur during different stages of sleep.

Deep NREM sleep is when long-term memories are established. Studies have shown the more deep NREM sleep during the evening, the more the subjects recalled the next day. Researchers could predict with high degree of accuracy a subject's recall of material studied based on the amount of non-REM deep sleep that subsequently occurred while the subject slept.

A direct observation of sleep resulting in formation of long-term memories has been observed utilizing MRI [91] [96] [97]. After participants had studied some material, and before they slept, they were placed in an MRI and tested on the material they studied. The region of the brain where most activity was happening was the hippocampus.

Performing the same test in the MRI the next day, after the participants had a full night of sleep, the neocortex was where the activity was observed and not the hippocampus. When we study, material is stored in the hippocampus. During deep NREM sleep the material is transferred from short-term storage in the hippocampus to long-term storage in the neocortex. Just as important, there is an erasure of the material in the hippocampus. This fits nicely with what we have seen with spaced learning. The spacing increases the number of nights of sleep and LTP that occurs, thereby increasing both the storage and retrieval strength of material you transfer to long-term memory.

Studies have shown that without sleep, there is a limit to what can be stored in the hippocampus [98]. As we learn, the hippocampus fills up and we cannot store anymore, or some overwriting of material can occur, which is called interference forgetting. The amount of erasure of material in the hippocampus during sleep, which frees up space for new learning, correlates with the amount of sleep spindles that occur during stage 2 NREM sleep. The amount of new material people could learn the next day correlated with the amount of sleep spindles occurring the night before.

Students often wait until the last minute to study for an upcoming exam, which is referred to as cramming and pulling all-nighters. Cramming, such as pulling all-nighters, is a very poor way to learn. Even if the motivation is grades, it is the learning that will get you those grades. Sleep is important, not only to be able to concentrate when taking an exam, but for transferring material to long-term memory locations in the brain and emptying the hippocampus so more material can be learned. Patient H.M., who we met in chapter 3, could not form new long-term memories because he had had part of his hippocampus removed. Patient H.M. didn't have that temporary storage space to hold new memories until sleep could move them to long-term storage locations in his neocortex.

The occurrence of sleep spindles increases during the latter part of sleep. Sleeping six hours instead of eight hours will disproportionately reduce the amount of sleep spindles you get and the subsequent amount your hippocampus is restored for learning the next day. This makes sense because you do not want to erase the material in the hippocampus until it has been written into long-term memory during the deep NREM sleep earlier in the night.

Another fascinating aspect of this long-term memory formation is that not everything in your hippocampus is moved to long-term memory. We code the material in the hippocampus as to its importance to remember [99]. Important material is transferred to long-term memory while unimportant material is not. One experiment that illustrates this was one performed by Saletin et al. [99]. Their research subjects memorized a list of words presented one-by-one on a computer screen. Following each word, either a large green R for remember, or a large red F for forget were displayed. Half of the participants took a 90-minute nap and half stayed awake. Both groups were tested on how many words they could recall and told to try to remember irrespective of the R or F that followed each word. The awake group recalled both sets of words equally. The sleep group had an enhanced recall of the words followed by the R and a suppressed recall of the words followed by the F. Furthermore, the more sleep spindles during a nap, the greater the efficiency with which they strengthened items designated for remembering and actively eliminated those designated for forgetting. I'm sure you have experienced better memory for things you are interested in, compared to things you are not interested in. You essentially are coding some things for remembering and some things for forgetting.

Figure 11.4 illustrates this memory process. While awake you are putting information into your hippocampus. This may be things you want to remember, what you are studying, and things you won't need to remember such as where you parked your car when you went to the grocery. During your initial deep sleep stages, the information coded as important in your hippocampus is transferred to long-term memory in your neocortex. In the last part of sleep, your hippocampus is erased to provide space for learning the next day.

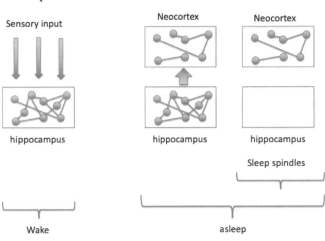

Figure 11.4 Illustration of forming long-term memories.

Besides formation of memories, during sleep the brain works to process and integrate what you learned the previous day with your existing mental models; sleep builds that latticework of mental models and forms a deeper understanding. After sleep, you can solve more complex problems than before. This is another reason why spacing your studying is so important, to give you more sleep episodes. This integration occurs during REM sleep, when you do much dreaming. The role of dreaming may be to make non-obvious connections between distance models in your brain. Earlier we learned that during REM sleep the neurotransmitter serotonin is blocked. In addition, the neurotransmitter noradrenaline is shut off during REM sleep. Noradrenaline plays a role in focusing our attention. The lack of noradrenaline during REM sleep allows the mind to wander and find these weak associations between mental models.

Brain waves during REM sleep, and while you are awake, are very similar. It is difficult, or even impossible, to tell whether a person is in REM sleep, or awake, from brain scans. However, MRI scans reveal differences between the awake and dreaming brain. The visual cortex, motor cortex, memory, and emotional areas are 30% more active during REM sleep, while the logical, rational, and reasoning areas of the prefrontal cortex shut down.

While awake, the brain is processing what is going on in the outside world. During REM sleep the brain is processing information learned the previous day and integrating it with things you already know. You are going over what you learned the previous day during sleep resulting in LTP. Incubation is occurring, a topic we discussed in chapter 6. Let's look at some studies that illustrate this deeper understanding that occurs during REM sleep.

Scullin et al. took a group of 102 undergraduate who had never studied economics and split them into two groups [100]. The first group watched a virtual lecture in the morning and 12 hours later took an exam on the material. This was the wake group. The second group watched a virtual lecture in the evening and 12 hours later, after having a full night's sleep, took the same exam as the wake group. This was the sleep group. On problems like the lecture material, which just required recall, the sleep group performed 8% points better than the wake group. Probably almost equivalent to a letter grade. Even more interesting, on novel problems, where an application of the material studied was required, the sleep group performed 32 percentage points better than the wake group. It has been found this deeper learning is correlated with the amount of REM sleep obtained the night before.

Another sleep example was a study by Wagner et al. [101]. The participants were taught how to solve a mathematical problem using a tedious method. They were not told of another, much simpler and quicker approach. There was a wake group, that studied in the morning and took an exam 12 hours later, and a sleep group, that studied in the evening and took the exam 12 hours later after a night of sleep.

It was found that 23% of the wake group discovered the simpler approach while 59% of the sleep group discovered the simpler approach. This indicates a deeper understanding of the concept behind solving these problems after a night of sleep. It is likely that during REM sleep connections are made between the different mental models in our heads. REM sleep is when we build our understanding of the outside world and is when creativity, innovation, and solving complex problems can take place.

We already encountered this role that sleep plays in problem solving and creativity in chapter 6 on incubation. Several anecdotes of artists' and scientists' creativity during sleep were presented. Let me present one more. During a troubling time in his life, Paul McCartney saw his mother in a dream, and she told him, "Let it Be." His mother's name was Mary. Hence the title of the song, "Let It Be" and the line in the song, "When I find myself in times of trouble, Mother Mary comes to me, Speaking words of wisdom, Let it be." College students will recognize this as the song played over the speakers during a football game, when a ruling on the field favorable to the home team is under review.

I had written part of the previous paragraph, but I was not happy with the wording. At 4:00 a.m. I woke and thought about the paragraph. I grabbed my iPhone and, in my sleepiness, dictated the wording to most of the paragraph. After learning how different our mind functions when asleep, (less focused and looking for connections no matter how weak between things we know), I often take advantage. If I stir and slightly awaken during the night, I think of something on which I have been working. Often, I will come up with a connection I would have never thought of when awake and more focused, or a better way of wording something.

Another study illustrated that even naps are beneficial for learning [102]. Participants studied a topic in the morning. It didn't matter if the topic was memorizing words, pattern recognition games, or material that contained deeper structure. One group took an hour-long nap, and the other group did not. The group that had an hour-long nap did 30% better on a test that was administered that evening. Studies of hunter-gatherer cultures have observed a biphasic sleep pattern, 7-8 hours in bed during the night and a nap of 30-60 minutes during the day. Maybe humans evolved to benefit from a biphasic sleep pattern, as the study of the benefit of napping for learning showed.

Alcohol is a sedative. After drinking, you mistake the resulting sedation with sleeping. Alcohol results in sleep fragmentation. You will wake many times during the night but not remember because the awakenings are brief. Alcohol is the greatest known suppressor of REM sleep [91]. What is the result on learning of suppressing REM sleep with alcohol? Probably a loss of that deeper understanding of the material you have studied that you would get with your normal amount of REM sleep.

This effect on learning of the reduction in REM sleep because of alcohol consumption was demonstrated by Smith and Smith [103]. The subjects were taught how to solve Wff'n'Proof logic tasks [104], which took about 50 minutes. The control group would not consume any alcohol during the eight days of the study. There were two groups that would consume 0.7g of alcohol per kg of body weight on just one day of the eight-day study. The group referred to as alcohol night 1 (ALN1) drank alcohol the same day they learned Wff'n'Proof logic. The group referred to as alcohol night 3 (ALN3) drank alcohol on day three after having learned Wff'n'Proof logic on day one. All three groups had about an 85% proficiency the day they learned Wff'n'Proof logic. Retesting occurred on the eighth day. The control groups efficiency was a little higher around 90%, which was probably within experimental error and the expected improved understanding with sleep. ALN1's proficiency had fallen to about 45% and ALN3's proficiency had fallen to about 55%. So, alcohol is very detrimental to the learning process even when consumed two days after the learning event.

The brain utilizes 20-25% of the oxygen we breath to burn 20-25% of our body's energy source of glucose. Burning fuel results in waste products. As we are awake, our brains are intensely active producing large amounts of metabolic waste products that build in our brain. It is during sleep that these waste products are purged, which wasn't discovered until 2012 [105]. This process of clearing metabolic waste products from the brain was named the glymphatic system, which functions for the brain like the lymphatic system functions for the body. When we sleep our brain cells shrink. This allows the CSF to flow in the spaces around arteries in the brain flushing out the metabolic waste products from between the brain cells. There is recent evidence the CSF drains into the dural venus sinuses to get into the lymphatic system [106] [107]. It is not hard to imagine that for our brain to function optimally during the day, we need a thorough removal of these metabolic contaminants from our brains. We need adequate sleep for this to happen.

One of the metabolic contaminants that is removed by the glymphatic system are amyloid proteins. One sign of Alzheimer's disease is a build-up of amyloid proteins that kill surrounding neurons. Epidemiological studies have confirmed a link between not getting enough sleep and the onset of Alzheimer's disease [108] [109]. Lack of sleep is just one risk factor for Alzheimer's disease, as we will see in the chapters on exercise and nutrition.

Although there is some purging of metabolic waste while awake, the rate of waste removal is 10-20 times greater during sleep [110]. This is why sleep deprivation is so dangerous. It results in brain damage and can possibly lead to Alzheimer's disease. Total sleep deprivation will eventually result in death. Brain damage and death are the reasons the Guinness Book of World Records no longer recognizes attempts to break the sleep deprivation world record. Subjecting rats to total sleep deprivation, Everson et al. [111] found they all died in 11 to 32 days.

There is a rare, fortunately, genetic disorder called Fatal Familial Insomnia, which usually begins around age 50, but has been diagnosed as early as age 21 and as late as the early 70s. It usually starts with a mild inability to sleep but progressively worsens. This inability to sleep is eventually fatal and there is no cure.

In chapter 2, we saw that surgical residents learned microsurgery better when the lessons were spaced. One factor is the role that sleep plays in developing motor skill memories, such as those used in surgery, playing a sport or musical instrument, typing, etc. Brain scans show that after sleep the motor memories are transferred to brain regions that are below consciousness [91]. In chapter 2, we saw that patient H.M. could still form long-term procedural memories without his hippocampus. It is not the hippocampus playing a role in procedural memories, but other brain regions. During sleep these muscle memories are placed in long-term memory. It is after this placement that you don't have to think about performing the muscle movement; the muscle movements become automatic. When you are learning to type on a keyboard, it is after sleep that you don't have to think when you see a t that it is hit with your left index finger. Instead, the movement becomes automatic. When the movements become automatic, your typing is smoother, faster, and less prone to error.

In 2000, after presenting a lecture on sleep to a general audience, Matthew Walker was approached by a gentleman who was a pianist. The pianist mentioned he often struggled with the fingering of parts of a new piece but found the next day he could play those parts flawlessly. The pianist inquired if sleep was involved. At the time it was not known if the pianist's observation was indeed caused by sleep, but it inspired Walker to investigate. Walker and Strickgold [112] had right-handed individuals learn a sequence of keystrokes with their left hands. They had the subjects continuously practice the sequence of keystrokes for 12 minutes. They were tested 12 hours later. As you can probably guess by now there were two groups. One that did not sleep and one that did. The awake group showed no improvement. The sleep group improved their speed by 20% and accuracy by 35%!

Walker and Strickgold [112] found that these automatic muscle memories are made during stage 2 NREM sleep, especially during the last two hours of sleep. Reducing your sleep by 25% and getting 6 hours, instead of 8 hours of sleep will eliminate most of your ability to commit the previous day's procedural learning to unconscious memory. Furthermore, Walker and Strickgold found that the more sleep spindles during stage 2 NREM sleep the more of the muscle movement was placed in unconscious memory.

Louie and Wilson have observed electrical activity in brains of sleeping rats that corresponded to electrical activity when the rats were awake and running a maze [113]. Microelectrode arrays were implanted into the hippocampi of four rats. The rats were then trained to run a circular maze and the electrical activity recorded when the rats were running the maze. The electrical activity of a rat running a maze is different than the electrical activity when a rat runs a different maze, or doing something besides running a maze. From the electrical activity, the researchers could tell where in the maze a rat was. The same electrical pattern exhibited by the rats when running the maze was also observed when the rats were sleeping! The rats were recalling the running of the maze. These patterns occurred during both deep sleep and during REM sleep. Maybe the activity during deep sleep corresponded to formation of long-term memories, and during REM sleep to building a deeper understanding of running the maze.

It appears that the formation of procedural memories in humans follows a similar process as seen with rats learning to run a maze. Regional cerebral blood flow measurements can be used to indicate hippocampal areas that are activated. This was done on the hippocampal regions of humans that were learning routes in a virtual town [114]. The same activity while awake and studying routes in the virtual town was observed during deep sleep. In confirmation with our earlier discussion, the greater the amount of such activity during deep sleep the better the performance in route retrieval the next day.

Several studies have been performed by Wamsley and colleagues on the effect of sleep on navigating a virtual maze. In the first study, the subjects were trained to navigate the virtual maze. There was a five-hour interval before testing. One group stayed awake, and the other group took a 90-minute nap. The awake group's performance navigating the maze improved by 25.6 seconds while the nap group's performance improved by 188 seconds [115].

In a follow up study, Wamsley et al. [116] showed an association with dreaming and improvement in times to navigate the virtual maze. The procedure was the same, five hours between learning and testing with one group awake and the other taking a 90-minute nap. The exception was that three times during the nap the subjects were awakened and asked if they had been dreaming, and what they had been dreaming about. Those who reported dreams that involved the maze improved their time navigating the maze by 91 seconds compared to only a 10 second improvement for those who did not dream about the maze.

Wamsley and Stickgold [117] have also looked at the effect of a full night of sleep on performance navigating the virtual maze. They found an association with dreaming of the task during all stages of sleep with improved navigation performance the next morning. Dreams may not be what is causing the mental processing to better understand and navigate the maze, dreams may just be a side effect of this mental processing.

Thomas Edison claimed he only slept 4-5 hours each night. Yet he did take advantage of the benefits of sleep for creativity with what he called his "genius" naps. Edison would sit in a chair with armrests and a pen and pad of paper next to him. He would have upside-down steel pans on the floor. He would sit with his arms on the rests with palms up and a steel ball bearing in each palm. After he was asleep, eventually the ball bearing would fall hitting the steel pan and waking Edison up. Edison would then write whatever he was dreaming about on his pad of paper.

In this chapter I was only able to touch on some of the various aspects, and importance, of sleep. To delve deeper into sleep, a superb book is *Why We Sleep* by Matthew Walker [91].

Chapter 12: Mindset

When Drew Brees set the record for most passing yardage in a career, the game was stopped for a brief ceremony. Drew went to the sidelines, where his family was, kneeled and told his children, "You can accomplish anything in life if you are willing to work for it." In an interview after the game Drew was asked "Do you remember what you said to them?" Drew responded, "It's probably what I tell them every night before they go to bed." Drew has what is called a growth mindset, and he knows it is important to instill a growth mindset in his children.

Do you believe intelligence is fixed or something you can develop? How you answer this question will tell what type of mindset you have. Carol Dweck, a professor at Stanford University, has been studying the mindset psychological trait and refers to two mindsets, fixed (entity theory) and growth (incremental theory) [118].

People with a fixed mindset believe that your level of intelligence and creativity cannot be changed. Putting effort into developing intelligence or creativity is a waste of time. A person with a fixed mindset, who is having difficulty with a subject, will not utilize a tutor as that will be perceived as not being smart. They are more concerned with proving their abilities. This causes them to give up early when they encounter difficulties. Fixed mindset people will self-sabotage. They will not sign up for a difficult class, even if it is something they are very interested in, because they are afraid of not doing well and appearing less intelligence. They will look for "easy" classes, so that they can get a good grade. They will do things that give them an excuse for performing poorly, such as partying instead of studying, so the reason they did poorly is not their intelligence. They are more concerned about the grade than learning.

People with the growth mindset believe that you can increase your level of intelligence and creativity. They are concerned with improving. Putting in effort is how you get more intelligent. Difficulties and hard classes are opportunities to learn a subject you are interested in. Growth mindset people will ask for help. It is not that those with a growth mindset don't believe that people have different native abilities. It is that they believe native abilities are dwarfed by effort. Your true potential is unknown, and only with time and effort can you see what you can achieve.

In chapter 17, I will talk about something I do in my classes that I call "concept point recovery (CPR)." It is an opportunity for students to look back at an exam they just took and recover some lost points. When they come in to recover points, I often have students tell me they don't look back to see what they did wrong on an exam; this would show them their flaws. This is the fixed mindset speaking. With a growth mindset you want to use a past test to discover what you did not know so that you can learn from it. After their first CPR session, these fixed mindset students often tell me how useful the CPR exercise was. They learned something they had not before. Hopefully this CPR experience helps to move them to a growth mindset.

Which mindset are you? Do you find it fun to undertake difficult tasks? To undertake things that will challenge you. Or do you avoid difficult tasks because you don't want to show weakness? Fortunately, it is easy to move from a fixed to a growth mindset, as we will see from some of the studies in this chapter.

Intelligent quotient (IQ) is a score obtained from a standardized test. The score is supposed to indicate human intelligence. The first IQ tests were developed by Alfred Binet [119]. Binet did not design his tests to measure intelligence, but to identify students who were not benefiting from the current educational system and in need of alternative education. Binet thought these types of tests were inadequate measures of intelligence.

IQ tests are designed so that the average score is 100 and the standard deviation is 15. A standard deviation of 15 means that the percentage of the population that scores 115 or greater is 15.9%. In 1984, James Flynn discovered that IQ test scores had increased by 15 points over the last 50 years [120]. In other words, if you took an IQ test from 1984 and scored a 100, your score on an IQ test from 1934 would be 115. If you could be transported back in time 50 years you would move from having average intelligence to being in the top 15.9% of the population in intelligence. This is known as the Flynn effect. The Flynn effect is believed due to a combination of factors. Health care and nutrition improved and became more accessible. People not only spent more and more time in school, but education changed. In grade school there was less rote memorization and more logical thought. People had to interact with a more and more complex world. Jobs kept becoming more cognitively demanding. All these things produce changes in the brain that make people more intelligence. More intelligent by one standard deviation, as measured by IQ tests, from 1934 to 1984. Intelligence can change. The point is your environment can change your level of intelligence indicating the correct mindset is the growth mindset.

This relates to the brain being remarkably plastic as we discussed earlier. Believing the mind can grow and change at any age is critical to instill the growth mindset. Neurons are born every day in the hippocampus and with use, exercise, and proper nutrition can grow and connect to other neurons. Exercise can result in formation of blood vessels, angiogenesis, to carry oxygen and energy sources to the brain. As we learn, dendrites grow and sprout and new synapses (synaptogenesis), the connection between neurons, occurs. As your neurons fire the existing connections (synapses) between neurons strengthen. Reading this book results in changes occurring in your brain! In people who have become blind, the brain rewires so that areas that were used for processing sight are now used to process sound or touch [15].

Some of these changes in the brain can be seen using magnetic resonance imaging (MRI). Woodlett and Maguire [121] conducted a study of subjects who were studying to be London taxi drivers. To obtain a license to drive a taxi in London, a test must be passed referred to as "the Knowledge." This test requires knowing the 25,000 irregular streets of London, most efficient routes between points, and locations of landmarks. It typically takes 3-4 years of study to pass the test. Previous MRI studies of London taxi drivers found they had more gray matter volume to their posterior hippocampi than non-taxi driving control participants [122].

The Woodlett and Maguire study was longitudinal [121], taking MRI scans of participants before and after studying for the test of the Knowledge. There were 79 trainees who were studying for the test and additional control participants who were not. Of the 79 trainees some would pass, and some would not pass, the Knowledge. So, there would be three groups, trainees who passed the test, trainees who did not pass the test or dropped out, and the control group.

39 of the trainees passed the test and 40 did not. Only 20 of the 40 who did not qualify would come back for post-study MRIs. The 39 trainees who passed the test showed significant increase in the volume of their posterior hippocampi after the 4 years of studying for the

Knowledge. The trainees who did not qualify, and the control group, showed no discernable change in their hippocampi. The Woodlett and Maguire study found direct visible evidence of growth of part of the adult human brain, the hippocampi that plays a major role in acquisition of long-term memory. Woodlett and Maguire had clear evidence that studying resulted in extra neurons and brain tissue in the posterior hippocampi! It is probable that the 40 of the original 79 who did not pass, or quit studying for, the Knowledge were not gritty enough; it wasn't because they were not capable. The implication is that with grit, and purposeful practice, anyone could grow their posterior hippocampi and become London taxi drivers. I suspect with enough grit, and knowing the appropriate approaches to practice, you can develop your brain to become whatever you want—engineer, surgeon, professor, novelist, etc.

Learning is a result of a growth mindset. Fortunately, it is not difficult to change your mindset. You do need to believe your brain can change and you can become more intelligent. People can be encouraged into a specific mindset. Praising someone's ability, or intelligence, will place them in a fixed mindset. They will think achievements are a result of innate talent. Praising someone's effort will place them in a growth mindset. They will think accomplishments and performance are a result of effort. Let us look at some studies that show what can result from developing a growth mindset.

The first study we will look at is work of Mueller and Dweck [123]. Mueller and Dweck did this study six times with different groups of fifth graders because they wanted to be sure of what they had observed. In their sixth study, their participants consisted of a diverse group of 48 fifth graders, 23 girls and 25 boys. Of these 84% were Caucasian, 8% were African American, and 8% were Hispanic. The children were given 10 moderately difficult problems from a non-verbal IQ test. The average number of questions answered correctly was 4.92. No matter what their score, all children were told they did well, scoring 80%.

The students were split into three groups. One group was praised for their intelligence, one group was praised for their effort, and one group received non-specific praise. The intention was to place one group in a fixed mindset, one group in a growth mindset, and the third group was the control group. The praise did have an observable effect on the students' mindsets. Children who were praised for their intelligence showed more interest in performance goals rather than learning goals.

Student praised for their effort showed more interest in learning goals rather than performance goals.

The three groups were then given 10 problems to work that were much more difficult than the first set of 10. No matter what their score, all children were told they did poorly, scoring below 50%. This second set of 10 problems was meant to give the children a sense of failure to see how they would respond. The groups were now given 10 problems of difficulty like the first set of 10 problems.

Children in the control group answered an average of 4.94 questions correctly. There was essentially no change for the control group. Children in the group praised for their intelligence answered an average of 4.38 questions correctly. Children in the group praised for their effort answered an average of 6.81 questions correctly. The group placed in a fixed mindset answered almost 2.5 fewer questions correct out-of-ten than the group that was put into a growth mindset. These were questions from an IQ test. A slight praise intervention put one group of children in a fixed mindset, slightly lowering their math IQ, while putting another group of children in a growth mindset, significantly increasing their math IQ. As mentioned, Mueller and Dweck repeated this experiment six times to be sure this striking result was real. Putting one group of children in a growth mindset and another group in a fixed mindset led to a 55% better performance on essentially a math IQ test for the growth mindset children compared to the fixed mindset children!

There was one additional interesting, or maybe troubling, observation. The children were told this study was going to be repeated with another set of students. They were asked to write a note to these children about their experience and to indicate their score. For the ability praised children, the group put in the fixed mindset, 40% lied about their scores and always in the same direction, higher! By praising students for their abilities, the researchers essentially turned 40% of them into liars.

Why did the fixed mindset children lie about their test scores? Because those scores reflected their intelligence, which they believe cannot change. They lied to appear more intelligent. Fixed mindset people are concerned with showing, not acquiring, abilities. Growth mindset children know their test score reflects their current math abilities and with effort they can improve.

Another study, by Eccles et. al. [124], also shows how a simple mindset intervention can have dramatic results. Entering seventh graders were divided into a control group and an intervention group. The control group had six sessions on study skills. The intervention group had six sessions, some on study skills like the control group, and some on mindset. The goal was to put the intervention group into a growth mindset.

Shown in table 12.1 are the average math grade point averages at the beginning (math GPA in sixth grade) and end of the study (math GPA in seventh grade). A few simple sessions on mindset resulted in the intervention group raising their math GPA while the control's group math GPA declined, resulting in a 0.31 higher average math GPA for the intervention group.

Table 12.1 Average Math GPA at end of 6th and end of 7th grade.

	End of 6th grade	**End of 7th Grade**
Control group	2.52	2.37
Growth mindset group	2.54	2.68

Another study by Grant and Dweck [125] shows how mindset affects the approach to learning and subsequent results. The study involved students taking a premed chemistry class at Columbia University. The students who take this course have a goal, one that many taking this premed chemistry course have been pursuing for a long time, to become medical doctors. The average grade in this class is a C+. The students taking this class have mainly achieved A's in previous classes. The participants were asked questions to determine their mindsets. Questions such as "Do you believe your intelligence is fixed or something you could develop?"

Those with a fixed mindset tended to do poorly. When interviewed, they indicated they studied by rereading the text and notes and trying to memorize how to solve problems. Techniques we know are poor for learning. Those with a growth mindset tended to do very well. When interviewed, they indicated they looked for themes and underlying principles. They were studying to learn, not to ace an exam; they usually did both.

Your character will reflect your mindset. With a fixed mindset nothing can be your fault. It is not uncommon for the fixed mindset to take credit for the work of others', or to lie to protect their greatness. We already saw how the children put into a fixed mindset lied about how many math questions they answered correctly. Since it is a public stage, examples abound in the sports world of poor sportsmanship because of a fixed mindset. John McEnroe's temper tantrums on the tennis court. Bobby Knight throwing a chair across the court when an opposing player is shooting a free throw because of Knight receiving a technical foul.

An example of someone with a growth mindset, displaying the highest of character, is Warren Buffett, the 92-year-old CEO and chairman of Berkshire Hathaway. Buffet is the greatest investor of all-time, yet he is extremely humble. Buffett was not good at, and had a fear of, public speaking. As evidence of his growth mindset, when in graduate school Buffett spent $100 to take a Dale Carnegie public speaking course. He knew it would serve him well to become a better public speaker. Buffett often speaks of his "circle of competence" when it comes to companies he invests in. He doesn't claim to be an expert on all industries and says, "Know your circle of competence, and stick within it. The size of that circle is not very important; knowing its boundaries, however, is vital." Berkshire Hathaway has purchased about 65 complete companies. He buys companies that have great management and insists they stay on and run the companies with little, or no, interference from him, a sign of someone with a growth mindset and character. Buffett's salary for running Berkshire Hathaway is $100,000 a year. His incentive is aligned with his shareholders, the performance of Berkshire Hathaway stock. Buffett often speaks of using the newspaper test to evaluate actions, "If an unfriendly reporter wrote about something he did, would he be ok with it?" He further says, "It takes 20 years to build a reputation and five minutes to ruin it."

I am sure you have encountered successful people with a fixed mindset. Or maybe you feel you have been successful so far with a fixed mindset. Eventually fixed mindset people will get to a level where it will require hard work and being able to deal with setbacks, where a growth mindset is required. Whether this happens in grade school, junior high school, high school, college, or beyond, it will happen; when you encounter setbacks, and need to work hard, you will be better able to handle it if you have already switched to a growth mindset.

"You can accomplish anything in life if you are willing to work for it," Drew Brees.

Chapter 13: Self-Control and Grit

"Never put off till tomorrow what you can do the day after tomorrow," Mark Twain. We are probably all guilty of procrastinating at times. The more self-control we have the less we will procrastinate. It takes energy to use your brain, no different than physical exercise, such as going out for a jog. It takes self-discipline, which is effortful, to not procrastinate. It takes grit to put in the sustained effort to space and interleave your studying. That does not mean learning cannot be enjoyable, just like people who routinely jog can enjoy that activity. (I exercise almost every day, as I will discuss in chapter 15, and it is something I find pleasure doing even though it is effortful.)

I have observed that most students use mass study, whether it is doing a homework assignment that they have known about for a week, preparing for an exam that they knew the date of the first day of class, or completing a project. Even though their intuition may be that mass study is better, because they haven't read this book, I suspect they do the mass study because of procrastination. (I do spend a few minutes in class early in the semester singing the praises of spaced study, but most students still wait until near a due date to get started.)

Self-discipline is the ability to resist a momentary diversion. You have an upcoming exam; you know you need to study. Some friends come by and ask you to go out with them. Self-control is that ability to resist this momentary temptation and tell your friends no. Grit is the ability to sustain an effort for months, years, maybe even decades to accomplish a goal. Grit is having passion and the perseverance to achieve a goal. **It takes both self-control and grit to become an expert at something whether that is being an engineer, physician, novelist, chess master, or virtuoso violinist**. In the last chapter on mindset, we learned with effort we can greatly develop our abilities. I hope to further convince you in this chapter that self-control and grit are more important than your innate talents in what success you will have, and that you can develop your self-control and grit. When we see someone who is very good at something—a Nobel prize winning scientist, a best-selling novelist, an athlete, a musician—we have a subconscious bias to attribute it to talent, that they are a natural. We have a range of innate abilities, but what we end up accomplishing has more to do with the effort we put in, and our ability to not quit when we run into difficulties; the amount of grit we have. Talent is an attribute we assign after the fact. When someone is a concert pianist, we attribute that to talent and ignore the decades of practice it took to get to that point. Maybe attributing others' achievements to talent is an excuse for us to avoid hard work, because the work is a waste of time, because we don't have the talent.

There is a famous study that was done at Stanford in Professor Walter Mischel's research group referred to as "The Marshmallow Test" [126]. The subjects were preschool children in a Stanford University nursery school. A child would be brought into a room that contained a table, chair, and a marshmallow on a plate on the table. (The children could choose the treat they wanted from an assortment that included marshmallows.) The child sat and the researcher told her that she could eat the marshmallow anytime. But if she could wait 20 minutes, until the researcher came back into the room, she could then have two marshmallows. The researcher left the room, and the child was observed through a one-way window.

Some children did not wait but quickly ate the marshmallow. Others tried to resist by covering their eyes, looking all around the room but not at the marshmallow, sitting on their hands, distracting themselves by singing, or talking to themselves. Of the 600 children who took part in the study, only 1/3 were able to wait the full 20 minutes to get their two treats.

The purpose of the Marshmallow Test was to learn what children would do to delay gratification. It proved to have much greater implications regarding self-control and predicting success in life. In a follow up study, when the children were seniors in high school, there was a direct correlation between SAT scores and their ability to wait as preschoolers [127]. Children who were in the top third of waiting scored 210 points higher on the SAT than students in the bottom third of waiting. Questionnaires to parents and teachers of these children indicate the children who waited longer were rated more intelligent, had more self-control and confidence, worked better under pressure, and were more goal oriented.

A decade later it was found that those who waited longer had achieved higher levels of education. When the children were in their mid-forties a follow up study of brain activity was performed using fMRI [128]. Those who waited longer as children showed more activity in their pre-frontal cortex, the region of the brain used in problem solving and self-control. In those who had had lower wait times, there was more activity in the ventral striatum region of the brain, an area involved in emotional responses of desire, pleasure, and addiction.

Although there were strong correlations between how long a child could wait for the second marshmallow and subsequent "success" in life, it does not mean if a child could not wait for the second marshmallow, they could not be successful. Self-control is a personality trait and can change. Also, context matters. A child may not have self-control to wait for a marshmallow, but they may when it comes to something they have a passion for, such as piano or science.

Mischel and his graduate students found they could control how long a child would wait for their treat reward, from seconds to the full 20 minutes, by priming the children's thought process. Telling the children to think how good the marshmallow is going to taste resulted in them not being able to wait. Telling the child to think distracting thoughts, such as thinking of the marshmallow as a puffy cloud instead of a treat, greatly increased the time a child could resist the treat. This is an important takeaway. Self-control, and self-control strategies, are things we can develop.

Self-control comes from the prefrontal cortex and is not fully developed until the mid-twenties. This is the most recently evolved part of our brain and is where planning, logic, problem solving, and resisting temptation are performed. It is the emotional part of the brain, the limbic system, which causes us to lose control and not wait for the second marshmallow. To delay gratification, you need your prefrontal cortex, your conscious thinking, to override your limbic system, your emotional response.

As with other human characteristics, it is difficult to separate how much of your self-control is inherited and how much can be developed. Both play significant roles. But as with any achievement in life, as we saw in the chapter on mindsets, it is hard to know how far you can ultimately develop your self-control, but it is likely you can greatly improve it.

Chronic stress degrades your cognitive abilities and hence your self-control. Most troubling is that if the stress persists it can lead to atrophy in the prefrontal cortex and the hippocampus [129]. When you are tired you have reduced self-control. When you must continuously exert self-control your ability to do so decreases. To help you resist those temptations, adequate sleep, reducing chronic stress, and not putting yourself in a position where you must constantly exert self-control will help you avoid temptations and stay on task.

There are strategies to help you resist temptation that will over time develop your self-control. One strategy is to anticipate the temptation and plan your response. If you have a homework assignment due the next day anticipate your friends trying to distract by asking you to go to a movie and already be prepared to tell them no. This approach also improves your self-control by developing the habit of sticking to and finishing your assignment. Your response to the temptation becomes automatic.

You should write down the tasks you have to perform and what times you will work on these tasks. A strong psychological influence that humans have is "commitment and consistency." Once you write down a plan, you are unconsciously influenced to fulfill that commitment and to be consistent with what you planned [130].

The culture around you can instill self-control. Being around people who have self-control will help. Look to make friends, or study partners and groups, with students in your class who exhibit self-control and work hard. You'll want to demonstrate that you can have as much self-control as they do.

As we will see in the chapter on meditation, meditation calms the emotional part of your brain and allows the pre-frontal cortex more control. Meditation will improve focus on the present and your ability to study. Meditation is much more restorative than sleep. We have seen that when you sleep, your brain is very active. When you are awake there is constant chatter in your brain. Only with meditation can you get your brain to a restful state.

As we will see in the chapter on nutrition, diet can affect executive function, which is the brain controlling your emotions, focus, and pursuit of goals. So, changing your diet, as will be described in chapter 14, can improve your self-control and grit.

Mischel's studies have shown that the more the children could delay gratification on the Marshmallow Test the more they believed they could control the outcome. They believed they had self-control. To improve your self-control convincing yourself that you can do it is a big step. Telling yourself that you have, or can have, self-control helps. Fake it until you make it! Every time you can say no to going out with your friends, so that you can stay home and study, the easier it will be for you to avoid temptation the next time. You must put yourself into a growth mindset when it comes to developing self-control.

One reason a person has a lack of self-control is they do not trust that the reward will be there. They take the instant reward of going to the movie with their friends rather than staying home and studying for greater rewards that may not be there later. Even if you believe the reward will be there in the future, you discount the value of that future reward compared to the value of that present reward. You must convince yourself that the efforts put into studying will translate into greater rewards later in life. You should envision yourself in the future with a completed degree and the life that results. This way your prefrontal cortex can convince you to say no to the distraction. You envision the success from the completed homework assignment, or the completed degree, which instills in you that the delayed gratification will result in a bigger reward later.

To help develop self-control use Jacobi's method of 'invert, always invert." Don't try to come up with ways of having self-control. Think of things that could derail your self-control and prevent those things from happening. You have a homework assignment due tomorrow. Anticipate a friend coming by to ask you to do something this evening, such as going to the movies. Already have a planned response to stop this derailment. Know what you are going to say to your friend, "Let's do it this weekend as I have an assignment I have to work on this evening."

I do not want to imply it is easy to develop self-control. If it were there would be fewer people addicted to alcohol, gambling, tobacco, drugs, etc. It is hard work and takes time because it is a culmination of small successes. But the encouraging point is that you can, over time, increase your self-control, just like going to the gym and lifting weights can improve your strength!

Oaten and Cheng have shown that a two-month program of self-regulatory physical exercise resulted in significant improvements in a wide range of regulatory behaviors [131]. Essentially improving the subjects' self-control. The study involved 24 sedentary students who volunteered to participate in exchange for a gym membership. The gym staff determined the best exercise program for each participant, which included aerobics and strength training. The participants kept journals of their daily habits and were given psychological tests every two weeks that measured intellectual control. There was significant improvement in the control exhibited in the psychological tests, and the participants reported improvement in a host of self-regulatory behaviors including a decrease in procrastination! We will learn of many more benefits to learning that result from exercise in chapter 15.

Will power is very much like a muscle [132]. The more you continuously use your will power the more depleted it becomes and your ability to resist temptation decreases. The participation of the subjects in the exercise program required exercising their self-control, going to the gym when scheduled to participate in these physical exercises. This use of their self-control to go to the gym strengthened their self-control, just like strengthening a muscle from use. The resulting stronger self-control was beneficial other times when they needed to have self-control. Such as when friends came by to ask them to do something, and they were able to resist to study instead.

When you are using your willpower to study, you should plan breaks to replenish your willpower, just like you take breaks between sets when you are weightlifting. Planning your breaks will also help you avoid giving in to unexpected temptations that will take you away from the rest of your study plan. Commit to not looking at texts, emails, or items on the internet until your break. The other benefit of these planned breaks is it results in periods of incubation, which we have seen is where your brain is subconsciously thinking about what you have been studying, a problem you have been trying to solve, or creating something new. This strength model of self-control resonates with our discussion above that you can improve your self-control, just like you can increase the strength of a muscle.

The strength model of self-control is not perfect. With the proper mindset you can indeed keep going, which you could not do with a physical task. Approaching self-control from a growth mindset and knowing you can improve your self-control, you will likely develop self-control beyond what you ever imagined.

It takes self-control to resist those momentary distractions. But it takes grit to sustain effort toward a goal for an extended period-of-time. That period-of-time is years in the case of pursuing a degree or could even be a decade, or more, in the case of pursuing a career such as a chess grandmaster, virtuoso violinist, surgeon, novelist, or entrepreneur. Success begins with failure, whether you are pursuing something in academics, the artistic field, or athletics. As an example, consider that the best basketball players make over 80% of their free throws. It is highly likely they missed the first free throw they ever attempted. It is likely they started out hitting a small percentage of their free throws. This is the case in any pursuit, you start out with failure. It takes grit to continue working at something, such as free throw shooting, for the years it takes to be among the best. It takes grit to keep trying something different until you finally figure out what works. It also takes a growth mindset that intelligence and skills can be developed. Infants cannot do anything. As they try things for the first time they fail. When they try to stand up, they fall repeatedly. Finally, they are successful for a few seconds and with continued work can finally stand without falling. They have developed that procedural memory, changes in the brain, for standing. The success of being able to stand began with failure, after failure, after failure. This is the case with everything we undertake. The infant is not troubled by the failures. But at some stage as we age, we start to become embarrassed when we make a mistake. This embarrassment probably originates from reactions of those around us, our parents, teachers, and peers. This pushes us into a fixed mindset and prevents us from pursuing challenging tasks. It is important as a parent, a teacher, or a coach, to be encouraging in every way, and show that making mistakes means we are challenging ourselves and putting ourselves in a position to learn, to get better.

When I teach, I just talk and write on my iPad, which is displayed on a screen. I do not use a perfected PowerPoint presentation. This way I am sure to make an occasional error. The students see that my errors don't bother me. Besides being an example of not being embarrassed by an error, the students see how I figure out that something is wrong, and how I go back and fix it. (I especially like when my class catches my error. I know they are not only listening but understanding what I am saying and writing!) I think this is an important lesson, my making an occasional mistake in class, and one of the many reasons I think PowerPoint, which has become ubiquitous at the college level, has been a step back for education.

I had an experience with a course as an undergraduate that set me back; it placed me in a fixed mindset. The course was on computer architecture and would have been very helpful with the first job I had right out of college, designing microcomputers at Intel. The instructor was the exact opposite of encouraging, especially for me. If a student asked a question in class, there were two types of responses from this instructor. He either acted as if the question was brilliant, or he ridiculed the student for asking an ignorant question. He embarrassed students who were having difficulty and striving to learn. As a result, I never asked a question when often clearing something up would have been very beneficial to help me follow the rest of the lecture. As a result, I didn't conceptually understand the material. Somehow, I ended up getting a B in the class, probably by just memorizing enough procedures to answer questions well-enough, even though I did not understand. (I would have much rather understood the material and gotten a C. It would have helped with the start of my first job! Instead, I had to learn that course's material on the job.) I am an introvert and was very shy and lacked self-confidence in college. This professor set me back; I have strived to never make a student feel the way he made me feel. This is an extreme example, but teachers, parents, and other adults can subtly, with facial expression and comments, cause students to feel embarrassed and move them along the scale from a growth to a fixed mindset.

Grit is the combination of having passion for something and the perseverance to see it through. You might have the passion, the enthusiasm, to be a novelist. You also need perseverance to pursue becoming a good writer and continue after repeated rejections from publishers. You may have the passion to become an engineer, medical doctor, scientist, mathematician, etc., but it will take perseverance to get through college to become these things.

Angela Duckworth, a professor at the University of Pennsylvania, has developed questionnaires that measure a person's grit. Prof. Duckworth has found that adults who have achieved an advanced degree (Ph.D., M.D., J.D., etc) are grittier than adults who have just achieved a four-year bachelor's degree, who are grittier than those who have received some college credit but no degree [133]. Prof. Duckworth looked at whether individuals had successfully completed a goal such as college graduation, completion of Green Beret training, high-school graduation, or becoming a successful salesperson. She found that comparing individuals whose other characteristics are the same, scoring on her grit scale is the difference between those who achieved their goals, and those who dropped out.

The importance of effort being as important, or more important, than innate talent has been recognized for a long time. In a letter to Francis Galton in 1869, Charles Darwin said, "I have always maintained that, excepting fools, men did not differ much in intellect, only in zeal and hard work" [134]. William James recognized that most fall well short of their potential because of lack of effort and in 1907 in the journal Science he wrote, "The plain fact remains that men the world over possess amount of resource which only very exceptional individuals push to their extremes of use" [135].

Two people with different levels of innate talents can develop the same skill with different levels of effort. With the same skill, it is likely the person who had to put in more effort to get to the same skill level will put in more effort utilizing that skill to obtain greater accomplishments.

Here is what Professor Duckworth's grit math looks like [133]

$$Skill = Talent \times Effort$$

$$Achievement = Skill \times Effort$$

So,

$$Achievement = Talent \times (Effort)^2$$

If you could double your talent, you could double what you could achieve. But talent is something we cannot change—it is that innate ability we have. But most of us could double our effort, which would result in quadrupling what we could achieve.

If you want to write novels, you first must learn the skill of writing. You might have to put in twice the effort as someone else to develop the same writing skills. But then, with the same writing skills, if you put in twice the effort to write novels, you will be the more successful novelist.

In the long run, it is often the one with the most grit, the one who practices and works harder, not the one who starts with more talent, intelligence, or ability, that prevails. It has been shown in many fields— chess, music, scientific research, sports, Go, surgery, and mathematics—that those who are ahead when they are just beginning, probably because of greater innate talent, are not the ones who end up at the top of these fields. The ones who ended up ahead, and were considered as experts, correlate with the amount of practice [136]. No one has come up with a way to test children to determine who will be the best musician, mathematician, tennis player, etc. That is because, in the long run, it is the work ethic that makes the difference. A study showed that the rankings of junior tennis players had no correlation to their professional success. They may have been ahead as junior tennis players, maybe because of more innate talent, but in the end, it was grit, the amount of practice, which made the difference [137]. Thinking that only logical people should go into math, athletic people into sports, or musical people should take up an instrument are excuses not to pursue something that you might get good at and enjoy.

Consider mathematics. In grade school some children will initially perform better either because of some slight differences in abilities or experiences the child may have had, such as playing games that require counting [138]. Based on these early performances, some children will be labeled gifted in math and some as not so good at math. This will then determine which children end up in an advanced math sequence and which children will take the minimum of math to graduate high school. Ultimately the better mathematicians may have come from those children who were ushered away from mathematics either by teachers, or because the child believed he was no good at math. A certain level of math is required to go into fields such as engineering, computer science, and physics. These fields will be closed to those who were told, or believed, they lacked math aptitude; but by utilizing a growth mindset combined with grit, they could have eventually surpassed those who had been labeled gifted at math.

People without grit will often quit when the task becomes difficult, or they encounter a failure. Depending on your talent level, encountering difficulties and failure could happen at the grade school to junior high school, junior high school to high school, or high school to college transitions. With grit you will keep working, or start working, when things become difficult and overcome inevitable failures. It happens at some point for everyone, and that is why success begins with failure. It is why grit will take you further than someone more talented but who does not have your grit.

There are many examples of people with grit and a growth mindset who kept pursuing their dream despite what might appear as overwhelming odds. As a sophomore, Michael Jordan did not make his high school basketball team but was placed on the junior varsity team. Jordan was only 5'10" at that point, but he had the grit to continue and arguably become the greatest basketball player of all time. Stephen King worked continuously on his writing starting as a teenager. By the time he was through college, he had written many stories. He had some success with publishing short stories, but he had to work as a teacher to support himself when he wrote his first novel. His first novel was Carrie, which was rejected 30 times. He did give up at that point throwing the manuscript in the trash. His wife showed more grit at that point digging it out and asking him to submit it to a 31st publisher, which was Doubleday, who published it. Thomas Edison's teachers told him he was too stupid to learn things. More than 1,000 of Edison's inventions were patented, many world-changing, because he would just not give up. He tried over 6,000 materials to find what would work best for the filament in his light bulb. My third-grade teacher told my parents that I would not amount to anything. That teacher was not aware of my grit. There is an appropriate quote from Winston Churchill to instill grit. You will often find it stated as "Never, never, never give up." The actual quote was "Never give in, never, never, never." But either way it instills the message.

A great example of someone showing grit, and a growth mindset, to become successful was in Angela Duckworth's book, *Grit: The Power of Passion and Perseverance*. This person needed five years to graduate from high school. He earned a C- in high school English and scored a 475 out of 800 on the English portion of the SATs, which put him in the lower 1/3 of students who take the SAT. Yet he wanted to be a writer, which clearly would seem impossible. There is no telling where you can end up with a growth mindset and grit. This person was John Irving. He has published 15 novels. Five of his novels have been made into movies. His novel, *The World According to Garp*, won the National Book Award and made into a movie. His novel, *The Cider House Rules*, was made into a movie and Irving received the Academy Award for writing the screen play.

Grit, like all personality traits, is a combination of nature and nurture. A recent study indicates a heritability of 37% for the perseverance component and 20% for the passion component of grit [139]. So, the biggest influence on how much grit you have is how much it has been developed. A good start is to envision yourself as someone who is gritty, someone who will put in the effort to accomplish their goals. You want to make grit part of you.

Robert Eisenberger has shown several experiments with animals and humans that industriousness can be learned [140]. You can learn that working hard will result in a reward. You can develop your grit. If someone is rewarded for working hard, then they associate working hard with a reward. But they will also associate a positive feeling with the experience of working hard! They will start to want to work hard because it feels good. In fact, you must learn that working hard feels good and results in rewards otherwise you will not do it.

To put in effort day after day, year after year, to accomplish something is difficult to do if you don't enjoy what you are doing. Warren Buffett, arguably the greatest investor of all time, says he "tap dances" to work [141]. Warren Buffett found match quality with investing. He has grit when it comes to investing. He has relentlessly read company's annual reports and financials for almost eight decades. Having grit doesn't mean one loves all the activities it takes to accomplish their goal. A concert violinist still practices routines that a beginning violinist practices. They probably aren't doing that because they love to play scales, but it makes them better at what they do love, playing a concert in Carnegie Hall. Attributed to several musicians is the quote, "If I skip practicing one day, I notice the difference. If I skip two days, the critics notice. If I skip three, the public notices."

Having a passion for something will help you develop grit to pursue that passion. But for most people that passion had to be developed. It doesn't just happen one day like a lightning bolt; it takes time to develop. You don't realize after your first session of a programming class that your passion is going to be computers, or after your first guitar lesson your passion will be performing. When something becomes a passion, the motivation to pursue it is all internal. You are no longer doing it to please a parent or a teacher or to receive a high grade. You also must search for what will become your passion. Do not hesitate to change your direction if that passion isn't developing, or you see something else that interests you. Just make sure you give a good try to whatever you undertake before changing direction. The knowledge you gain won't be lost. It will just be another mental model you will have in your latticework of mental models to tap into on your other pursuits.

You may have a passion for more than one activity to pursue. As we saw, many Nobel prize winners have additional pursuits unrelated to their science. You must try things. Most of us don't initially know what that pursuit will be for which we will develop a passion. But we do know pursuits where we won't develop a passion. For those activities for which you have some interest, you must pursue, for a while, to see if that passion starts developing. It takes a sufficient time to learn the intricacies and to become good at aspects of that activity before a passion will develop. It also helps to be around people who have interests in this activity. These people are your teachers, classmates, and friends who share a similar interest. When you pursue an activity, also pursue as friends those who show interest in the same activity.

If something is really turning into a passion, you won't get bored with it. You get bored when there is a lack of novelty. With a passion, you are always learning something new or taking your pursuit to the next level. When I teach a course that I have been teaching for decades, I don't get bored. Every semester there is a point where I have a moment when I realize I never thought of a concept in this way before. A student asks a question that I have never encountered. I think of a new, simpler way of presenting something. I think of a new demonstration I can construct that would help illustrate a concept. You won't get bored with your passion because you will always be finding these new intricacies. William James recognized this over 100 years ago. James wrote, "And the maximum of attention may then be said to be found whenever we have a systematic harmony or unification between the novel and the old. It is an odd circumstance that neither the old nor the new, by itself, is interesting; the absolutely old is insipid; the absolutely new makes no appeal at all. The old in the rim, is what claims the attention—the old with a slightly new turn. No one wants to bear a lecture on a subject completely disconnected with his previous knowledge, but we all like lectures on subjects of which we know a little already...." [22]. It is remarkable how much James new about learning and human nature.

You can develop grit by making it a habit. The way you make something a habit is you make it a ritual. You plan your time. You can set a time where you will study, or practice, every day such as 7:00-8:00 p.m., then a 30-minute break followed by another study session from 8:30-9:30 p.m. By having a set time to study it helps you avoid distractions. You know you will indulge your temptations at other times, such as during your 30-minute break or after your last study session.

Most people buy a piece of exercise equipment and then never use it. I have a Nordic Track, rowing machine, elliptical, treadmill, indoor exercise bike, road bike and weights. I have had to replace two flywheels on my elliptical and one on my Nordic Track because I have used them for decades and worn them out. I exercise almost every day, as I have for four decades. I have made exercise a habit by having a ritual. My daily ritual is to get into work by 7:00 a.m. and leave for home at 3:30 p.m. to exercise. I have gotten to where I enjoy the hard work of exercising and that feeling of accomplishment, and exhaustion, when I am done. (In chapter 15 we will discuss the huge benefits to learning and the brain that come from exercising.) I am also always looking to understand more about how best to exercise and to correspondingly modify my routines. I am still learning about exercise, my body's reaction to that exercise, and trying new exercises. If I get held up at work and don't leave until 4:30 p.m., I find it much harder to make myself exercise once I get home. My ritual has been disrupted. As William James (chapter 8 of *Talks to Teachers*) stated, "There is no more miserable human being than one in whom nothing is habitual but indecision,…….., and the beginning of every bit of work are subjects of express volitional deliberation" [22]. What James was telling us, which he knew over 100 years ago, is that you want to ingrain your habits, when and what you will work on each day. You don't want to start your day not knowing when and what you are going to work on.

I approached writing this book as a ritual. When I got to work it was the first thing I started, and I would spend two hours on it. Starting a book is a daunting prospect. It is amazing what can be accomplished by developing a habit of working on something a little bit at the same time every day.

In his book, *Developing Talent in Young People*, Benjamin Bloom presents his study of 120 intensely talented individuals [142]. These individuals came from all endeavors, a mathematician, research neurologist, pianist, sculptor, swimmer, etc. Bloom found a common thread on how they rose to the top of their fields. Bloom found that their work ethic and passion, their grit, had more to do with them rising to the top of their fields than their talent. Bloom found that to develop this passion, to be able to have the grit to pursue an endeavor has three stages. The first stage was trying things to find that interest, which we discussed earlier. The second stage was developing self-discipline to continue to pursue that passion. The final and longest stage was developing a larger purpose, a purpose outside of oneself.

I have been teaching for 39 years. I feel I was a good teacher for the first 20-plus years. When my daughter became a student at the university where I teach, I developed a greater sense of responsibility to the students in my class. My daughter was a student in someone's class and my students were someone's sons and daughters. I greatly increased the effort I put into my teaching. I developed 50 demonstrations to illustrate course concepts. I created videos of all course material for students to be able to rewatch course topics. I developed something called Concept Point Recovery (discussed in detail in chapter 17) that gives students an opportunity to recover points they lost on an exam by demonstrating they had gone back and learned the concept. I had experienced Bloom's third stage; teaching had become a calling.

I mentioned that Warren Buffett is considered the greatest investor of all-time and that he has been pursing investing for almost eight decades. Eight decades exemplifies true grit. If you listen to him talk at annual meetings, or read his writings, he has a strong sense of responsibility to his shareholders. For Buffett investing has become a calling.

This third stage, developing a larger purpose, happens with your gritty pursuit. Your purpose will be to serve your students, patients, clients, customers, readers, audience, an organization, etc. Purpose is powerfully motivating, so it makes sense that the greater your sense of purpose in what you are doing the grittier you are.

In a 1997 publication of their study on how people view their work, Wrzesniewski et al. found that 1/3 view their work as a job (a necessity to earn money), 1/3 as a career (focus on advancement), and 1/3 as a calling (fulfilling and socially useful) [143]. Occupation did not matter. For instance, they found that for the 24 college administrators they interviewed 1/3 viewed their work as a job, 1/3 as a career, and 1/3 as a calling. Where you are in your work is not fixed. As you pursue your work you can become more satisfied. If you become competent in your work, and go through the motions, you won't increase your level of satisfaction. Instead, you could put effort in to further developing the skills necessary for your work, so you become better at it. You look for intricacies in your work. You figure out small changes in what you do, or suggestions for tweaking the job, to improve the contribution to the organization and your interest in what you are doing. You can go from just having a job, to a career, to a calling. As I mentioned earlier, my job changed from a career to a calling after 20 years!

It takes a growth mindset to be gritty. **You will not persevere if you don't believe that the failures that occur when you push yourself to get better are part of the learning process.** In fact, grit and growth mindset have been found to be mutually reinforcing [144].

It has been observed that as we mature, we become more conscientious, responsible, caring, open, extroverted, and grittier. That is certainly my experience. Growing up I was a shy, unsure, introvert. But I had a growth mindset. I was also gritty. My growth mindset and grittiness probably came from my grandmother. She came to the US in her teens from Poland. I still remember sitting at her kitchen table when I was preschool age drinking coffee with her; yes as a child I drank coffee! She was always stressing the importance of education and working hard. The way she talked to me must have instilled my grit and growth mindset. I could learn to do things with effort. Interestingly, my mother had two sisters and each of the three sisters had a son who got a Ph.D. My cousins and I were the first in our family to graduate from college. My grandmother played a major role.

In junior high school I was placed in the regular math sequence, not the advanced sequence. This meant I would not be able to take calculus my senior year. I took two regular math courses one semester, received A's, proving I was capable. I was allowed to move to the advanced math sequence and able to take calculus my senior year. That was a success because of my grit and growth mindset. But I was still terrified of talking, especially in large groups or in front of a class. I dreaded the idea of being valedictorian and to have to make a speech. I made sure I got a B in a class to prevent that from happening. I also thought people just sat down and wrote something like a valedictorian speech, which I knew I could not do. I didn't know that speech writing required spacing and incubation to come up with the concept of a speech and to put it into succinct words. I have since accepted projects that I had no idea how I was going to accomplish. I would only be able to make a little progress. When I would come back to the project, I was able to make a little more progress, possibly due to the incubation that occurred. By starting early and spacing my efforts, I was able to accomplish what at first seemed like a daunting undertaking. This book is a perfect example, taking many years and continuous work to complete.

All through college, I was uncomfortable joining a group of people already talking. I was very self-conscious when meeting someone new. I was terrified of asking questions in class, let alone giving a presentation. I would sit near the back of a class. But I persevered and felt I could get there. I had the grit to change. I left my first job as an engineer at Intel to go work on a Ph.D. because I wanted to become a professor. I knew this would involve having to become more confident. As a Ph.D. student I would have to make presentations to my research group and eventually at scientific meetings. If I was successful, and became a professor, I would have to get up in front of a class, maybe a very large class, several times a week to teach. By going back for a Ph.D., I knew I was going to be putting myself into a position where I would be very uncomfortable and needed to develop new skills to succeed. It would take grit.

The evening before my wife and I were to leave California to head to Purdue for me to start graduate school, we were having dinner with a group of people from my wife's job. I was not yet comfortable with this group, so I rarely spoke. One of them decided he had to tell me there was no way I was going to be successful at what I was going to try to do, be a professor. I rarely spoke, so how was I going to get up in front of a group and make a presentation or teach a class? Unlike the experience I had had in the course on computer architecture, instead of this person setting me back, it made me more determined to achieve my goal. I had become a little surer of myself but still had a long way to go.

I went from a person who was reluctant to initiate interactions with new people to one where I get up in front of 50 people several times a week to teach a class and sometimes present seminars to much larger classes. Having a growth mindset and being gritty allowed me to completely change my characteristics. (Something I had been told would not be possible for me.) There is no telling where you can go with a growth mindset, self-control, and grit. I still feel a little awkward at times when I meet people, but I do not hesitate to initiate interactions. I have developed circuitry in my prefrontal cortex that allows me to quiet and overcome the fear response from my amygdala.

Another thing that will help you develop grit is participating in one or two extracurricular activities. Grit takes practice and committing to an extracurricular activity for at least two years is good for engendering grit. You picked an activity because it has some interest for you. It is an activity that could be fun but challenging. There will be a person guiding the activity such as a coach, instructor, advisor, or student officer who will help you develop follow through. Studies show that participation in one or two extracurricular activities result in better academic and psychological development—better grades, less alcohol and drug use, more self-confidence and self-esteem [145]. The longer you participate in these activities, especially multi-year participation, the more grit you will develop. You are probably also developing skills that are complementary to your academic pursuits. It has been found that those who participate, for at least two years, in an extracurricular activity are more likely to graduate from college, to have a job, and to make more money [146]. Accounting for all other variables—grades, SAT scores, etc.—those students who participate in a high school extracurricular activity for multiple years and advance significantly in that activity (become an officer, win a significant event, etc.) are significantly more likely to graduate from college with honors [147]. Pursuing an extracurricular activity develops your perseverance and teaches you how to follow through on hard things. You will be more successful in college because of the work ethic developed from these extracurricular pursuits.

Once you commit to something you need to follow it through. You commit to going to college, you go to all your classes, and you show up on time. (Actually, be early; it is about respect, details, and excellence.) When my daughter was a college student she told me, "Dad, I go to all of my classes, but all the instructors just read their PowerPoints to us and they provide those PowerPoints to us ahead of time." My daughter has much more grit than I do not missing those non-fulfilling classes. Maybe her grit is from participating in many extracurricular activities in school, including competitive tennis, which she did from age 10 to 18.

When you join an extracurricular activity, pick a particular college, or join a company, you are surrounding yourself with a culture. If that culture is working hard to improve, it will instill you with grit. The way the group does things will become the way you do things. You will not want to let them down, so you will work hard. You will want to be competitive with them, so you will work hard. You will want grit to be part of your identity.

John F. Kennedy said, "We choose to go to the moon in this decade and do the other things, not because they are easy, but because they are hard, because that goal will serve to organize and measure the best of our energies and skills, because that challenge is one that we are willing to accept, one we are unwilling to postpone, and one which we intend to win." John F. Kennedy had grit and he was recognizing, or instilling, the grit culture it would take to get to the moon.

You will thrive if you undertake hard things that you enjoy. Struggling, and making progress, will engender confidence to keep trying harder and harder things.

Chapter 14: Nutrition

You might be surprised to find a chapter on nutrition in a book on how to learn. If you were reading a book on exercise, or a sport, such a chapter would not be surprising. For you to learn, and then to use what you have learned, you need to optimize your brain. That is, you must practice things that provide for a healthy brain, nutrition being one of those along with exercise, sleep, and meditation.

A billion neurons utilize 6 calories per day. With 86 billion neurons in the human brain, the energy used in the brain is 516 calories per day. (Details of brain energy calculations can be found in Appendix A.) The human brain, which averages about 3 pounds, is 2% of the body's weight yet it consumes 20-25% of the body's oxygen and energy sources (mainly glucose). In other words, >20% of the oxygen you breath, and >20% of the foods you eat, go to fueling your brain. A human brain is very expensive from an energy standpoint to operate. Per pound, the brain uses 10 times the energy as the rest of the body. 90% of the energy use in the brain is to continuously recharge neurons for signaling. Nutrition is as important, or even more so, to brain health and efficient operation as it is to a training athlete. Of all the organs in the body, the brain is the most susceptible to damage from poor nutrition. Recently the number of Americans killed by their diets has surpassed the number killed by smoking! [148]

The effects of diet on the brain have been visually observed by Lisa Mosconi et al. [149]. Mosconi looked at MRI images of 50 participants whose age ranged from 25 to 70 years. On average, those who followed a Mediterranean diet (whole grains, fruits, vegetables, seafood, beans, and nuts) typically had visibly much healthier brains then those who followed a more Western diet (red meat, sugar, processed foods and low in fish, vegetables, and fruits). On the Western diet there was clear evidence of brain atrophy, regions where neurons were lost [150]. In Mosconi's brain MRIs dark areas are regions filled with fluid and not neurons. Brains from those following a Western diet typically had visibly less areas with neurons, and much greater areas with fluids, than the brains from those following a Mediterranean diet. It was also observed that those on the Western diet had a greater amount of amyloid plaque than those on the Mediterranean diet. Amyloid plaque is observed in the brains of those who have Alzheimer's.

We will see that proper nutrition not only optimizes the functioning of our brains, but proper nutrition also protects us from age-related cognitive decline and dementias such as Alzheimer's [151]. The understanding of nutrition is a complex, and hotly debated field. This is exasperated because of special interest groups, especially the food industry, influencing research and government guidelines. There are many vastly different diets—Mediterranean, paleo, keto, low carbohydrate, high carbohydrate, DASH, MIND, etc.—with studies in respected medical journals to support whatever you want to claim about nutrition. There is also variability between people when it comes to effects of a particular food. But there are foods, such as sugars and trans-fats, which should be avoided as much as possible and some foods that are clearly good for your body and your brain, which will be discussed. This chapter is just a start on your nutrition education and on eating better for your brain's health and functioning.

The human brain is 80% water compared to 60% water for the rest of the body [152]. Water plays many functions in the brain. Water is involved in every chemical reaction in the brain, water cushions the brain, and water is involved in the waste product removal by the glymphatic system. It has been observed that if you feel thirsty, your cognitive processing will be slower [153]. Research has shown drinking water before performing cognitive tasks improves performance. Drinking water is probably the easiest nutriment to provide to your brain, but don't think consuming any fluid counts. Caffeinated beverages will dehydrate you. Soft drinks and juices, as we will see, do harm because of the sugars they contain. Milk is highly processed and contains sugars. Get your water by drinking water. Spring water is best because it is from rain and snow that has been filtered through rock, from which it has picked up vital nutrients.

How much water should you drink? People are various sizes, ages, and perform different physical activities, which impact the water needed. The best way is to let your body tell you. When you urinate, your urine should be a pale yellow [154].

Early hominids were small and not made for chasing game; meat was hard to obtain. But early hominids lived near water, which provided energy dense food—fish, shellfish, and bird eggs. Humans, and human ancestors, have been around for about 6,000,000 years. Homo Sapiens appeared about 300,000 years ago. For most of this time humans lived in hunter-gatherer societies; humans evolved to eat a hunter gatherer diet. Agriculture based human societies began about 12,000 years ago. Modern humans rarely eat the foods consumed by our ancestors— vegetables, fruits, seeds, and nuts. Studies of still existing hunter-gather communities show that 65% of calories come from plant sources and no more than 35% from hunted meat.

When modern humans do consume these plant-based foods they have often been highly processed—canned, frozen, juiced, or with chemicals added. For 200 years the food industry has developed these technologies of food processing. This has resulted in foods with long shelve life and that are addictive, which increases consumption and profits. (One familiar ad campaign used the slogan, "You can't eat just one.") The meats our ancestors ate had much healthier proportions of omega-3 to omega-6 fatty acids than the beef, chicken, butter, and farmed fish that most of us eat, because of what is used to feed these animals. These processed foods not only lack the nutrition found in unprocessed foods, but consumption of these processed foods can be harmful, especially after years, or decades.

We have seen that 80% of the brain is water, and hence the need to stay hydrated for proper functioning. The next largest component at 11% of the brain's weight is fat. (55% of what is left after removing the water.) This is not the fat that we are familiar with, the energy storage fat (adipose or white fat). There are no stored energy sources in the brain. The fat in the brain is structural fat. The insulating sheath called myelin that is wrapped around nerve cell axons is made up of these structural fats and proteins, and it provides for electrical insulation. Neurons are surrounded by membranes composed of fats, like omega-3 fatty acids, that protect the neuron but allow for nutrients and signals to flow in and out.

Shown in figure 14.1 are the structures of saturated, monounsaturated, and polyunsaturated fats. A saturated fat has only single carbon bonds so it is saturated in the sense no more hydrogen could be added. A monounsaturated fat has one double carbon bond. If this bond became a single bond and two more hydrogen atoms were added, it would become a saturated fat. The hydrogen atoms are on the same side of the carbon atoms in the double bond. This is referred so as the cis configuration and there is a bend in the molecule at the cis bond. A polyunsaturated fat has more than one double carbon bond with the hydrogen atoms on the same side of the carbon atoms in the double bond.

Saturated Fat (all single carbon bonds)

Monounsaturated Fat (one double carbon bonds)

Polyunsaturated "Omega-3" Fatty Acid (more than one double carbon bonds)

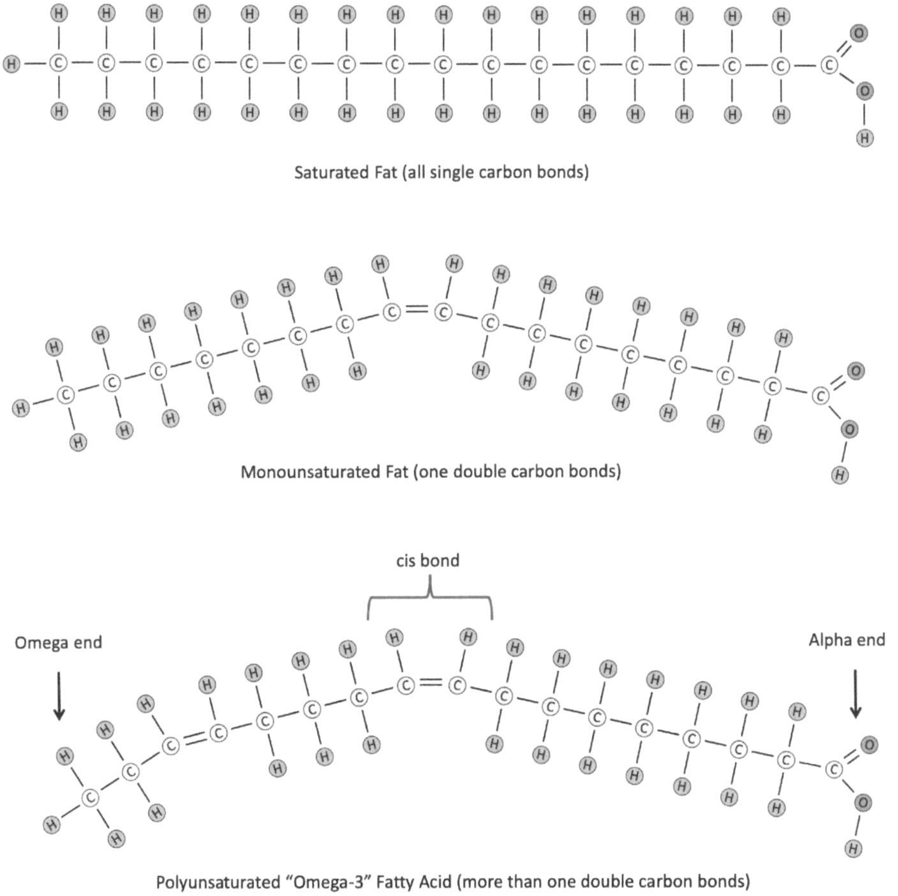

Figure 14.1 The structure of saturated, monounsaturated, and polyunsaturated fatty acids.

A trans-fat is shown in figure 14.2. A trans-fat has the hydrogen atoms on opposite sides of the carbon atoms in the double bond, the trans configuration. With the hydrogen atoms on opposite sides of the carbon atoms in the double bond there is no bend at this point in the fatty acid.

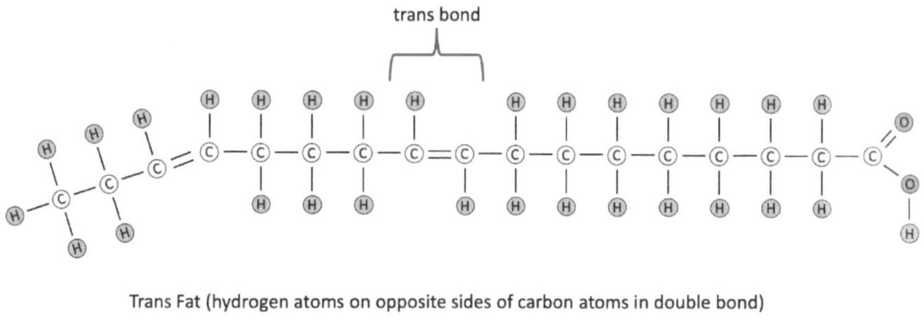

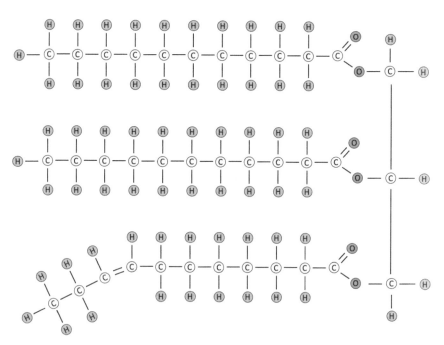

Trans Fat (hydrogen atoms on opposite sides of carbon atoms in double bond)

Figure 14.2 A trans fatty acid. (Hydrogen atoms on opposite sides of carbon atoms in the double bond.)

The main way saturated, monounsaturated, and polyunsaturated fats are stored in biological systems is in the form of triglycerides. A triglyceride is a glycerol, a three-carbon molecule, to which three fatty acids are attached. The attached fatty acids can be any combination of saturated, monounsaturated, and polyunsaturated. Show in figure 14.3 is a triglyceride with two saturated fats and one monounsaturated fat.

Figure 14.3 Triglyceride composed of two saturated fats and one monounsaturated fat.

A less common way fats are stored in biological systems is as a phospholipid. A phospholipid is a glycerol molecule with only two fatty acids attached, the third attachment being a phosphate group. Cell membranes contain two layers of phospholipids.

The blood-brain barrier decides what fats are allowed into the brain. While you are still growing nerve cells, which continues into your teenage years, the blood-brain barrier lets in saturated fats. When we are fully matured, saturated fats are blocked from the brain as your brain can make any saturated fats required. (There are a few minor exceptions.) The brain can also manufacture all the monounsaturated fats it requires. So saturated and monounsaturated fats are referred to as non-essential since the brain can manufacture these fats as needed. (Of course, the components to make these non-essential fats come from the foods we eat.) The fats that the brain requires, supplied from our diets, are polyunsaturated fats (PUFAs) such as omega-3s and omega-6s, which are the most abundant fats in brain cell membranes. These are called essential fats, because our bodies cannot manufacture them, we must get them through the foods we eat. The blood-brain barrier allows flow of PUFAs into the brain. That is, if our diet is supplying PUFAs. The brain makes more complex fats from these PUFAs, phospholipids and sphingolipids, which comprise 70% of the fat found in the brain.

The structure of omega-3 and omega-6 PUFAs are similar, but their regulatory roles are opposite. A PUFA has an alpha end and an omega end. In an omega-3 PUFA, the first carbon double bond is between the third and fourth carbon atoms from the omega end. In an omega-6 PUFA, the first carbon double bond is between the sixth and seventh carbon atoms from the omega end. The PUFA depicted in figure 14.1 is an omega-3 PUFA.

Shown in table 14.1 are the regulatory roles with which omega-3 and omega-6 PUFAs are involved. There must be a balance between these responses as both are necessary. Omega-3 PUFAs help with blood fluidity, so you don't develop blood clots that can lead to a heart attack or stroke. But if you cut yourself, you need the platelet aggregation that omega-6 PUFAs are involved with to clot and stop the bleeding. Omega-3 PUFAs cause vasodilation, so your blood pressure is not too high. Too much vasodilation and you would faint from low blood pressure. Omega-6 PUFAs cause vasoconstriction. Too much vasoconstriction and you suffer from high blood pressure. Omega-3

PUFAs inhibit cell proliferation preventing tumors. Omega-6 PUFAs promote cell proliferation for growth and to repair tissue damage. Omega-6 PUFAs are needed for inflammatory responses when your body has an infection or a wound. Omega-3 PUFAs are needed for an anti-inflammatory response, to turn off the inflammatory response. It is important to provide your body, and brain, with a balance to these responses through your diet. Proper neuron communication requires this balance. If your diet is providing too much omega-6 PUFAs compared to omega-3 PUFAs, there will be chronic (continuous) inflammation that can damage the brain over time, as will be discussed later when the main source of chronic inflammation, sugars in our diet, is discussed.

Table 14.1 Regulatory roles of omega-3 and omega-6 polyunsaturated fatty acids.

Omega-3 PUFAs	Omega-6 PUFAs
Anti-inflammatory	Pro-inflammatory
Vasodilation	Vasoconstriction
Blood fluidity	Platelet aggregation
Inhibit cell proliferation	Promote cell proliferation
Immunosuppression	Immunity
Pain inhibition	Pain transmission

Humans evolved on a diet that had about the same amount of omega-6 and omega-3 PUFAs [155]. Today the ratio of omega-6 to omega-3 PUFAs in the American diet is greater than 25 to 1! [156]. This is a source of chronic inflammation that leads not just to Alzheimer's, but other diseases—cancer, cardiovascular, and autoimmune. Reducing the ratio of omega-6 to omega-3 PUFAs from 25 to 1 to much lower ratios, such as 4 to 1 or lower, will not only improve your health and longevity, but also your cognitive functioning.

Two types of omega-3s come mainly from animal sources, cold-water, wild-caught fish such as salmon, fish roe, grass-fed beef, and pasture-raised eggs; these two are eicosatetraenoic acid (EPA) and docosahexaenoic acid (DHA). DHA is the most important structural component of brain cells. This DHA can be in the form of a triglyceride or phospholipid. DHA in phospholipid form is taken up ten times better than DHA in triglyceride form. Only 1.5% of the DHA in fish is in the phospholipid form. However, in fish roe 38-75% of the DHA is in phospholipid form making fish roe the best source of DHA.

From plants we get the omega-3 PUFA acid alpha-linolenic acid (ALA). Unfortunately, ALA must be processed by your body into EPA and DHA to be useful, which is inefficient. Between 8-20% of ALA is converted to EPA and between 0.5-9% is converted to DHA [157]. Sources of ALA are flax seeds, walnuts, Brussel sprouts, and soybeans.

As mentioned, we consume too many omega-6 PUFAs compared to omega-3 PUFAs. Foods that contain a high ratio of omega-6 to omega-3 PUFAs, and should be avoided, are grain-fed beef, farmed fish, and these oils: safflower, sunflower, canola, corn, grapeseed (often hidden in salad dressings), rapeseed, peanut, vegetable, and soybean. (For salad dressing I always opt for olive oil and vinegar, much healthier than processed salad dressings.) Foods with a good ratio of omega-6 to omega-3 PUFAs are cold-water, wild-caught fish and fish roe. Wild caught salmon has an omega-6 to omega-3 ratio of 1.4 to 1 while farmed salmon has an omega-6 to omega-3 ratio of 20 to 1 [158]. If you are going to eat beef, eat grass-fed beef. Grass-fed beef has an omega-6 to omega-3 ratio of 2:1 while grain-fed beef has an omega-6 to omega-3 ratio of 9:1.

When you eat eggs or poultry, you want them pasture raised. Caged chickens are fed a commercial, nowhere near their natural, diet. They also live their lives under stressed conditions, and you should not want to support such cruelty. Commercial feed, and stressed conditions, do not result in the healthiest foods to consume. Free-range is a huge improvement. Free-range chickens have some access to outside space, but there is no uniform standard. If the free-range chicken is Food Alliance Certified, the birds do not live in cages and have at least eight hours per day of access to outdoor vegetation covered areas and 1.23 square feet of floor space. If the free-range chicken is American Humane Certified, the chickens have access to at least 21.8 square feet of outdoor space per bird. Pasture raised is the best designation. Pasture raised chickens have regular access to large grass or vegetation covered outdoor space—pasture. Again, there are different certifications, but the certified humane label indicates the chickens have 108 square feet of outdoor space, as well as indoor space for shade and cover. Pasture raised chickens have regular access to feed on grubs and insects, their natural diet, resulting in healthier birds.

PUFAs are delicate and their mere extraction will cause damage, such as creating some trans fats, the worst kind of fat to consume, which we will discuss in a moment. Foods are often fried in oils with high ratios of omega-6 to omega-3 PUFAs and the food absorbs the oil. There is a danger beyond the high ratio of omega-6 to omega-3 PUFAs in these absorbed oils. These PUFAs are very delicate and are easily damaged by heat becoming free radicals, a reactive molecule. (Even without heating, which greatly increases the damage to these oils, they are susceptible to being damaged.) Once a PUFA is damaged it is not food anymore, but a toxin. These free radicals can cause harm to molecules in the body such as lipids, proteins, DNA, enzymes, hormones, and brain cells. Avoid oil-fried foods. These oils also appear in most processed foods. In the US 8-10% of total calories come from these dangerous oils.

Brain-Derived Neurotropic Factor (BDNF) is a molecule that promotes neuron formation in the hippocampus, and generation of nerve cell dendrites. DHA omega-3 PUFAs, along with exercise (as we will learn in chapter 15), promote the formation of BDNF. You can think of BDNF as brain fertilizer. Not only is BDNF a powerful plasticity promoter in the brain, there are also indications that high levels of BDNF may prevent Alzheimer's and other types of dementia [159]. Post-mortem brains of Alzheimer's victims show lower BDNF levels than those of age-matched controls [160]. BDNF may also be the explanation for greater brain volume with age for those who consume fish [161].

Researchers have seen improved executive function with omega-3 PUFA supplementation [162]. Other researchers have observed improvement in executive function of 7-9 year old children with lowering of the ratio of omega-6 to omega-3 PUFAs in their diets [163]. Other researchers saw a 26% enhancement in executive function for adults who were given omega-3 supplements compared to a control group [164]. In addition, they saw an increase in gray matter in the brains of those taking the supplements. **A step in improving your self-control and grit, discussed in the previous chapter, may be to change your diet so that you are getting more omega-3 PUFAs.**

Although some of the studies cited used extracted omega-3 PUFA supplements, it is always better to consume these substances in their original form—cold-water fish, grass-fed beef, and pasture raised eggs. Extracting the oils can lead to damage of the oils, and it is possible there are nutrients that are not being extracted, which aid in the process that omega-3 PUFAs perform in our bodies and brains. Besides, as a source of omega-3 PUFAs, eggs are just an overall perfect source of nutrients. An egg contains all that is required to develop a body, including a brain and nervous system, which makes eggs an excellent food.

The myelin sheath around nerve cells contains monounsaturated fats, fats that contain only one carbon double bond. This sheath not only protects the nerve cells but improves the speed and efficiency with which electric signals travel along the nerve cell. Monounsaturated fats are much more chemically stable than PUFAs. Extra-virgin olive oil (EVOO) is a MUFA, an oil that is safe after it is extracted from its source. Other sources of MUFAs are avocados, avocado oil, macadamia nuts, wild salmon, and beef, which is almost 50% MUFAs.

A six-year study looked at the effects of consuming MUFAs on cognition. Subjects were separated into three groups. The control group ate a low-fat diet. The other two groups ate a high-fat version of the Mediterranean diet, with one group consuming a liter of EVOO per week and the other group consumed nuts, like almonds, walnuts, and hazelnuts. The control group showed cognitive decline after six years. Both groups on the Mediterranean diet showed cognitive improvement after six years, with a little more improvement for the group that had the high EVOO consumption! [165]. Olive oil also contains vitamin E and phenolic compounds, which are antioxidants and anti-inflammatory.

Saturated fats have only single carbon bonds. They are the most stable of the fats, so they don't degrade and become harmful when used for cooking as PUFAs do. The body uses saturated fats in cell membranes and in the manufacture of various hormones. To indicate the importance of saturated fats, it is the most abundant fat in human breast milk.

We get saturated fat from beef, pork, chicken, butter, cheese, coconut, and olives. In fact, EVOO is 15% saturated fat. It is best to consume beef and butter from grass-fed beef so that you get the appropriate ratio of omega-6 to omega-3 PUFAs.

A high level of saturated fats in the blood stream has been linked to increased risk for dementia [166]. It is natural to assume consuming food high in saturated fats is the cause. But most fat in the blood stream is produced in the liver. Studies show that high levels of fat in the blood stream did not occur after eating high-saturated fat diets, but after eating high-carbohydrate diets [167]. It is likely the combination of a diet that is high in saturated fats and sugars is detrimental to brain health, as has been seen in a study that showed such a diet resulted in inflammation and reduction of BDNF in the brains of rats [168]. When you see studies that indicate diets high in saturated fats are detrimental to your health, you should check to see if the diets in the studies were also high in carbohydrates and sugars. The brain does not need saturated fats after adolescence. It cannot hurt to eat a low-saturated fat diet; you'll still get enough saturated fats.

Trans fats are PUFAs that have been chemically processed to stay solid at room temperature. They became popular because you can hydrogenate cheap vegetable oil and change it to a saturated fat. But not all the PUFAs are changed to saturated fats, hence the term partially hydrogenated. The amount of hydrogenation depends on the final consistency desired, such as for use in margarine. What happens first is the cis bonds in the PUFA, where the hydrogen atoms are on the same side as the carbon atoms in the double bond, change into a trans bond, where the hydrogen atoms are on the opposite sides of the carbon atoms in the double bond. This removes the bend that was there when it was a cis bond. Now the carbon double bond can be broken and replaced by an addition of two hydrogen atoms: one bonded to each carbon atom.

Trans fats are absolutely the worst fat you can consume. If the packaged food contains less than 0.5 grams of trans fat per serving, such as 0.49 grams, the manufacturer is allowed to say 0 grams of trans fat. So, when you see hydrogenated or partially hydrogenated on the label, even if the label says 0 trans-fats, you know the food contains trans fats. Often this is your only indication the product contains trans fats. Consuming trans fats lowers your high-density lipoprotein (HDL) levels, the good cholesterol, and raises your low-density lipoprotein (LDL) levels, the bad cholesterol, in your blood. Trans fats are highly atherogenic—they cause fatty plaque in arteries. Trans fats increase inflammation. Trans fats can cross the blood-brain barrier where they stiffen neuron membranes and have been linked to increased risk of Alzheimer's and brain shrinkage [169]. Trans fats are often used in restaurant deep fryers because they don't have to be changed as often. Trans fats are added to processed foods because they increase shelf life, and they add a rich buttery texture. Packaged foods, cakes, doughnuts, cookies, crackers, margarines, salad dressings, ice cream, non-dairy creamer, snacks, and nut butters contain trans fats and should be avoided, or at least your consumption greatly decreased.

The way trans fats cause atherogenesis is that they lower your HDL levels, and raise your LDL levels, in your blood. Lipids are insoluble in water so they cannot be sent directly into the bloodstream. Cholesterol is a lipid that is used by all the cells in our body. Cholesterol is not burned for energy like some other fats in our bodies. One important use of cholesterol is in forming and maintaining all our cell structures. Plants do not contain cholesterol; it is only found in animals. But all the cholesterol needed is produced in our livers. Since lipids are hydrophobic, they are first packaged in structures called lipoproteins. The lipoprotein contains the hydrophobic cholesterol, which can enter the bloodstream. There are several lipoproteins. LDL is the major cholesterol transporting lipoprotein in our bloodstream and is responsible for delivering cholesterol to the cells that need it for growth or synthesis of hormones. The cells that need cholesterol completely uptake the LDL molecule and disassemble it. If there is more LDL in the bloodstream then needed, the LDL just stays in the bloodstream. Prolonged time in the blood stream makes LDL molecules susceptible to oxidation and alterations so cells will no longer accept them. These damaged LDL molecules are surrounded by macrophages, a type of white blood cell, die, and are then the cause of initiating atherosclerosis. A diet that provides antioxidants is helpful in preventing LDL oxidation. LDL is vital in delivering cholesterol to our cells, but it is referred to as the bad cholesterol for what happens if it oxidizes. HDL is involved in reverse cholesterol transport. HDLs acquire excess cholesterol from circulating LDL, peripheral tissues, dead cells, and macrophages from the arterial wall. The HDL then transports this excess cholesterol back to the liver for elimination. This removal of excess cholesterol is why HDL is referred to as the good cholesterol.

The blood-brain barrier blocks cholesterol from the blood stream. All the cholesterol in your brain was manufactured there. Most of the cholesterol in your brain was produced early in your life, the majority in your first few years of life, when your central nervous system was developing. By adulthood, production of cholesterol in the brain declined to a very low level [170]. Cholesterol is a major structural component of myelin, the insulating sheath around nerve cell axons. Our central nervous system is about 2% of our body weight but contains 25% of the cholesterol in our bodies, with 70% of the cholesterol in our brains located in this insulating myelin sheath.

Why talk about the effects of cholesterol in the blood stream, if the cholesterol in your brain is produced there? Because your brain is dependent on your cardiovascular system to deliver fuel, oxygen, nutrients, and repair molecules. For your cardiovascular system to stay healthy, you want a low total cholesterol with a high ratio of HDL to LDL. As general guidelines, you want your LDL to be < 100mg/dL, your HDL > 50 mg/dL, your triglycerides < 100 mg dL, and your total cholesterol < 170 mg/dL. What we have been describing for the health of your brain so far, a diet rich in omega-3 PUFAs and a low (4 to 1 or less) omega-6 to omega-3 ratio, is also a heart healthy diet. It has also been observed that saturated fats and trans fats increase your cholesterol levels. We already know trans fats are toxins and should be eliminated from our diets. It would not hurt for most Americans to decrease their intake of saturated fats. Only 15% of the cholesterol in our bodies comes from the cholesterol in the foods we eat. 85% of the cholesterol in our bodies is manufactured in our livers and other organs. If you are a vegan, since cholesterol is not found in plant foods, your liver can make all the cholesterol you need.

There are over 100 different neurotransmitters in the brain. These neurotransmitters are created from the foods that we eat. They are created as a communication is needed to be sent between neurons. Then they disappear. They are involved with your mood, learning, memory, and cognitive ability. Some neurotransmitters you may have heard of are dopamine, serotonin, GABA, glutamate, epinephrine (adrenalin), and norepinephrine. Neurotransmitters will respond rapidly to a change in our diets. **So, your mood and cognitive ability depend on what you eat**. Neurotransmitters are made from amino acids, so they come from the protein that we eat. There are essential (our bodies cannot manufacture them and they must be obtained from our diet) and non-essential (our bodies can synthesize them) amino acids. Besides amino acids for making neurotransmitters, you need choline, vitamin C, B-vitamins, zinc, iron, omega-3 PUFAs and vitamin D.

The following table lists some neurotransmitters, their function, and foods that provide the building blocks for them.

Table 14.2 Neurotransmitters and nutrients that provide the building blocks.

Precursors/Neurotransmitters	Function	Food Source
Glutamate	Muscle excitation, Nerve signaling, learning and memory	Turkey breast, soybeans, eggs, sesame seeds and pumpkin seeds
Tyrosine	Precursor to dopamine	Turkey, eggs, soybeans
choline	Precursor to acetylcholine	Meat, eggs, grains, turkey, soybeans, chickpeas, lentils
Gamma-Aminobutyric acid (GABA)	Regulates communication between brain cells	Germinated chia seeds, kimchi, sourdough, yogurt, fermented soybeans
Serotonin	Stabilizes mood, aids sleep and digestion	Bananas, walnuts, pineapple
Tryptophan	Precursor to serotonin	turkey, eggs, soybeans, white beans, mung beans, split peas, some nuts and grains

Carbohydrates are sugar molecules. Starches and fiber are referred to as complex carbohydrates. A starch is a complex form of glucose units (residues), in either a linear form of glucose residues, called amylose, or a branch form of glucose residues, called amylopectin. Your body breaks starches down into glucose. Any cell in your body can use glucose for fuel. Examples of foods that are starches are potatoes, rice, bread, pasta, and corn. Your body cannot digest the complex carbohydrate fiber, but fiber plays an important role in regulating digestion of glucose. Sugars are referred to as simple carbohydrates. Examples of sugars are glucose, fructose, sucrose, dextrose, maltose, and lactose.

With the advent of agriculture, there was a great change in the human diet from the one in which our bodies and brains evolved. There was a great increase in carbohydrate consumption. Even more recent is the consumption of carbohydrates in the form of refined sugars. Sugar started to become available in the early 1800s. By 1900 the average American consumed 25 pounds of sugar per year. It is now estimated that the average American eats 160 pounds of sugar each year in various forms, especially sucrose and high-fructose corn syrup (HFCS). Refined sugar is now in everything, not just in candies, cakes, ice creams and donuts. It is put in processed foods to improve shelf life. It is found in condiments, crackers, bread, soft drinks, juices, pizza, etc. Since the human body and brain did not evolve to consume such large quantities of sugar, it should not be surprising these are essentially toxins.

In the food industry there is something known as the Bliss Point. When a new product is being introduced, focus groups are fed the product. There is a variation in added sugar in the product between the various focus groups. The Bliss Point is the concentration that optimizes deliciousness as determined from the focus groups. The Bliss Point results in you consuming large quantities of sugar whenever you eat a processed food item.

In the US 34.2 million people, 1 in every 10 people, have diabetes mellitus and 88 million adults, 1 in 3, are categorized as pre-diabetic. Diabetes mellitus is a group of diseases where there is too much glucose in the bloodstream. For simplicity, I will just use the term diabetes as is commonly done. In type 1 diabetics the body doesn't make enough insulin. In type 2 diabetics the body cannot use insulin properly. 90-95% of people with diabetes have type 2 diabetes. Most cases of type 2 diabetes can be prevented. Dementia is now sometimes referred to as type 3 diabetes because many cases can be prevented with the same practices that can prevent type 2 diabetes. Shown in figure 14.4 is the rapid growth in diabetes in the US between 1958 and 2015. From 1% of the US population having diabetes in 1958 to 7.5% in 2015! It is believed the increase is all due to diet.

Number and Percentage of U.S. Population with Diagnosed Diabetes, 1958-2015

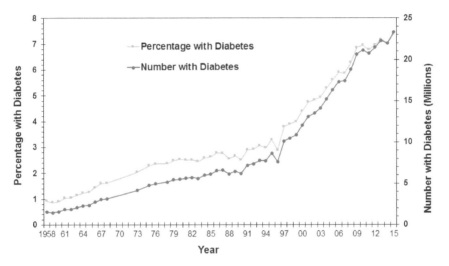

CDC's Division of Diabetes Translation. United States Diabetes Surveillance System available at http://www.cdc.gov/diabetes/data

Figure 14.4 Percent of people with diabetes in the US as a function of year.

Table sugar (sucrose) is 50% glucose and 50% fructose. HFCS is 55% fructose and 45% glucose. (HFCS can have different ratios of fructose to glucose, the most common being HFCS-55, which I will just refer to as HFCS.) HFCS was developed in 1957, economic production began about 20 years later, and HFCS became the sweetener of choice in the United States in the 1980s.

Glucose is absorbed directly into your bloodstream from the small intestines. As the glucose levels rise in your bloodstream, your pancreas responds by releasing insulin into your bloodstream. Insulin signals your cells to uptake glucose from your bloodstream, where it can be metabolized to provide energy. Excess glucose can be stored as glycogen molecules in your liver, and skeletal muscles, for later energy needs. Glycogen is a large molecule containing 2,000 to 60,000 glucose residues. A glycogen molecule is essentially branches of glucose residues in the shape of a ball with a protein at the center. The protein initiated the formation of the ball of glucose residues.

About 100 grams of glycogen is stored in the liver and 500-770 grams in the muscles. The amount in the muscles depends on muscle mass, the fitness of the muscle, and diet. (The way diet effects the amount of glycogen in your muscles is that you need to consume carbohydrates to supply glucose to your muscles and liver for glycogen production.) The glycogen in a muscle needs to be used in that muscle for energy; it cannot be released into the bloodstream to be used in other muscles. Hours after you eat, and your blood sugar levels are decreasing, the pancreas will now release glucagon into your bloodstream. Glucagon signals liver cells to convert glycogen back into glucose and release it into your blood stream. In this way insulin and glucagon work together to maintain a constant glucose concentration in your bloodstream.

Fructose must be processed in your liver. The liver converts fructose to glycogen to replenish glycogen stores in your liver. Once the liver can store no more glycogen, additional fructose is processed into fats. Some of these fats will remain in the liver. High consumption of fructose can be toxic to your liver eventually resulting in non-alcoholic fatty liver disease (NAFLD). Some of the fats produced in your liver from fructose will be pumped into the bloodstream in the form of triglycerides for storage in adipose tissue for energy use later. Insulin is a one-way indicator. When insulin is high, adipose tissue will accept lipids (fats) for storage but not release lipids into the blood stream for use as an energy source. Cognitive deficits are seen with NAFLD, with a more severe cognitive deficit observed as the NAFLD increases in severity.

We evolved consuming small quantities of sugar in berries that also contain fiber, water, and other nutrients. (Fiber slows the digestion preventing spikes in blood glucose concentration.) Unfortunately, our brains pleasure centers react strongly to sugar. A study of rats showed that 94% of them will choose sugar over cocaine [171]. Sugar is addicting, but cocaine is more addicting than sugar. The rats are choosing sugar over cocaine because the time to peak dopamine levels is 2 seconds with sugar and 60 seconds with intravenous cocaine [172].

Typically, your five liters of blood contain 4 grams of glucose, slightly less than one teaspoon. A 12-ounce coke contains 12 teaspoons of sugar. Assuming the coke is sweetened with HFCS, this results in 5.4 teaspoons of glucose quickly dumped into your bloodstream and 6.6 teaspoons of fructose your liver must process! Your body did not evolve to process such large quantities of simple sugars as in a 12-ounce coke, or any of the other high sugar content foods. The rapid rise in blood glucose levels from sugar consumption results in your pancreas releasing high levels of insulin into your bloodstream. Over time, your cells will react to the constant excess of insulin by becoming resistance to this process of letting glucose enter, and your pancreas will wear out from having had to over-produce insulin. The result is higher blood glucose levels and eventually type II diabetes. But the higher sugar levels in your blood stream do harm long before you reach the stage of having type 2 diabetes. Even with blood glucose in the normal range, blood glucose levels on the high end of that normal range have been linked to brain shrinkage [173], reduced neuroplasticity, and cognitive impairment [174]. Cognitive impairment has been found in nondiabetic middle-aged adults with signs of insulin resistance [175].

Large concentrations of excess insulin and sugar cause chronic inflammation all though your body. Inflammation is a good thing when it is an acute response to an injury, but the chronic inflammation from sugar consumption is not. The inflammation response is to repair injury and fight bacteria. With chronic inflammation the body is not responding to an injury. Chronic inflammation is attacking your healthy body tissue. Inflammation causes swelling with the result being compression and restricted blood supply, which damages nerves. This is why diabetics develop peripheral neuropathy, which in some cases can lead to infection and limb amputation. You may be aware that diabetics can lose eyesight because of the resulting nerve damage. Chronic inflammation is slowly damaging the nerves in your brain.

A study at UCLA trained two groups of rats to run a maze. Both group's drinking water contained fructose, but one group also received omega-3 PUFAs. The group that also received the omega-3 PUFAs outperformed the other group. The group that did not receive the omega-3 PUFAs showed a decline in synaptic activity [176]. Nutrition is complex where one component, omega-3 PUFAs, can somewhat protect from another detrimental component, sugar.

Inflammation is a good thing when you have an injury or infection. Chronic inflammation is not. It leads to damage to your immune system, raises blood pressure, cholesterol, and triglyceride levels and leads to nerve damage, pain, and dysfunction. Neuroinflammation reduces our brains neuroplasticity. Neuroinflammation is especially detrimental to the new neurons that are born every day in the hippocampus; we know the hippocampus is a critical area for forming explicit memories. The American diet is a major factor in chronic inflammation. We have seen the large ratio of omega-6 to omega-3 PUFAs in foods leads to inflammation. The lack of antioxidants and other nutrients that help control inflammation are lacking in the American diet. But sugar may be the worst toxin we ingest because high blood sugar levels incite inflammation in blood vessels and nerves. High blood sugar levels damage the brain. One study that tracked 2,067 adults for 6.8 years found that the higher the blood sugar level the higher the risk of dementia [177]. It has been found that people who consume junk foods do not do as well on memory tests as people on a healthier diet.

Glucose and fructose also participate in a process called glycation, the attachment of a sugar to a protein or lipid, with fructose being about 10 times more reactive than glucose. These compounds then form Advanced Glycation End Products (AGEs), a highly reactive molecule that is a gerontotoxin (aging toxin). AGEs cause inflammation. AGEs have been implicated in the aging process and many degenerative diseases such as diabetes, atherosclerosis, chronic kidney disease, and Alzheimer's [178]. AGEs will affect your cognition long before you show symptoms of these degenerative diseases. Adults with high levels of AGEs show loss of cognition, memory, learning, and brain plasticity [179]. People who eat a high-carbohydrate diet have more AGEs than those on a low carbohydrate diet. AGEs can also result from preparation of foods in dry, high heat—roasting, air frying, grilling, and broiling, especially at temperatures greater than 350 °F. The browner, more charred, the more AGEs created from cooking. If there are grill marks, AGEs have formed. You should not eat charred, burned food.

Remember our discussion of the glymphatic system that functions when we sleep to remove metabolic contaminants? Insulin interferes with the functioning of the glymphatic system. That is why it is important not to eat 2 to 3 hours before going to sleep, when the glymphatic system would be most active. Also, elevated glucose levels result in glycation of amyloid protein in the brain, leaving a plaque that is observed in brains of those who had Alzheimer's.

Another source of sugar to be aware of is fruit. Our ancestors ate fruit, but it was only available during certain times of the year and was not genetically engineered like today's fruits are to be high in sugar. Examples of high-sugar fruits are grapes, figs, dates, mangos, bananas, and pineapple. But there are plenty of other fruits that are low in sugar such as berries (blueberries, raspberries, blackberries, and strawberries), coconut, avocado, olives, and cacao. Plus, berries are packed with flavonoids, a group of phytonutrients. Flavonoids are found in all fruits and vegetables and are the source of the vivid colors. Flavonoids are powerful antioxidants, with benefit to the immune system, and they also are anti-inflammatory [180]. In a long running study, it has been seen that those who ate the most berries had MRI brain scans that looked 2.5 years younger [181]. Chocolate is made from cacao, which is a berry, and contains cocoa flavanols, which have been shown to improve blood flow in the brain and reverse cognitive aging [182]. But you do not want to consume large quantities of sugar when you eat chocolate to get the beneficial flavanols. Look for chocolate that is at least 85% cacao.

Our brains rely exclusively on glucose for energy. An adult brain uses about 62 grams of glucose every day. We do need to provide sources of glucose in our diet, but not in the high simple sugar content of foods that our bodies did not evolve to consume—cakes, candies, donuts, soft drinks, fruit juices, processed foods, sugary coffee drinks, etc. The food sources of glucose should be ones that don't cause a spike in blood glucose levels. They should be low-glycemic index/glycemic load (explained below), high-fiber foods. (The body can produce glucose from fats and proteins.)

Our brains use insulin to signal cells to uptake glucose, but also to influence neural plasticity, long-term memory storage, and functioning of neurotransmitters like serotonin and dopamine [183]. When there is too much insulin, to protect themselves, cells reduce the number of insulin receptors. The reduction in these receptors results in the brain not hearing the insulin signal, resulting in reduced cognitive functioning.

The glycemic index (GI) ranks foods on a scale of 1 to 100, based on how quickly they cause blood glucose levels to rise when consuming an equal quantity of carbohydrate. The GI calibration is set with glucose at

100. (Sucrose, which is 50% glucose and 50% fructose, has a GI of 65.) It would take 0.5 cups of sugar, 48 five-inch spears of broccoli, 11 medium-sized carrots, 11 cups of cashews, 3 cups of mashed potatoes, or 2.25 cups of white rice to consume 100 grams of carbohydrates. Since an equal quantity of carbohydrate can mean vastly different servings of one food compared to another, the Glycemic Load (GL) was introduced to take this into account.

Glycemic Load = (Glycemic Index X Carbs in a serving)/100

You want to get your carbohydrates from foods that are low on the Glycemic Index and/or glycemic load to prevent that rapid rise in blood glucose levels. A good time to eat carbohydrates is after you have had a vigorous workout. The exercise depletes the glycogen stored in your muscles and liver, making them ready to quickly take up the glucose in your bloodstream.

Fiber in our diet has many benefits. Fiber is a complex carbohydrate, but one our bodies cannot digest. For our discussion of blood glucose levels, fiber improves blood glucose control by slowing down the absorption of nutrients. This slows the increase in blood glucose level in the blood stream. The liver and cells have time to process the glucose, preventing large peaks in blood glucose level and the corresponding high levels of insulin from the pancreas. Some foods that are high in fiber are broccoli, berries, apples, beans, avocados, whole grains, and nuts. Fiber has many other health benefits, such as lowering your chances of developing colon cancer, improving your digestion, and promoting beneficial gut bacteria.

Protein, fat, and carbohydrates are macronutrients, things our bodies require in large quantities. Vitamins and minerals are micronutrients, things our bodies require in small quantities. Vitamins are important for our immune systems, and for synthesis of neurotransmitters in our brain. Vitamins are essential for the health of our brains and to protect against the development of dementia. Vitamins C and E are antioxidants that remove free radicals. A free radical is a molecule, or atom, with an unpaired electron. Free radicals are created by the body's chemical processes, such as metabolism. Free radicals can also be created by absorption of radiation, inflammation, and pollutants. Since >20% of our metabolism is in the brain, free radicals are especially a concern for the health of the brain. A free radical wants to form a bond with another atom. The free radical scavenges the atom from another molecule without an unpaired electron, and then is no longer a free radical. But the molecule it has scavenged an atom from is now damaged and a free radical. This new free radical scavenges, and hence damages, another molecule that becomes a free radical. In this process cells, DNA, proteins, etc. are damaged. This chain reaction continues until it is stopped by an antioxidant.

When a molecule loses an electron, it is said to be oxidized. This is what happens to a molecule that reacts with a free radical. When a molecule gains an electron, it is said to be reduced because its charge becomes more negative. When a free radical reacts with a molecule it is reduced and is no longer a free radical. When Vitamin C or E encounter a free radical, the free radical is reduced, and the vitamin C or E are oxidized, becoming free radicals! But not all free radicals have the same reactivity. It is something too complicated to explain here, but the unpaired electron in vitamin C or E, once they become a free radical, is spread out around the molecule making the vitamin C and E free radicals very unreactive. Vitamin C and E are called antioxidants because they stop the chain reaction of oxidation by free radicals that destroy molecules in the body.

Our bodies cannot manufacture most vitamins, so they are considered essential and need to be supplied by our diet. (Vitamin D can be manufactured by skin cells with exposure to sunlight and vitamin B7 can be manufactured by gut bacteria.) Vitamins readily cross the blood-brain barrier. There are 13 vitamins, A, C, D, E, K, and 8 B vitamins. Vitamins A, D, E, and K are fat soluble, which means the body can store these vitamins for future use. The B vitamins and vitamin C are water soluble, which means the body cannot store them; they must be supplied every day through diet. You can get an adequate supply of all vitamins from meat, except for vitamin C, which you can get from fish roe and eggs. Fresh fruits and vegetables are a good source for many vitamins. You should be getting your vitamins from food. Many studies show that vitamin supplements do not work and may even cause harm [184] [185].

Green leafy vegetables—spinach, arugula, kale, and romaine— should be consumed every day. They contain nutrients like vitamin K, folate, and phytonutrients. Phytonutrients are not essential, but they help prevent disease. Phytonutrients fight inflammation and oxidation; they are found concentrated in berries. Dark chocolate, which should be

>85% cacao, is a source of some of these phytonutrients—flavanol and resveratrol. In plants, phytonutrients protect against germs, fungi, and bugs. Other vegetables that provide phytonutrients are bell peppers, Brussels sprouts, asparagus, broccoli, and carrots.

One of the main neurotransmitters is acetylcholine, which requires the essential nutrient choline to manufacture. (In chapter 1 we learned that acetylcholine is essential for neuroplasticity, learning, to occur.) Alzheimer's patients exhibit a shortage of acetylcholine. The body can produce choline, but only about 10% of what you require. Diet must provide the other 90%. The best source of choline are egg yolks, fish roe, and brewer's yeast.

We know that neurogenesis occurs in the adult hippocampus. It has been shown that a diet of soft foods inhibits the formation of these new neurons. A diet that requires crushing and grounding enhances the formation of these new neurons in the hippocampus [186]. So nuts, raw vegetables like broccoli, carrots, and celery not only deliver useful nutrients, somehow the chewing of these foods enhances neurogenesis. Also, resveratrol (found in dark chocolate), omega-3 PUFAs, blueberries, folic acid, flavonoids, curcumin, and intermittent fasting have been shown to enhance neurogenesis. Whereas high saturated fat, high sugar, alcohol, and vitamin E, D, and B deficiencies inhibit neurogenesis.

Intermittent fasting is when you reduced the window during which you eat. An example of intermittent fasting would be not eating for 24 hours twice per week. Another, which I do because I find it easy to follow and it doesn't impose difficulties on others, is fasting 16 hours each day. I won't eat after 8:00 p.m., I skip breakfast, and I don't eat again until around noon. As mentioned above, this promotes neurogenesis [187]. It also results in depletion of glycogen stores in your liver, and your body must switch to burning fat stored in adipose tissue. Early humans encountered stresses such as the ones encountered with intermittent fasting. So human cells evolved to respond with enhanced functionality and resilience to such stresses [188]. Humans are antifragile systems that improve with slight stresses, as opposed to fragile systems that are permanently damaged by slight stresses, as will be discussed in chapter 15 on exercise.

Some minerals are essential, and important for regulating brain fluids and hydration, and signal transmission in nerves. These minerals are magnesium, zinc, copper, iron, iodine, selenium, manganese, and potassium. You should obtain these minerals from eating plants. Do not take supplements to obtain them as some of these essential minerals, such as iron, copper, and zinc, can be toxic in too large of quantities.

We all have a different genetic make-up. But our environment and lifestyle have a huge influence on how our genes get expressed. **Proper nutrition is especially important when we are young, and our bodies and brains are developing.**

A diet that has been developed with brain health in mind and adheres to much of what I have talked about in this chapter is the MIND diet [189]. MIND is a diet developed at Rush University Medical Center. The MIND diet is a combination of the Mediterranean diet and the DASH diet. DASH stands for dietary approaches to stop hypertension. MIND stands for Mediterranean-DASH Intervention for Neurodegenerative Delay. Unlike most diets, the purpose of the MIND diet is not weight control. The MIND diet is based on research to improve cognition and to protect against Alzheimer's. Although the MIND diet does not focus on weight loss, it does involve portion control.

The original MIND study [189] showed a 53% reduction in Alzheimer's risk for those who followed the diet strictly, and a 35% risk reduction for those who followed it moderately. It also concluded those on the MIND diet had brains that were 7.5 years younger! The MIND diet has been shown to result in a lower risk of all-cause mortality over the 12-year study [190].

The MIND diet is described in the following two tables. It conforms with what was discussed in this chapter.

Table 14.3 Foods to eat on the MIND diet.

Food	Servings	Comments
Green leafy vegetables	1 or more servings per day 1 serving = a cup raw	Romaine, spinach, kale, arugula, endive, Swiss chard, dandelion greens, and all the leafy herbs*
Vegetables	1 or more servings per day 1 serving = a cup raw	Asparagus, broccoli, Brussels sprouts, cabbage, cauliflower, carrots, green beans, onions, snow peas, bell peppers, sweet potatoes, bok choy
Nuts	5 oz per week	Almonds, cashews, pistachios, and walnuts. I would add seeds to this list—sesame, chia, flax, etc.
Fruits	3 or more servings per week 1 serving = ½ cup	Blackberries, blueberries, raspberries, and strawberries
Beans/Legumes	4 or more servings per week 1 serving = ½ cup	Chickpeas, lentil, black, pinto, garbanzo, and cannellini beans
Whole grains	3 serving per day 1 serving is ½ cup or 1 slice	Whole grain bread; brown, forbidden, black or wild rice; quinoa; barley; whole grain pasta; whole grain cereals
Fish (fish roe is an even better source of omega-3 PUFAs than fish)	1 or more servings per week 1 serving is 3-5 oz, but not fried	Cold water, preferably wild caught, fish like salmon, cod, tuna, halibut
Poultry, preferably pasture raised	2 or more servings per week 1 serving is 3-5 oz	Chicken or turkey breast, skinless and not fried
EVOO	2 TB per day	

*opt for EVOO and vinegar, regular salad dressings have sugar and trans fats

Table 14.4 Foods to avoid on the MIND diet.

Food	Servings	Comments
Red and Processed meats	3 or less servings per week 1 serving = 5, or less, oz	Beef (grass fed), pork, lamb, cold cuts, hot dogs, bacon*
Butter or margarine**	1 or less teaspoon per day	Use EVOO instead, but if you use butter have the butter come from grass-fed cows
Cheese	2 oz or less per week	
Deserts***		Brownies, cake, candy, cookies, donuts, ice cream, milk shakes, pie, pop tarts
Fried or fast foods	1 time, or less, per week	Potato chips, crackers, fast food restaurants
alcohol	Wine, no more than 1 glass per day	Red wine does contain resveratrol and other polyphenols, but alcohol is not brain friendly
Foods containing trans fats		Potato chips, biscuits, rolls, crackers, cold cuts, hot dogs, brownies, cake, candy, cookies, donuts, ice cream, milk shakes, pie, pop tarts
Extracted polyunsaturated oils		(peanut, safflower, sunflower, canola, corn, grapeseed (often hidden in salad dressings), rapeseed, vegetable, and soybean because the extraction creates trans fats

*Other than the grass-fed beef, I would recommend avoiding these other meats because of the trans fats they contain or poor omega-6 to omega-3 PUFA ratios

**I would avoid margarine as it contains trans fats.

***An exception is 2 oz of a >85% cacao candy bar, which provides flavonoids and is a brain healthy treat.

Don't forget to stay hydrated, but by drinking water. Most other liquid drinks—soft drinks, juices, cappuccinos—are filled with things that are not good for your health, such as sugar. An exception is green tea. Green Tea is particularly high in concentrations of flavonoids, which are powerful antioxidants with benefit to the immune system and they also are anti-inflammatory [180]. Green tea provides 272 to 1144 of micromole of antioxidant power/g of dried tea leaves, more than double that of other teas [191].

The foods mentioned to avoid in this chapter, and in Table 14.4, are not 100% at-all-times simple to avoid. These are foods you should not eat all the time, but if you occasionally indulge that is fine. If I am at a birthday party, I do not refuse when they serve the cake. If you are only indulging in the foods on the avoid list on occasion, it should not impact your brain health.

If only ice cream and pizza were health foods, I could live on just those two food items! If you find the MIND diet too difficult to follow, any movement of your current diet towards the MIND diet will provide benefits to your cognition and long-term brain health. I am still in the process of improving my adherence to a better diet. Unfortunately, I learned about nutrition, and began working my way to improving my diet, after I was 50.

Chapter 15: Exercise

As Rodolfo Llinas pointed out, only creatures that move around require a brain [192]. Brains developed to enable mobility. For predators to hunt prey and for prey to escape. As often happens, an evolutionary development finds other uses; humans use their brains to create mental models. It is not surprising that something that involves motion, such as exercising, will be good for the brain. There are strong biological connections between the body and the brain. Physical activity, especially strenuous physical activity, enhances the health and performance of the brain just like exercise enhances the health and performance of the body.

After you have exercised, you are primed for learning. You feel better after having just exercised; you are more focused, less tense, and invigorated. Your senses are heightened and ready to focus on the activity of study. Exercise not only increases neurotransmitters, which improves communication between neurons, it improves the balance between neurotransmitters. Attention deficit hyperactivity disorder (ADHD) is caused by an imbalance of neurotransmitters in the brain, especially dopamine. Exercise has been shown to have a moderate, to sometimes large, effect on symptoms such as attention, hyperactivity, and impulsivity in children with ADHD [193]. Through this increase in the neurotransmitter dopamine with exercise, there will be a corresponding improvement in your motivation.

The positive effect of exercise on cognitive flexibility has been observed even after just a single session of moderate exercise of 60% of maximum heart rate [194]. Cognitive flexibility is the ability to shift thinking between different concepts, consider multiple concepts simultaneously, and come up with creative ideas, not just recall of information. In Netz's study, fourteen men and forty-five women ages 50 – 64 years were split into three groups, a group that would exercise at 60% of maximum heart rate for 35 minutes on a treadmill, a group that would exercise at 70% of maximum heart rate for 35 minutes on a treadmill, and a control group that would watch a nature movie for approximately 35 minutes. To assess cognitive flexibility, the alternative use test was given to the groups before, and 5-minutes after, there 35-minute sessions. (The alternate use test consisted of the subjects being asked to come up with as many alternate uses as they can for a common object within 90 seconds [195].) The control group's pre and post test results showed no change. The exercise groups demonstrated measurable increases in cognitive flexibility. If just one exercise session can result in a measurable improvement in cognitive abilities, imagine what a lifetime of exercise will do for you!

The brain utilizes over 20% of the body's oxygen and glucose (energy source). The way oxygen and glucose get to the brain is through the circulatory system. Every 7 minutes your entire volume of blood flows through your brain. The better your cardiovascular health, the better your brain will function. Exercising not only improves the circulatory system inside your body, but also inside your brain, allowing for efficient delivery of oxygen, fuel in the form of glucose, and chemicals known as myokines, which are discussed below.

Your skeletal muscles play an important role in the health of your body and brain. When we discussed nutrition, we learned that when we eat and glucose enters our bloodstream, the glucose is taken up by our muscles and liver, where it is stored as glycogen for later use. In an average person, muscle composes 40% of the body weight, making muscle the largest organ in the human body. Five times as much glycogen is stored in the skeletal muscles as in the liver, and even more if you increase your muscle mass with exercise. Once in the muscle, glycogen cannot be released into the bloodstream as glucose; it must be used by that muscle. Strenuous exercise will use up glycogen in our muscles, opening a place to store glucose coming from our next meal. (Not to mention resulting in fresh glycogen in the muscles and not glycogen that has been there for years, or even decades, as in the sedentary.) When the body needs more energy, the glycogen is released from the liver as glucose into our bloodstream. Increasing your muscle mass, and depleting the glycogen in your muscles and liver, both of which occur with exercise, allows your muscles to quickly soak up the glucose in your bloodstream after a meal. As we saw in the chapter on nutrition, quickly eliminating the increase in glucose after eating is good for your body and brain.

Muscles are not just for pushing and pulling. Muscles release hundreds of different substances, known as myokines, during exercise. Myokines have been identified that promote healthy blood vessel walls, speed up the body's ability to burn fat, fight development of cancer, control blood sugar levels, and help build strong bones. Some myokines are released during aerobic exercise (cycling, swimming, and jogging) and some are released during anerobic exercise (strength training and intervals) [196]. Therefore, it is important to incorporate both aerobic and anerobic activities as part of your exercise program. Myokines travel through the circulatory system to the brain, where they play roles in the health and functioning of our brains.

An improved cardiovascular system results in lower resting blood pressure and a corresponding lower strain on your blood vessels including those in your brain. Vascular endothelial growth factor (VEGF) is a myokine released during exercise. VEGF triggers the production of endothelial cells, which are not only used for repairing existing blood vessels but are used for building new blood vessels; essentially increasing your vascular network, including the network in your brain. This increased vascular network also provides for added protection due to the redundancy. For instance, alternate paths to deliver blood to regions of your brain if there is a blockage.

Another important myokine is insulin-like growth factor, IGF-1. IGF-1 is produced in the liver, but it is also produced in the muscles and released by the muscles during exercise. During exercise, IGF-1 aids delivery of glucose, for energy, to your muscles. The IGF-1 that crosses the blood-brain barrier has other functions in your brain that aid learning. IGF-1 aids in the strengthening of connections between neurons, neuroplasticity, and neurogenesis [197]. This was an evolutionary development, for instance so that you could recall the location of food or predators. In the brain IGF-1 promotes the production of the neurotransmitters serotonin and glutamate. IGF-1 also causes production of receptors for a very important myokine released during exercise; brain derived neurotropic factor (BDNF).

When BDNF is added to a neuron in millicel inserts (like a petri dish), the neurons were found to sprout new axon branches, dendrite branches, and dendrites [198]. In the brain, BDNF is crucial for the survival of neurons that are born every day in the hippocampus. BDNF has been referred to as "brain fertilizer." This role for BDNF will be discussed further below.

From an evolutionary point of view, a lack of exercise is abnormal, so it is not surprising that exercise has learning benefits. Even a single exercise session has been shown to measurably increase levels of neurotransmitters such as dopamine, serotonin, and epinephrine. After an intense work out session, I find my thought processes feel crisper. This is, in part, caused by the increase in neurotransmitters with exercise; the brain is functioning at its best. When you are learning, new connections are forming, and existing connections strengthen, between neurons. Exercise enhances the brain's ability to make these new connections.

As mentioned, neurogenesis occurs in the hippocampus of the adult mammal brain. Exercise has a profound effect on the genesis and survival of these neurons. In a study of effect of exercise on neurogenesis in the hippocampi of adult mice, a control group was kept in a cage without an exercise wheel and the other group in a cage with an exercise wheel. Mice like to run and given an exercise wheel they will run 4-5 km a day. Observed were significantly more neurons generated in the hippocampi of the mice that were are allowed to exercise [199]. For these new neurons to survive, they need to be used. The neuron must fire its axon to survive and integrate with other neurons. You should always be participating in learning activities to stimulate, and ensure survival, of these continuously generated neurons. Studying after exercising is especially beneficial. Working also involves using your brain, and stimulating these new neurons to survive, which may in part explain the decreased risk of developing dementia with continuing to work [200].

The mice that were allowed to exercise also demonstrated greater cognitive abilities. A container of opaque water had a platform in one corner one centimeter below the surface, so the mice could get out. With repeated placement in the water, the mice who had exercised were better at remembering where the platform was to escape the pool.

How do we know exercise will do the same for the adult human hippocampus? In his book *Boost Your Brain* [201], neurologist Majid Fotuhi, M.D., Ph.D. shows MRI scans of the hippocampus before and after a vigorous exercise regimen clearly showing growth, even to an eye untrained at reading these images. Remember the studies of London taxi drivers presented in chapter 10 on Mindset, where growth in the hippocampi was observed resulting from study of the Knowledge [122] [121]? This hippocampi growth led to improvement in long-term memory.

It is not just the hippocampus that can grow with exercise. Colcombe and colleagues [202] did a six-month study with 59 adults who were between the ages of 60-79 and 20 adults who were between the ages of

18-30. The aerobic exercise group started with reaching 40-50% of their maximum heart rate, increasing to 60-70% over the six-month study. The control group participated in whole body stretching and toning activities. There were three one-hour sessions each week. For the older cohort, there were significant increases in white and gray matter with fitness training. The resolution in this study was not sufficient to determine what comprised the growth. Arthur Kramer, whose lab was at the University of Illinois where the studies were performed, believes the increases seen were the growth of vascular structure, neurons, and connections between neurons. No such increase was observed in the older adults who just participated in toning and stretching. There was no change in brain matter between the exercise and stretching/toning groups for the younger adults. As we age, exercise appears to become even more important for the health of our brains; further studies are needed to determine at what age exercise could prevent loss of brain mass.

As I write this, I am in the middle range of the older age group in this study. This result is of importance to me as I still learn every day. I cannot imagine when I won't be interested in learning every day. The act of writing this book is a learning experience. Not only as I research what is known about learning but getting better at writing as I put the chapters together. When I teach classes, even a topic I have taught for decades, I find I still learn something new every semester. I also learn new ways of presenting material so that my students can better grasp it. I will continue to exercise vigorously to maintain my mental capacity as long as I can.

Sarcopenia is the loss of muscle mass and strength with age. Sometime after we turn 30, we start to lose muscle mass. An inactive person will lose between 3% and 5% of their muscle mass each decade. It is considered a disease. It is highly preventable with physical activity, especially strength training. Loss of muscle mass is very detrimental to our health and to our brains. As our muscle mass is reduced, so is the source of myokines, such as BDNF, VEGF, and IGF-1. Our skeletal muscles contain 50-75% of the body protein and is the prime reserve of amino acids. This makes the skeletal muscles critical when it comes to fighting infections, healing injuries, and preventing chronic diseases such as diabetes and Alzheimer's. The reason a hip fracture is so serious for an elderly person is the lack of skeletal muscle to provide repair materials. Fortunately, by adopting a lifelong exercise routine, you can maintain your skeletal muscles, your health, and your brain function throughout your life.

Besides loosing muscle as you age without strength training, if you don't do cardiovascular training, there will be a decrease in blood flow in your brain, with a corresponding decrease in cognitive abilities [203]. Three groups, each of size 30 subjects, were followed for four years. At the beginning of the study, they were all nearing 65, retirement age. Group 1 continued to work for the four years of the study while groups 2 and 3 retired. Group 2 participated in regular physical activity while Group 3 did not. Throughout the four years of the study, Group 3 exhibited continual declines in cerebral blood flow while both Group 1 and Group 2 maintained their cerebral blood flow throughout the four years. At the end of the four-year study, those who continued to work, and the active retirees scored better on cognitive tests than did the inactive retirees.

The benefits of exercise to academic performance have been demonstrated with the physical education program in the public school district of Naperville, IL [204] [205]. The original motivation to the changes implemented in the physical education program was the decline in fitness, and increase in obesity, of children in the US. Phil Lawler, a physical education teacher at Madison Junior High in Naperville, realized that in gym classes students were mainly standing around, waiting for their turn at bat, waiting for the snap of the ball, etc. He decided to revamp the curriculum to introduce physical fitness, health, and wellness to address this decline in fitness and increase in obesity. Typical team sports were changed to increase participation. Soccer consisted of four on four with smaller goals and no goalie. To score a goal, the offensive team had to have all four players beyond mid-field. Basketball consisted of playing three on three, volleyball four on four. These changes to soccer, basketball, and volleyball were so everyone had to be constantly active, no one could just stand around. In addition, students were taught about fitness, and engaged in vigorous exercise using treadmills, ellipticals, stationary bikes, rock climbing, dance classes, and weight machines. Heart rate monitors were used so students could keep their heart rates at 70-75% of maximum for 30-45 minutes, and their heart rates could be tracked to monitor improvements. Students were graded on improvement in their fitness, not in comparison to their peers.

At the same time this new physical education program was being put in place, the high school was looking at data to determine the reasons some students were struggling with their academic work. It was determined the students struggling were poor readers. To address this, a course was created, Literacy class, for freshman, which would replace an elective choice for freshman. Because some parents were concerned about the loss of an elective, students could opt to take their required physical education course before school started, hence it was referred to as "Zero Hour."

There were 16 students enrolled in the first offering of this literacy class. Nine of them decided to take Zero Hour physical education (PE), so they could take an elective, and seven opted out of the Zero Hour PE. The literacy class was scheduled for the first period, immediately after the Zero Hour PE course. The Nelson-Denning test was used to assess the students' reading levels at the beginning, and end, of the literacy course. The nine students who participated in the Zero Hour PE course improved their reading level by a half year more than did the seven students who did not participate in Zero Hour!

The next year every student who was in the literacy course was put into what they began to call Learning Readiness Physical Education (LRPE) the period before the literacy course. Again, the improvement in reading skills exhibited were comparable to the ones the year before for the students who had been in Zero Hour PE. For the following year, some students who were behind in math and not ready for algebra, took a course called "Introduction to Algebra." Some of the students in Introduction to Algebra were enrolled in LRPE the period before their Introduction to Algebra class. After completion of the Introduction to Algebra class, the students took an algebra ready test. The students who were in LRPE performed 90% better than students who had not taken LRPE.

LRPE is now utilized throughout the Naperville, IL public school system. This not only results in probably the fittest population of students, but the serendipitous finding it also resulted in the best performers academically, improved attendance, and improved behavior. Naperville eighth graders ranked first in the world on the science section, and sixth in the world on the math section, of Trends in International Mathematics and Science Study in 1999. These are tests on which US students typically perform poorly.

We know what was happening to improve the academic performance in the Naperville public school district. A meta-analysis of 59 studies from 1947 to 2009 concluded there is a significant positive effect on cognition from physical activity [206]. After LRPE, there was an increase and balancing of neurotransmitters that primed the students' brains for learning. The students' brains were being flooded with BDNF to nourish the newly created neurons in the hippocampus. BDNF and IGF-1, produced by the exercise, were helping the formation of connections between neurons as the students were learning. The students were building new blood vessels, essentially increasing the vascular network in their brains that enhanced the delivery of oxygen and fuel to their brains.

Naperville is an affluent community, which by itself increases academic performance. That LRPE results in a significant boost, and significant improvement, in academic performance has now been seen in other less affluent communities where such programs have been instituted.

LRPE is not your typical gym class but learning how to monitor and maintain health and fitness. I have been active for four decades participating in activities like Tae Kwon Do, cycling, weightlifting, high intensity intervals, rowing, and cross-country skiing. I have done it because I feel good afterwards. I am pleased to learn the bonus side benefits for my cognitive abilities! If you can learn to be active in grade school or high school, it is known that you are more likely to be an active adult. We all have a different genetic make-up. But our environment and lifestyle have a huge influence on how our genes get expressed. Proper exercise, as with LRPE, is especially important when we are young, and our bodies and brains are developing.

Your exercise should be varied. Aerobic exercise, such as running, cycling, and rowing, will improve your cardiovascular system, which supplies oxygen and glucose to your brain. Aerobic exercise increases and improves the balance of your neurotransmitters, releases myokines into your blood stream, and has been shown to improve cognitive function. Strength training increases your muscular mass and releases myokines into your blood stream. Doing exercises that involve complex motion—martial arts, dance, and basketball—develops complex circuitry in your brain as you learn, as you develop the mental models, to do these activities. The movement and attention regions of your brain overlap and learning new movements in activities like martial arts and dance will help improve your attention.

Every semester I have several students in my class tell me about their exam anxiety. Exam anxiety may not directly impact how much these students learn in my class but can affect their class grade through their performance on exams. Grades can subsequently affect their learning because it might eliminate future learning opportunities. They may not get into the graduate school or professional program they would like. Even worse, they may be dropped from their current program and need to find a less demanding major, or they may not even graduate.

Anxiety is fear. It is a memory of danger. This memory of danger, and the anxiety response, is coming from the amygdala. To combat this anxiety requires control from the prefrontal cortex. It has been found that exercise is just as effective as drugs in controlling anxieties. I would contend exercise may be even more effective because it gives us more of a sense of control over our anxiety. Exercise improves the prefrontal cortex control of the amygdala [207]. Exercise increases the concentration of anti-anxiety neurotransmitters [208].

When we start to feel anxious, our heart rate increases, our blood pressure increases, our breathing becomes more rapid, and our muscles become tense. These are also things that occur when we exercise. That is why, in the past, it was believed exercise should be avoided for those who had severe anxiety. But when these symptoms are brought on by exercise, we learn that they are not necessarily going to lead to something bad happening. You recognize that these symptoms can be a good thing when brought on by exercise; something you purposefully brought on. When you go into an exam, and these symptoms start to present, you know they are not necessarily something bad and you can stop them from bringing on panic [209] [210]. In addition to exercise retraining your brain that increased heart rate, blood pressure and breathing can be a good thing, exercise results in many physiological reactions that ameliorate anxiety.

When we experience anxiety, there is an increase in the stress hormone epinephrine. Epinephrine binds to muscle spindles, increasing the tension in our muscles, making them ready to explode into action, and increasing blood pressure. Exercise blocks epinephrine from binding to these muscle spindles reducing muscle tension and lowering blood pressure. This results in a diminishing of that feeling of anxiety. The effect lasts well beyond the exercise episode, but it is important to exercise frequently to maintain this benefit. Over time, with improved conditioning, your body isn't as likely to go into the stress response from minor stressors, such as going into an exam.

We have learned that exercise produces BDNF. We know that BDNF plays a crucial role in growth of neurons and formation of synapses. With exercise our brains are primed to form connections to cope with the onset of anxiety. BDNF will also increase our levels of serotonin, which triggers a good feeling. Besides serotonin, exercise increases our levels of dopamine, endorphins, and oxytocin, all four of what Loretta Raziano Breuning in her book, *Habits of a Happy Brain*, [211] refers to as the happy chemicals.

Serotonin causes a feeling of being respected by others, a sense of pride. It has a calming effect on the amygdala. Dopamine brings on that feeling of joy when you find what you are seeking. Endorphins increase the feeling of well-being and blocks pain. Although I exercise alone, there is a real benefit to exercising with a partner or group. When you are exercising with other people, you produce oxytocin. Oxytocin produces a feeling of comfort in your social alliances, a very positive happy feeling.

When we exercise, heart muscle secretes atrial natriuretic peptide (ANP), which crosses the blood-brain barrier [212]. In the brain, ANP attaches to receptors in the hypothalamus that results in a calming effect. ANP reduces the secretion of epinephrine, a hormone that is secreted in response to stress; lowers the heart rate; and reduces that anxious feeling.

For students who come to me and mention they have test anxiety, I highly recommend that they take up exercise. The more frequent the better. It can be especially helpful if they can exercise the day of an exam, or before any other potentially stressful event, such as making a presentation, being interviewed, etc. Besides the physical effects of reducing stress, exercise is a distraction, it takes your mind off the upcoming event.

A memory is forever, but we can get our brains to invoke other memories to avoid triggering an anxiety response. One suggestion is to simulate the testing experience, but in a controlled non-threatening environment. If you can acquire previous exams for the course you are going to have an exam, take that exam in conditions as close as possible to the actual exam. This includes doing the practice exam where you will be taking the real exam if possible. This will be a non-threatening experience. At your actual exam think of the memory of this practice. Close your eyes and take slow deep abdominal breathes. When you become anxious you start to breathe rapidly, and often with shallow breathes. This results in expelling too much carbon dioxide, which lowers your blood's pH level. This triggers your brain to cause your muscles to constrict, making the condition worse. Slow deep breathing will ensure that you do not reduce your carbon dioxide levels, and in the extreme case, prevent you from hyperventilating.

This is a good lead into our next topic, meditation and breathing!

Chapter 16: Meditation and Breathing

Meditation is an important activity for the health of the brain. When we are awake, there is constant chatter in our heads. We have seen that during sleep our brain is very active. Information is moved from the hippocampus to long-term storage sites, the hippocampus is erased to make room for the next day's learning, and deeper understanding occurs during the REM portion of sleep. Meditation is more restorative than sleep. It is only through meditation that we can completely rest our brains. At least attempt to!

Meditation can also change the structure of our brains. A study at Harvard was performed on 16 healthy adults who had never meditated [213]. The subjects had weekly meditation classes and averaged three hours of meditating per week for eight weeks. MRI scans of their brains were performed before, and after, the eight weeks of meditation. Observed was increased gray matter around the hippocampus and a decrease in gray matter around the amygdala. We already know the importance of the hippocampus to learning. We will see that the amygdala triggers the fight or flight stress response.

A study at UCLA looked at the effects on brain structure from long-term meditation using MRI techniques [214]. The 50 subjects who were active meditators ranged in age from 24 to 74 years, and their years of meditative practice ranged from 4 to 46 years. There were also 50 in the control group who never practiced meditation, but otherwise were closely matched to the active meditators—age, education, and gender. In both sets of subjects there was age-related loss of gray matter, but the decline in brain gray matter with age was less with the active meditators. The gray matter being the actual neurons in the brain. The meditators also had more gyrification, folding of the cortex, than the non-meditators.

A study was conducted at the University of Pennsylvania Medical Center to see if meditation influenced cerebral blood flow. The study involved 12 advanced meditators and 14 non-meditators. The researchers found that advanced meditators had significantly greater blood flow in the prefrontal cortex, parietal cortex, thalamus, putamen, caudate, and midbrain regions. These areas of the brain support attention, regulation of emotion, and autonomic function [215].

A purpose of meditation is to become aware of the present moment. There are many ways to meditate. Let me describe two simple techniques. Find a comfortable chair, sit upright with your feet flat on the floor and your back straight. You want to breath normally, but to be sure to breath with your abdomen and not your chest. To insure you are breathing abdominally, place one hand on your abdomen and the other on your chest. As you breath, the hand on your abdomen should move out and in, while the hand on your chest does not move. Close your eyes and then for the next 10 minutes try to focus just on your breath. If you haven't meditated before, you will probably only go about 30 seconds before your mind wanders and you are thinking of something else. At some point you will realize you are thinking of something else. Bring your attention back to your breath. It is ok for this to happen. It is part of the process. Each time you realize your mind has wandered, just bring your attention back to your breath. You should be just observing—your breath, your mind wandering, refocusing on your breath—not judging.

Another form of meditation, of being in the moment, can be done with rhythmic exercise such as when you are walking, running, cycling, or rowing. Breath abdominally and be mindful of each step, each peddle, or each stroke. Realize when your mind wanders and bring it back to focusing on the step, peddle, or stroke.

You can also look to join an organization to learn about meditation. If you are at a university, chances are there will be one or more clubs related to meditation and mindfulness that you could join.

Meditation is strength training for your brain. You improve your ability to control the mental chatter in your head, which improves your ability to focus, and it calms you. Proper breathing is part of the meditation process to provide oxygen to your brain. The abdominal breathing you do during meditation is how you should always breathe. Periodically during the day, you should notice how you are breathing. Many people do not breathe properly. If it is not abdominal breathing, but shallow chest breathing, you should make a conscious effort to change to abdominal breathing. Eventually you will automatically breathe correctly, even when not consciously thinking about it.

When you breath shallowly, the air does not get to the bottom of your lungs. There is more blood flowing at the bottom of your lungs, and the bottom of your lungs have 70% of the alveoli, the tiny air sacs where oxygen and carbon dioxide are exchanged between the blood and the lungs. This results in the bottom of your lungs being able to transport 40 mL of oxygen per minute, while the top part of the lungs can only transfer 6 mL of oxygen per minute, to your blood stream [216]. Breathing properly results in more oxygen into your blood stream to fuel every cell in your body, including those in your brain!

There is another very important health benefit from abdominal breathing. We introduced the glymphatic system, the system for removing metabolic waste from the brain. In the rest of your body, you have the lymphatic system for transporting wastes and toxins to the liver and kidneys for removal. The lymphatic fluid moves in response to your muscle movement. A particularly important muscle for this "pumping" is your diaphragm, the muscle used in deep abdominal breathing, because 60% of your lymph nodes are right below your diaphragm [217].

The oxygen to your brain comes from the air you breath. It has been found that the quality of the air you are breathing can impact your cognitive abilities. Carbon dioxide also crosses the blood-brain barrier. This is a concern, not only when you are meditating, but whenever you are breathing. If the air you are breathing has increased levels of carbon dioxide, there will be a comparable increase in carbon dioxide, and a commensurate lowering of the oxygen level, in your blood. This results in less oxygen being delivered to your brain. This is a concern because as the level of carbon dioxide increases in your brain you become sleepy, and your cognitive abilities decrease.

The level of carbon dioxide indoors is higher than it is outdoors. As buildings have become more airtight to reduce energy losses, the levels of carbon dioxide we breathe have increased. Most humans spend 90% of their time indoors breathing these higher levels of carbon dioxide. Humans did not evolve breathing these higher levels of carbon dioxide.

Additionally, the air in buildings contain volatile organic compounds (VOCs). These VOCs come from hundreds of sources. Examples are cleaning products, pesticides, outgassing of building materials and furnishings, permanent markers, glues, adhesives, etc. The levels of VOCs will therefore be much higher inside buildings, up to 10 times, than outside.

Allen et al. [218] performed a study with 24 individuals with different carbon dioxide level exposures. All 24 participants were exposed to the same environment each of the six days of the study. After 6 hours in the rooms, the participants cognitive abilities were tested in the same room. The Strategic Management Simulation software tool was used to administer the 1.5-hour assessment [219].

Cognitive scores were 15% lower on days when carbon dioxide exposure was moderate, ~945 ppm (parts per million), and 50% lower on days when carbon dioxide exposure was high, 1,400 ppm. All days but one, the VOC levels were around 50 ppm or lower. On one day the VOC levels were 10 times higher, while the carbon dioxide level was moderate, which resulted in the worse performance on the cognitive test.

Ten seconds without oxygen to our brains and we are unconscious. The results of Allen et al. [218] are not surprising; a reduction of oxygen to the brain adversely affects cognition. It is imperative to keep your exposure to carbon dioxide at 600 ppm or lower. (The current atmospheric carbon dioxide level is around 420 ppm and climbing.) You should make sure there is a periodic supply of fresh air by opening windows for a few minutes several times a day. To ensure minimal contribution to carbon dioxide inside have regular maintenance on your heating, ventilation, and air conditioning. Keep indoor plants that use the carbon dioxide and release oxygen into the room. No smoking inside. Utilize exhaust fans, especially in the kitchen to remove smoke and carbon dioxide released during cooking. Spend more time outside. I know the weather may not always permit it, but if you can, do some studying outside. This not only exposures you to better air quality, as we learned earlier, varying your study environment improves your learning.

Besides the brain structure changes mentioned above, meditation can have a very positive effect on our autonomic nervous system (ANS). The ANS is the part of your nervous system that functions unconsciously. It includes your blood pressure, heart rate, heart rate variability (HRV), breathing, and digesting. HRV is the variation in time from heartbeat to heartbeat. This is illustrated with the EKG in figure 16.1. The heart rate shown is 60 beats per minute. If all you knew was that the heart rate was 60 bpm (beats per minute), you would expect a heartbeat every 1,000 ms. But over the 6 beats of the EKG shown in figure 16.1, the time between beats varied from 910 to 1,100 ms. HRV is a measure of this variation.

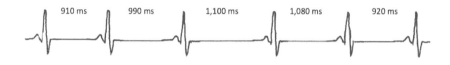

Figure 16.1 Illustration of heart rate variability (HRV).

The two main parts of the ANS are the sympathetic nervous system (SNS) and the Parasympathetic Nervous System (PNS).

When the SNS is active your body is responding to a stressor. Your respiration increases, your heart rate and blood pressure increase, and your digestion ceases. This is a fight or flight response, which will be discussed in detail below.

When the PNS is active it reduces the body's energy consumption. Your respiration, heart rate and blood pressure decrease, and your digestion increases. This allows you to recover from stressful situations. This is a rest and digest response.

Your HRV indicates the balance between your SNS and PNS. The SNS is sending a signal to increase your heart rate while the PNS is sending a signal to decrease your heart rate. In balance these competing signals result in a high HRV. If you are under chronic stress, your ANS is out of balance, with the SNS dominating, leading to a low HRV. When in balance you have a more resilient stress response. You will better respond, and adjust, to stressful situations. Studies show that with meditation you can increase your HRV, effectively training your ANS to better handle a stressful situation. This will help with anxiety you might encounter when you are taking an exam, giving a presentation, or being interviewed.

Since meditation can help balance our ANS, and help us handle stress, meditation will help alleviate the brain destruction caused by chronic stress. The stress response evolved to deal with immediate life-or-death situations. But humans can evoke the stress response just by anticipating something might happen. This can happen to students when they are taking an exam, making a presentation, being on an interview, or when they are thinking of such upcoming activities. If you continuously, chronically, evoke the stress response from your thoughts, the result will be adverse health issues, even if what you are anticipating never happens, or is not something that warrants a stress response. The physical response is the same whether the stress is coming from being pursued by a predator, or just thinking about a stressful situation. The stress response is all about getting your muscles ready for action.

Stress can be beneficial. It prepares us for a challenging task at hand, making us alert and focused as we go into an exam, start a public talk, or start an athletic competition. Stress becomes a problem when it is overwhelming. We may freeze and not be able to function. If it is chronic, our body and brain may not have time to recover. Whereas when we do have time to recover, we can become stronger from the stressful event.

Our stress response can range from mild, to the severe form known as the fight, flight, freeze or fawn response. For simplicity I will just refer to it as the fight or flight response as is commonly presented. The amygdala is the region of the brain that determines the severity of the stress from sensory inputs and our bodies subsequent response. These responses to stress are automatic. The amygdala sends a signal to the hypothalamus, which through the autonomic nervous system controls our stress response. The hypothalamus sends a signal to the adrenal glands to release epinephrine, a hormone. The release of epinephrine into the blood stream elevates the heart rate, blood pressure, and breathing; blood vessels in the skin constrict to reduce bleeding in the case of a wound; and muscle tension is increased preparing you for action. The airways in the lungs open to allow uptake of more oxygen.

There is increased oxygen provided to the brain by the faster heart rate, faster breathing, and open airways, which increases alertness. Your digestive system shuts down to conserve energy for in the extreme cases, fighting or fleeing.

After this initial surge of epinephrine, the hypothalamus activates the second stage of the stress response involving the adrenal and pituitary glands, so it is known as the HPA axis.

The hypothalamus signals the pituitary and adrenal glands to release hormones. Some hormones also act as neurotransmitters. Endorphins are released by the pituitary gland to minimize pain. Norepinephrine and dopamine are released by the adrenal glands so that you are sharply focused on the issue at hand. Cortisol is released by the adrenal glands and plays several roles. Cortisol signals your liver to start converting glycogen to glucose, but it inhibits uptake of glucose by nonessential parts of the body, so there is plenty of fuel for your brain and muscles to deal with the threat. This means your digestive, immune, and reproductive systems shut down. With sufficient stress, you become impervious to pain. Cortisol also signals your body to start converting protein into glycogen and storing it as fat to replenish energy stores. Therefore, constant stress will result in an increase in fat around one's abdominal region.

Earlier we learned of the role that the hippocampus plays in making long-term memories. There are cortisol receptors in the hippocampus, and the cortisol response from stress plays a role in searing the stressful event into our memories. These stress hormones cause an increase in the neurotransmitter glutamate. This increased level of glutamate enhances the firing between synapses, which more readily results in long-term potentiation (LTP). LTP is the strengthening of connections between neurons that occur with continued firing of those neurons. But having constant elevated levels of cortisol will kill neurons in the hippocampus. This effect is seen when cortisol is put in a petri dish with neurons. The neurons wither and die.

This stress response was useful when humans lived in a land of saber-toothed tigers and marauding tribes. Fortunately, that is not the case today for most of us. But we still react with this fight or flight response to non-lethal situations such as giving a speech, a work deadline, or taking an exam. The stress response does help us deal with these activities. It becomes a health, and brain, issue if it doesn't dissipate or is constantly recurring.

A fragile system is one where stress will cause damage. An antifragile system is one where stress, at least up to a point, will result in an improvement of the system [220]. Any system can be damaged with too much stress. Humans are antifragile systems. When you exercise by lifting weights, you do some damage, such as to your muscles. The body not only repairs the damage, but your muscles become stronger.

Occasional small stresses can result in the brain becoming better prepared to handle future stresses. If you continue to do public speaking, those feelings of stress become less, or quickly dissipate, as you start speaking. Because teaching a college class required me to do three 50-minute lectures each week, I have no feelings of "butterflies in my stomach" anymore when I teach a class or present a seminar.

Chronic stress, where the brain does not have time to repair and come back stronger, is detrimental. Chronic stress is very damaging to the body and brain. Stress raises blood pressure. Chronic high blood pressure damages arteries. Such arterial damage can lead to heart attacks, strokes, and decreased oxygen to the brain. The increased cortisol levels result in increased abdominal fat. Abdominal fat leads to high cholesterol, inflammation, heart disease, stroke, and diabetes.

Even without sensory input you can create stress. Worrying about something such as whether you will be able to find a job after graduating or the bombardment of events around the world, such as wars and global warming, can stress us. If such worrying becomes constant you can put yourself into a condition of chronic stress, which is detrimental to your health and to your brain.

The purpose of our stress response is to get us to act; fight, flee, or when fighting or fleeing is not an option, to freeze. We can influence our mental condition with what we do with our bodies. It is therefore not surprising that exercise will help alleviate stress, yet another benefit to our brains of exercising. The next time you feel stressed, try participating in some strenuous physical activity.

When I was working on my Ph.D., I would often feel stressed after a meeting with my thesis advisor. After such a meeting, I had a Tae Kwon Do class immediately following; I serendipitously discovered that after Tae Kwon Do the stress feeling had dissipated. Thereafter whenever I had a bad day, as soon as possible, I participated in a session of Tae Kwon Do, or some other strenuous physical activity, to relieve the stress.

Meditation is another way to relieve stress; to restore your inner calm and peace [221]. You can invoke meditation wherever you are, to address stress. You don't need to be at home, in the usual place, where you meditate. If you are in a waiting room, riding a bus, etc. you can just close your eyes and focus on your deep abdominal breaths. Even if you only have a few minutes, it will not only help you in the moment, but continue to help after you are called from the waiting room or get off the bus.

Meditation is one of the easier suggestions in this book. For some reason, it is one I have had difficulty with consistently doing. I hope the act of writing this chapter will inspire me to take those 10 minutes each day, when I am waiting or walking somewhere, to meditate, to help grow and maintain my brain, and to eliminate stress. It helps to make the practice a ritual; set a time each day when you will do your 10 minutes of meditation.

Chapter 17: Concept Point Recovery

Many students tell me that after they receive their graded exam, they don't spend much time looking at it, especially if they did poorly. This is missing a great learning opportunity, a purposeful practice. Recall our earlier discussion of how chess players become chess masters. They look back at games they played, especially games they lost, to figure out what they did wrong, and what would have been better moves. This is exactly the approach you should take when you get a graded exam back. I know it can be painful to look at an exam with much red ink on it, but using your growth mindset, you know that you can get better. The purpose of taking a class is to learn, to develop mental models. These mental models will help you in future courses, where you will need to call on these mental models, and in life, where you will have to apply these mental models in your job.

In this chapter, I am going to describe an activity that I use in my classes that encourages students to look at a graded exam and have the opportunity to learn a concept that they were missing when they took the exam. This chapter describes something teachers can do to help their students learn. But it is something students can do on their own to enhance their learning, even if they are not recovering points.

During my freshman year, a small group of us were studying for our calculus final. We were in a small study room on our dorm floor. It had a table, about four chairs, and a chalk board. There were three or four of us. (It was 52 years ago, and I can distinctly remember two, Jeff and Chris, who were there but there might have been another.) I recall being at the chalk board most of the time explaining, or showing, how to work a problem. I aced that final. I was surprised the others did not do as well as I. They seemed to understand everything I was doing at the chalk board. I was engaged in active learning, teaching, while they were engaged in passive learning, naïve learning. This may be part of the reason I came up with the concept in this chapter. As Richard Feynman said, "If you want to master something, teach it. The more you teach, the better you learn. Teaching is a powerful tool to learning."

As mentioned, teachers and students view exams as assessment exercises. Although that is the main purpose of exams, they are also learning activities. Taking an exam is a retrieval exercise, which enhances memory and interrupts forgetting. Working a problem on an exam can be an elaboration exercise where you must figure out which concepts to use, and how to apply these concepts, to the question being asked. When exams are returned, spending minimal time examining, and figuring out, what you did wrong is a missed learning opportunity. The activity described in this chapter results in additional student learning, from an exam already taken. The activity results in a student learning a concept that they had not learned for the exam. The incentive for the student is the possibility of recovering points lost on the exam. I refer to this activity as Concept-Point-Recovery (CPR).

I employ this technique at the college level. At a large public university many classes do not require attendance, just that you turn in the required work and take exams. Of course, it is in student's best interest to attend class, but many will attend sparingly. In some cases, instructors impose penalties for not attending class to force students to attend, but this is not common practice. At University College Dublin, the average attendance rate is 56% [222] and I feel that is representative of what I have observed. With CPR, I offer an incentive, rather than a penalty, for attending class. After each exam, if the students have attended at least 80% of the lectures, they have an opportunity to recover missed points on one problem. The student has 15 minutes to explain, as if she were teaching a classmate, the concept behind the problem on which she is trying to improve her score. If an exam consists of 10 problems, the possible point recovery is small enough so as not to influence the effort students put in preparing for an exam. But this opportunity to recover up to 10% of the exam points has many positive impacts.

Occasionally I will have a student raise a concern that my policy is not fair. With a 10-question test, with each question being worth 10 points, the number of points each student can recover will vary from 0 points for a student who scored perfectly, to 10 points for a student who missed all the points on one problem. For an individual test, it is not fair. To make it fair would be to not have CPR, in which case everyone, except someone scoring perfectly, would be worse off. (On my exams, typically there are only a couple of students who score perfectly out of 50-60 students, and it is not unusual for no student to get a perfect score.) CPR only helps everyone; it does not punish anyone. It just helps some more than others. Over the course of a semester, with three exams, most students should benefit from CPR.

The best way to understand a concept is to figure out how to explain it. With the CPR teaching episode, the student receives no points if all the student does is rework the problem. The student must be able to explain the concept behind the problem to recover lost points. This concept, which was a weakness, now becomes a strength. In addition to students learning better when they try to teach a topic, there is a psychological drive to learn the material to regain lost points. Prospect Theory shows that humans exhibit greater sensitivity to losses than to equivalent sized gains [223]. Therefore, most students will put in considerably more effort to learn material to recover lost points on an exam than they did to learn the material for the original exam. I have observed that some students, who had no idea how to work a problem on an exam, are experts on the topic when they come in for their CPR teaching session. Some students have told me they have started to tutor because of the learning benefits they experienced from figuring out how to teach a concept.

An exam should be a learning opportunity, not just a method of assessment. Most students do not spend much time reviewing a past exam; to recover their lost points this review is required. If students had difficulty on several problems, they would probably spend time looking at the concepts on all of them to figure out on which one they should do their CPR teaching session. Students have commented how useful they have found spending time reviewing their graded exams and the posted solutions with the intent of being able to teach the topic behind a question.

Many students experience anxiety taking an exam, which will affect their performance reinforcing their anxiety. During an exam, if students know they will have the opportunity to recover all lost points from one problem, there should be some alleviation of their anxiety. If a student is having difficulty with a problem, the student can move on to finish the other problems without becoming anxious because they know they can recover the lost points later.

I incorporated the CPR teaching sessions in a junior level course on Electric and Magnetic Fields called Electromagnetics I. This course is a mathematically intensive course using vector calculus. All the equations can result in the course being a mathematical abstraction to the students with no understanding of the concepts. It takes considerable effort on the part of students to develop mental models of what these equations represent, which is essential to do well in the course. For the students to be able to teach the concept behind a problem, they must develop these mental models. To teach the material, the students cannot just memorize a procedure, or solution to a particular problem. They must understand the concept behind the equations.

Some students are clearly nervous when they come in for their first CPR teaching session. They become much more comfortable as they gain experience from their one-on-one CPR teaching sessions. These sessions are good preparation for the students for when they are asked to explain a technical concept during a job interview. It is another exercise in reducing their anxiety.

The opportunity to recover lost points is a positive way to greatly improve class attendance. Unless a student has attended at least 80% of the lectures, they are not eligible to recover lost points on an exam. So instead of punishing students for not attending class, the opportunity to recover lost points provides an incentive for class attendance. This attendance policy results in greater than 90% attendance, instead of the slightly more than 50% attendance that would be typical. I like to think a student gets a benefit from attending my classes!

Another benefit of the CPR teaching session is students who had not come to office hours before the first exam, start coming to office hours after their CPR teaching session. The opportunity to recover lost points is sufficient incentive to schedule their fifteen-minute session in my office, after which they feel comfortable dropping in during office hours.

There is the occasional student who comes to their CPR session with little understanding of the course material. This affords an opportunity, early in the semester, to counsel this student, who might otherwise never come to see me, languish, and end up failing the course.

The three fifteen-minute sessions during the semester (for a three-exam course) result in my better knowing the students. The students feel there is a faculty member who cares about them as an individual. A recent Gallup-Purdue poll showed the importance for students' life after college from having been actively engaged with a faculty member, and these sessions foster such engagement [224]. I have much more to say about the role of relationships to success in college in the next chapter.

The students who are successful with their CPR have taken a concept that they may have had no understanding of and became competent enough to be successful with their CPR. This convinces them they can learn this concept with the appropriate effort. This helps them develop a growth mindset. It is also a form of purposeful practice. They are studying their weakest concept, not studying something they know.

There has been a significant, and measurable, effect on the students' performance on the exams and the final course GPA because of the additional learning that occurs with the teaching sessions. As in most courses, but especially Electromagnetics I, students are not ready to learn the material for the next exam unless they know the material covered on the previous exams. There are three exams and a final in Electromagnetics I. As the course progresses, the material in Electromagnetics I becomes conceptually more difficult, and requires comprehensive knowledge of all previous material. The result had been that each exam had a lower average than the previous exam, typically by 3 to 5 percentage points. With three exams and a final, there was a significant decrease observed in students' understanding of the material as the semester progressed. To prepare for their CPR teaching sessions, the students must go back and learn material they did not previously. The result has been improved exam performance; there is no longer a decline in exam averages as the semester progresses.

There has been considerable interest in introducing active learning techniques at universities. CPR is a very simple to implement active-learning technique. Any instructor wishing to incorporate this technique into their class can instantly do it. For a class size of 60 students, with three exams during the semester, the investment in instructor time is about 40 hours during the semester. For larger classes, or instructors who do not want to invest this time, teaching assistants could be utilized.

Chapter 18: Relationships

A job occupies a large portion of one's life. Personal identity is usually tied to one's job. The Gallup Employee Engagement Index categorizes employees as engaged, not engaged, and actively disengaged. If you are engaged in your job, you are enthusiastic in what you do. As Warren Buffett has said he "tap dances to work." He is engaged. If you are not engaged, you can be productive and happy with your work, but not emotionally connected to your work. To you it is not a significant part of your identity. If you are disengaged in your work, you are physically there going through the motions, just waiting for retirement because you are unhappy at work.

Education is the path to your job. But you want your education to lead to not a job, but a vocation. You want to want to go to work, to tap dance to work, because you are happy with what you do. You want work to be self-motivating, not something you have to do for a paycheck.

Gallup surveys show that only 30% of Americans are engaged in their jobs. I have been fortunate that most of my life I have had jobs where I tap dance to work. But I did have a job for three years where I would place myself in the not engaged camp, and the difference in happiness between an engaged job and a not engaged job is staggering. I cannot imagine what it would be like to be in a job where I would be disengaged. Relationships—peer-to-peer, student-to-faculty, and student-to-staff—are key to student success and ultimately ending up engaged with what they do in life [225].

I know from all the students I have had in class over the last 39 years, they are in school to get a good job. They may not realize yet that a good job, besides a source of income, needs to be something that will be engaging. They should seek a career where they want to go to work every morning. They do the job not only for the money they receive in return for working, but because it brings happiness and fulfillment.

A 2014 Gallup-Purdue Index Report was the first attempt to determine if college graduates had great jobs, great lives, and what factors in college were critical to obtaining them [226]. This initial poll included interviews with 30,000 U.S. graduates from every type of college, large and small; public and private; highly selective and not. Of those surveyed who were employed full-time, 39% were engaged, 49% were not engaged, and 12% were disengaged.

Surprisingly, the institution did not matter, as far as ending up with a great job, and a great life. There were six experiences in college that were identified as important for enhancing chances that the graduates had a great job and life. The six experiences, with the percentage of participants who strongly agreed they had had that experience, are shown in table 18.1. In addition, the increase in odds of the participant being engaged at work are shown.

Table 18.1 Undergraduate experience that let to being engaged in one's career.

Undergraduate Experience	% Strongly Agree	Odds of being engaged at work
I had at least one professor that made me excited about learning	63%	2 times higher
My professors cared about me as a person	27%	1.9 times greater
I had a mentor who encouraged me to pursue my goals and dreams	22%	2.2 times greater
All three	**14%**	2.3 times higher
I worked on a project that took a semester or more to complete	32%	1.8 times higher
I had an internship or job that allowed me to apply what I was learning in the classroom	29%	2 times higher
I was extremely active in extracurricular activities and organizations while attending college	20%	1.8 times higher
All three	**6%**	2.4 times higher
All six	3%	

After the Purdue-Gallup poll showed the importance of mentoring on student success, Purdue added mentoring as a required component to be included, and weighed, in the process for promotion of faculty members. Publishing papers and research grants still dominate the reward and promotion process. But at most research universities, such mentorship is not considered at all, is not incentivized, and only occurs if faculty members feel a sense of responsibility to mentor. Fortunately, there are such faculty on every campus. Students should actively, and aggressively, seek out that mentorship.

This is an important message for both teachers and students. At least for the last 16 years, I have incorporated activities in my teaching that would lead students in my classes to indicate they strongly agree they obtained several of the six items. The CPR activity, described in chapter 17, results in a one-on-one interaction with students, often students who would never seek me out during office hours. In my course-instructor evaluations students often respond that the CPR activity indicates that I care about them. Pre-covid I would meet with groups of about 4-5 students each week for lunch in my office. This was an informal meeting that students left feeling a professor cared about them; often the discussion focused on mentoring issues. Since my classes are large, typically in the range of 50-65 students, I have a way where I get an interaction with most students at the end of each week. I call it a reflection exercise that is worth 1-point. There are 15 weeks in the semester. So, it is not too onerous on the students, they only must do this 10 of the 15 weeks to get the maximum number of points. I ask them to keep it brief, only a couple of sentences, since I must read, and usually respond to most of them. The reflection can be questions they have, things they have learned the past week, material they found difficult/confusing, things they liked about the course that week, connections they see between the material and other courses, etc. In some cases, it allows me to answer questions students have about the material, which they would not have taken the initiative to ask without the requirement of these reflection exercises. It gives me feedback each week if there is general confusion about something; what worked, and what didn't work, that week. So, an additional benefit is it improves my teaching. Some students are reluctant to ask questions or seek help. They are more willing to if it is in the form of these reflection exercises. Since the first week of my classes contains much review, for the first week's reflection I use it to initiate this relationship building. I provide my students with a short paragraph about myself and ask them to reciprocate.

For educational success, it is critical to develop relationships. This can be especially difficult if one is at a large research university. A massive campus, and large class sizes, can be intimidating, especially for shy and introverted students. Students can feel like imposters and that they should not be there. This is where relationships are important. Relationships help you feel you belong. They provide support that you need when you are stressed or having difficulty, which everyone will have at some point, especially during a college career.

Many of the six items in table 18.1 are things students can actively pursue. If you are in college, you should make it a goal to meet one faculty member each semester. This can result in you finding that mentor, getting encouragement from a professor, and knowing a professor cares about your success.

Let me mention another reason why you need to get faculty to know you. Let me motivate it with something similar that I needed to do. When a faculty member is up for promotion at a university, they need letters of support for promotion from persons outside their institution. The more prestigious the letter writer, the more valuable the letter will be perceived. I made it a point at each conference that I attended to meet at least one person who would be viewed as a prestigious recommendation. I had to force myself to do this, because I am a shy introvert. This led me to the piece of advice I am always giving students, try to meet at least one faculty member each semester.

Meeting faculty can be challenging if you are at a large state university, where your smallest class may be 50 or more students. In a large research university like the one where I teach, students can go through the whole undergraduate program without a faculty member knowing who they are. When students are looking for a job, or applying to graduate schools, they need references from faculty members. That is why I advise our undergraduates to try to meet one faculty member every semester; to have a faculty member who knows you and might be willing to be listed as a reference on your resume. The best way to do this is to go to the faculty member's office hours. You are not only cultivating a future reference, but you can also be clearing up issues you have with the course material. In addition, when it is time to determine grades, if the faculty member knows you, and how hard you work, you may be given the benefit of the doubt when final grade cutoffs are determined. It might also lead to an undergraduate research experience. You never know where those opportunities might come from, and it is often when you are not expecting them.

From 1869 to 2004 we had the Schools of Engineering at Purdue. Unfortunately, a Dean of Engineering felt that our name should be changed to College of Engineering (CoE). I always liked how we were different from other universities and used schools instead of college. I feel that emphasized the education mission. The individual departments are still called schools, such as the School of Electrical & Computer Engineering (ECE), School of Mechanical Engineering, etc. Since relationships are so critical to our undergraduate education mission, the CoE has many programs that foster relationships. I will describe two CoE programs.

The two CoE programs are Engineering Projects in Community Service (EPICS) and Vertically Integrated Projects (VIP). These are two opportunities for students to pursue projects for more than one semester that fulfill degree requirements. EPICS is a team design project where students partner with a community organization to address needs of that organization. As an example, I was a mentor for a team that developed an exhibit on nanotechnology for a children's museum. This was a two-year project. Some students participated for the full four semesters, but the commitment is only one semester at a time for the students. VIP is a program where undergraduates can earn academic credit working on a research project with a faculty member, and the graduate students and post-doctoral students of that faculty member. The undergraduate students can be involved with the VIP project for multiple semesters. Both EPICS and VIP began as programs in ECE. They were so successful they were expanded to be CoE programs. Currently there are about 600 students who participate in EPICS, and 400 students who participate in VIP, each semester in the CoE at Purdue. There are now over 32 colleges that have EPICS programs, and EPICS programs can be found at many K-12 institutions. There are likely similar programs at your school, whether you are at the K-12 or college level. You should look for opportunities to engage in projects that are longer than a semester. Many programs of study automatically incorporate such an activity as an undergraduate thesis or capstone design requirement. If your program does not require such an activity, there may still be opportunities like EPICS and VIP at your institution.

Although much of your study will be solo purposeful practice, having friends in your courses to study with can be beneficial. Just don't neglect the individual work you have to put in, and don't turn these study sessions into just social activities. If you are trying to explain course material to someone else, that process can result in a better understanding of the material. Often, I have an experience when I am teaching, of seeing things in a slightly different, clearer way. There is evidence that verbalizing material improves your understanding of it. The explaining of technical material in study groups will also prepare you for job interviews, where you will be asked technical questions.

There can be mistakes in textbooks, mistakes in solutions given for old exams or homework, and the lecturer may have said something incorrectly. A study group is a good way to verify that there is indeed an error in the material, and not in how you are thinking. A study group is a good way to get information you may have missed during class, written down incorrectly, or learn of other study resources a member of your study group has found.

Having a relationship-rich environment will greatly increase your chances of success when pursuing an education. These relationships should be with your teachers/faculty, peers, and staff. I have found that many undergraduates fear coming to my office hours, missing an opportunity to build a relationship with a faculty member. They view professors as intimidating authority figures, although I am anything but that. At a large state university, you will encounter faculty who will not be overly welcoming. But that should not discourage you. You will encounter faculty who will be welcoming; who could become that needed reference when pursuing a job or applying to graduate school; that person you seek advice from; or that someone whose research group you join. I have had students I have come to know who have become comfortable enough to seek help with non-academic issues. Sometimes they just needed to talk to someone. Other times I was able to point them to the resource needed to help them navigate their difficulties. This would not happen if they did not develop a relationship with me.

Earlier, we saw that Angela Duckworth's research indicated that participation in extra curricula activities was an indicator of future success in college. The Gallup-Purdue poll shows active participation in extracurricular activities while in college was an indicator of future success after college. This could partially be due to the relationships that develop from these activities. Relationships with faculty advisors, coaches, and peers. Even if these activities were not directly related to academics, such as sports, student government, or clubs, relationships develop that can be sources of advice. Colleges are rich with extracurricular activities. At Purdue University there are over 1,000 student organizations and clubs. Finding an activity of interest and building rich relationships is possible for everyone. And if not, it is easy to start a new student organization/club. Most of those over 1000 student organizations at Purdue were founded by students! I had a student in my class on Electromagnetics who created an organization to put on plays. Something completely unrelated to the technical field she was studying. I wish I would have known how important it was to take advantage of activities outside my technical field when I was an undergraduate.

Another highly effective example for relationship building is an organization we have in my department, Electrical & Computer Engineering (ECE), called the ECE Student Society (ECESS). If your school does not have such an organization, faculty, staff, or students could initiate one. We did not always have this organization; it was started about 10 years ago. ECESS is a "Student led organization focused on creating professional and social opportunities for all ECE students." ECESS was conceived and spearheaded by one of our student advisors, Angela Rainwater. Any student, staff member, or faculty can get something like ECESS started, if your department does not already have such a program. Not only does ECESS result in relationship building with other students, but also with faculty, and staff such as student advisors.

Our ECESS accomplishes its mission with 9 committees. I will mention a few of the committees and their roles. The act of just joining one of these committees is relationship building.

The first one is Ambassadors. This is a committee that showcases ECE to prospective students, families, and visitors. They do this by giving tours of our department and making presentations. Ambassadors also host faculty candidates when they come to interview. For new students who will be participating as ambassadors, there is formal training for the tours and presentations. Being an Ambassador helps to develop presentation skills, the ability to interact with visitors, and to answer their questions. The Ambassadors also host a welcome back to students at the start of the Fall semesters.

The next committee is the Boiler podcast. These podcasts cover what is happening in ECE, from interviewing faculty about their research to students talking about their struggles.

The Community Outreach Committee organizes ECE students to participate in events for the local communities of West Lafayette and Lafayette. For example, working at the animal shelter or raking yards for people who cannot do it themselves. This committee also has events at local schools to introduce general engineering concepts, such as courses on Python programming.

The Faculty Outreach Committee connects ECE students with faculty in informal settings. Every month a faculty-student lunch is hosted. Faculty can talk about their research and the courses they teach, and students can convey their experiences in ECE. These events help students understand professors and professors understand students. These events help develop faculty-student relationships outside of the classroom. Even more casual social events are hosted for faculty and students, such as game and bowling nights.

The Women in ECE committee focusses on empowering women in ECE and making connections to other women in the major. They hold outreach, networking, and social events. This helps with making friends, finding study partners and mentors. Events are held where women ECE alumni come back to meet with, talk to, and make connections with current students.

The Social Committee organizes social events for ECE students. These events are a way for ECE students to connect, develop, and destress. Some themed events are done in collaboration with student organizations in other engineering disciplines.

The Spark Challenge Committee puts on a one-day event, but it is one of the largest events. The Spark Challenge is a campus-wide, corporate-sponsored event that is hosted by ECE. It is an opportunity for ECE undergraduates to present their projects to peers, faculty, and corporate partners. The projects presented are usually senior design projects. This event fosters networking with corporate partners and potential employment opportunities. The event has over 600 visitors, 30 participating teams presenting their projects, and 21 judges.

The Multicultural Affairs Committee's purpose is to empower students from all backgrounds, cultures, and identities. They do this by putting on events that have a cultural theme. They initiate collaborations with cultural centers on campus for some of these activities. These events are opportunities for all ECE to learn about other cultures. One advantage ECE has is that we are already very multicultural, so there are usually students connected to these other cultural centers to initiate the collaboration.

The ECE Mentoring Committee connects upper class ECE students, juniors and seniors, with First Year Engineering (FYE) students who are interested in ECE. This is a way FYE students can learn what it is like being a student in ECE, how to best prepare for entering ECE as a student, and to make friends in ECE.

During the first week of the Fall semester, ECESS holds a weeklong welcome back for ECE students consisting of different games, events, and resources. Some of the activities held this welcome back week are meet faculty with coffee & donuts, outdoor games with frozen custard, movie night with pizza, a pancake lunch, Escape Room, Paint Night, and WECE friendship bracelets. (Apparently, they have not read chapter 14 on nutrition!)

ECE at Purdue is very large with over 100 faculty and 2,000 undergraduate students. So, an organization like ECESS is very important for relationship building. But such an organization can be effective in any size department. It does not have to be of the same magnitude or cover as many different activities.

Besides getting involved in a program like ECESS for relationship building, as we learned from Angela Duckworth's work, active involvement in such an extracurricular activity engenders grit.

Earlier I mentioned our program of undergraduate teaching assistants (UTAs). This is also a relationship building program that greatly aids our undergraduate education mission. In our department, ECE, we employ over 200 UTAs each semester. Their role, and how they are hired, varies from class to class. There is a formal application process where potential UTAs can indicate courses they are interested in UTAing, how they performed in those courses, and why they want to UTA. Faculty and lab staff can then indicate who they are interested in as UTAs for their courses. I select UTAs from this list for my course, but I also ask students I have had previous semesters, students I have gotten to know well, if they would be interested.

The pay is usually not the main reason our undergraduates want to be UTAs; they are not paid that well! They do it because it is relationship building with faculty and lab staff. It is a way to retain information they learned, and improve their understanding of the material, as teaching is how you really learn. They do it as a sense of responsibility to our department and their fellow students. The UTA program also builds undergraduate-to-undergraduate relationships. With the large number of UTAs, we greatly increase the amount of contact between learners and teachers, between the students in a course and the UTAs for that course. Many undergraduate students are too intimidated to go to their professors for help. They may be more willing to seek help from graduate teaching assistants, but most are willing to seek help from UTAs who they see as peers.

In the Fall of 2022 semester, ECE launched a new mentorship program to connect our students with alums, industry partners, faculty, and other ECE students utilizing an online app called TaskHuman. Mentors who participate provide a profile so perspective mentees can find specific types of mentors. Mentors provide availability directly through the TaskHuman app, times when students can message, call, or set up a meeting time. Alums can also just hop on the app, and students can hop on the app to see who is available. Examples of topics include, but are not limited to, work-life balance, careers in industry, careers in academia, interviewing tips, entrepreneurship, advice on electives, hot areas in industry, what it is like "on the job," how to get involved in research projects, co-op opportunities, law school options, etc.

Too often students view their education as a series of steps. To get their degree they must earn a certain number of credit hours. Each semester they take a certain number of courses towards this goal. Each course is a hurdle to get credit hours towards their semester goal. In each course there are assessments (exams, homework, presentations, etc.) that determine if you pass (your grade) and get those credit hours. Going to school to learn is somehow lost to all these transactions. Relationships inspire students to learn. Relationships help students to look at their time in school as much more than credit hours, as a path to meaning and purpose, to learning, and personal development. The CPR activity that I described in chapter 17 serves two purposes. Students feel that someone cares about them because of the effort put in to provide them the CPR opportunity. Plus, CPR emphasizes the learning aspect, although recovering points is the initial motivation for students to participate.

During the 13 years I served as Associate Head for Education, I would talk with new faculty about teaching. The range of teaching concerns from new faculty included how many courses they would have to teach, what are best practices for teaching, and how do they get good teacher evaluations from the students. My advice was if you care about the students' learning, then you will become a good teacher and the students will recognize you care, and it will be reflected in your evaluations. Building relationships with students is also a reflection of the faculty member caring about the student and the student's learning. It is not always possible, because our classes can approach 100 in size, but I suggest to new faculty they should learn the names of as many of the students in their class as possible. When a student raises their hand with a question, call on them by name. Not only for that student, but for all the students, the instructor is creating a welcoming environment, and building a connection with her students, by using their names.

Pre-Covid I used to meet with groups of 4-5 students in my class each week for lunch. This was a great relationship building exercise and a great aid to learning names. Since the students fill my classroom, I hold evening exams so that students can sit in alternate seats. I use a seating chart and I use the exam time to memorize as many names as possible. After the first exam, I walk around the class handing back exams; I can see they are wondering how I know everyone's name! More than once I have seen a student in the hallway and I say Hi John or Hi Jackie and they incredulously respond, "you know my name!?" Another aid to learning names, which I haven't tried yet, is to have the students make name tents. It should then only take a few weeks to learn everyone's name if the class is not too large.

An important aspect of developing relationships is becoming comfortable in school and not feeling isolated. I was the first generation in my family to graduate from college. It was an intimidating experience for me arriving and starting college. I was a shy introvert and unsure of myself. I would sit in the back of the classroom; I would never ask questions. I was afraid of asking questions. I felt that everyone else knew what was going on and I would appear like I didn't belong there—imposter syndrome. I never developed relationships with faculty or the other students in my class, which would have made me more comfortable. I now know better, and I don't hesitate to admit I don't know something and to ask someone to explain it to me; an attitude that would have been very useful when I was back in school. Although much of learning is an individual endeavor, being able to ask for help when needed can be the difference between succeeding and floundering. That is where relationships are key, having peers, faculty, and staff you feel comfortable asking for help.

As I mentioned in the chapter on mindset, there are instructors who foster the imposter syndrome feeling with their adverse response to a student's question in class. They are the exact opposite of encouraging. They make the student feel that what they are asking is something they should already know, instead of encouraging the student to ask such questions and strive to learn. If you are an instructor, please try to be sensitive to students who are struggling, yet still have enough courage to ask a question in class. Unfortunately, students will encounter such instructors. It is hard, or impossible, not to let it discourage and embarrass you. Keep looking elsewhere for help, such as other students, instructors in other classes, or staff, such as advisors. Eventually you will overcome imposter syndrome and know you belong.

Chapter 19: Summary

Spaced Studying

Spaced studying involves multiple study sessions with at least a day between sessions. When you are studying, material is placed in the hippocampus. Once the material is in the hippocampus additional studying does not reinforce it. When you sleep the material is transferred from the hippocampus to long-term storage sites in the neocortex. During the time between study sessions, you continually lose the ability to retrieve the material you have in long-term storage. The retrieval is reconstituted, and made more durable, by studying after this forgetting has taken place. Spacing also provides opportunities for incubation to occur.

Incubation

After you have studied and are doing something else—taking a walk, playing a sport, sleeping, etc.— incubation occurs. Your brain subconsciously works on what you were studying and finds associations between your mental models. You have probably all had that experience where there was a problem on an exam you had no idea how to solve it. Then a few hours after the exam, when you are no longer thinking about the exam, how to solve that problem comes to you. That is an example of incubation, and something you want to happen when you are studying, not when you are taking an exam! Incubation can help you solve your homework problems if you start the homework in time to allow for periods of incubation, not start the day before your homework is due! Incubation also helps when you are working on a large project. If you are writing a term paper, start early so that you have periods of incubation. You will come back to your paper with new ideas, better ways of wording a section, etc. Incubation is another reason why your studying should be spaced—to allow for multiple incubation periods.

Interleaving

Interleaving is when you mix subjects, and mix the topics in a subject, as you are studying, rather than block study one topic before moving on to the next. Interleaving feels like a less efficient method of studying than block studying. But with interleaving you are gaining a deeper understanding of the material. You are learning to recognize the topics. On exams, questions are not going to be grouped by topic. You must recognize from the question the topic that is being asked. With interleaving you are developing that ability. Interleaving also works with different subjects. You don't want to just study algebra one day. You want to work on algebra, language, history, etc. That way you also build up connections between your different subjects. You are developing a latticework of mental models.

Vary Where You Study

Ideally, you want recall of material you have learned to be independent of where you studied. This requires you to vary the location of where you study. Do some of your studying in your room, the library, a coffee shop, at your friend's place, outside, etc.

Sleep

Sleep is very critical to the learning process. Adequate sleep is essential for optimal functioning of your brain. When you sleep, what you have been studying during the day is transferred from the hippocampus to regions in your neocortex. Your hippocampus is also erased during sleep to make room for new learning the next day. This is why staying up all day and night to prepare for an exam does not result in strong learning. Your hippocampus has limited storage, so you end up overwriting some material you have already studied. Without a sleep session the material is never transferred to long-term storage. Furthermore, during sleep your brain works to process and integrate what you learned the previous day and to find weak connections between your mental models. This allows for a deeper understanding of the material and the ability to solve much more complex problems. Sleep is also when creativity can occur.

Mindset, Self-Control, and Grit

It is very important you realize, where you end up will depend more on your effort than innate talent. If you believe you lack talent in some area, it will be a self-fulfilling prophecy; you won't put in the effort to develop talent in that area. You need to develop a growth mindset, instead of a fixed mindset. A belief that you can get better with effort, and that it is not known how proficient you can eventually become with sustained effort.

Self-control is the ability to resist momentary temptations. Grit is the ability to sustain effort for a long time to achieve a goal. Both self-control and grit can be developed. I know I have a lot more self-control and grit than I did when I was a student. I therefore know you can improve your self-control and increase your grit. (I often lament that I wish I had the self-control and grit I have today when I was a student.) Anticipate attempts to distract you from your work and already have a response prepared. If your friend calls to ask you to do something be prepared to say "No, I cannot; I am working on a homework assignment due tomorrow. Let's do it Saturday." Set a study schedule that you will follow during the semester. Do not wake up each day and wing it. Surround yourself with a culture of grit. Make friends with people that have self-control and grit. Choose a college to go to where students work hard. Take a job in a company that has a culture of grit. Choose an extracurricular activity and stick to it to develop grit. If you can participate in the extracurricular activity for more than a year and accomplish something significant, such as becoming an officer, winning a competition, etc., the better for developing grit. Tell yourself you are gritty.

Purposeful Practice

To learn, or develop a new skill, you need to work at the limit of your ability. Your study session, or practice, needs to be hard; not just going over things you already know or can do. You need to study to understand concepts, not just blindly memorizing procedures. This is called purposeful practice. Testing is an excellent type of purposeful practice. When you are studying, such as reading your text or notes, you should pause, look away, and recall what you have been reading. You should spend at least 50% of your study time in this recall mode. Afterwards, you should take out a blank sheet of paper and pencil, write down what you can remember. These are forms of self-testing.

I give my students several copies of past exams as study material. I tell them once they have studied, under conditions like they will encounter when they take the test—the same amount of test time with closed book and no notes—take one of the sample tests. After this exercise, do not look at the solutions. Wait until the next day. Give time for incubation to occur. Now look at the sample test again to see if you can work some of the problems you could not before. If you can now solve them, this results in a much deeper learning than if you looked at the answers to see how the problems were solved. There will be problems that require you looking at the answer key; that is ok because you are working at the limit of your knowledge. Now do the same thing with the next sample test. (Clearly you will have to start much sooner than the day before the exam to do this purposeful practice.) It will take self-discipline and grit to do this. Every semester I have a student tell me the sample exams were much easier than the test they were given. I have been teaching for 39 years; if my exams were indeed getting harder each semester, they would be impossible to answer! I ask them if they followed my suggestion of taking the exam under the conditions of their actual exam. The answer is always no!

Relationships

Building relationships is critical to success as an undergraduate in college. These relationships include peer-to-peer, faculty-to-student, and staff-to-student. Universities continuously strive to improve their rankings. The type of things that influence rankings are size and funding of research programs, size of the endowment, number of faculty who are members of national academies, and student selectivity. Once you are at a university, these things only have a minor, if any, impact on your success. When you are looking at colleges be mindful of those with programs that help build relationships and have programs that will engage you, such as EPICS, VIP, and ECESS that I discussed in chapter 18. Having such opportunities will not only lead to success in college, but as the Gallup-Purdue poll has shown, an engaged career and satisfaction in life [226]. In fact, a study from the Stanford Graduate School of Education found that engagement in college is more important than where you attend [227].

Epilog

I wish I had known the information in this book when I had been growing up, while I was still in school. Knowing what is important, and better yet not important, regarding learning. Difficulties, and the occasional failure, are necessary to truly experience learning, because you are working at the limit of your knowledge or abilities. Grades are not necessarily a reflection of your true learning. We all believe that if we grasp a concept easily or get top grades by whatever means necessary—cramming, memorizing—then we are successful. To truly learn a concept and be able to use it critically, you need an understanding of the concept. Understanding is learning. Blindly memorizing a procedure is not. You will get very good grades if you approach school from the aspect of really understanding.

To optimize your brain for this educational journey requires being challenged, a growth mindset, grit, adequate sleep, proper nutrition, exercise, meditation, and good social relations. If I had been exposed to this information when I was younger, it would have enhanced my learning when I was in school. If you are currently in school, you can take advantage of the information in this book. But your educational journey should last a lifetime, not just during the formal part of your schooling. If you are reading this book and are more advanced in age, learning is never too late. Learn something new every day, whether it is a new cooking method, taking up a challenging form of exercise, learning a new language, or just adding a new word to your vocabulary; it will be rewarding. I intend to learn throughout the rest of my life. I look forward to the struggle of mastering endless new concepts.

Bibliography

[1]   C. S. v. Bartheld, "Myths and truths about the cellular composition of the human brain: a review of influential concepts," *Journal of Chemical Neuroanatomy,* vol. 93, pp. 2-15, 2018.

[2]   S. Herculano-Houzel, The Human Advantage: A New Understanding of How Our Brain Became Remarkable, Cambridge, MA: MIT Press, 2016.

[3]   T. Xu, X. Yu, A. Perlik, W. Tobin, J. Zweig, K. Tennant, T. Jones and Y. Zuo, "Rapid formation and selective stabilization of synapses for enduring motor memories," *Nature,* vol. 462, pp. 915-919, 2009.

[4]   H.-q. Li, M. Pratelli, S. Godavarthi, S. Zambetti and N. C. Spitzer, "Decoding Neurotransmitter Switching: The Road Forward," *Journal of Neuroscience,* vol. 40, no. 21, pp. 4078-4089, 2020.

[5]   D. Hubel and T. Wiesel, "The period of susceptibility to the physiological effects of unilateral eye closure in kittens," *Journal of Physiology,* vol. 206, no. 2, pp. 419-436, 1970.

[6]   J. Altman and G. Das, "Postnatal Neurogenesis in the Guinea-pig," *Nature,* vol. 2145, pp. 1098-1101, 1967.

[7]   G. Kempermann, H. Kuhn and F. Gage, "More Hippocampal Neurons in Adult Mice Living in an Enriched Environment," *Nature,* vol. 386, pp. 493-495, 1997.

[8]   P. Eriksson, E. Perfilieva, T. Bjork-Eriksson, A.-M. Alborn, C. Mordborg, D. Peterson and F. Gage, "Neurogenesis in the Adult Human Hippocampus," *Nature Medicine,* vol. 11, no. 4, pp. 1313-1317, 1998.

[9]   B. Draganski, C. Gaser, G. Kempermann, H. G. Kuhn, J. Winkler, C. Buchel and A. May, "Temporal and Spatial Dynamics of Brain Structure Changes during Extensive Learning," *The Journal of Neuroscience,* vol. 26, no. 23, pp. 6314-6317, 2006.

[10]   W. James, The Principles of Psychology, 1890.

[11]   K. A. Ericcson, W. Chase and S. Faloon, "Acquisition of a
       Memory Skill," *Science,* vol. 208, pp. 1181-1182, 1980.

[12]   W. Chase and H. Simon, "Perception in Chess," *Cognitive
       Psychology,* vol. 4, pp. 55-81, 1973.

[13]   J. Soni and R. Goodman, A Mind At Play: How Claude
       Shannon Invented the Information Age, New York: Simon &
       Schuster, 2017.

[14]   G. Boole, An Investigation of the Laws of Thought, on Which
       are Founded the Mathematical Theories of Logic and
       Probabilities, 1854.

[15]   N. Doidge, The Brain That Changes Itself: Stories of Personal
       Triumph from the Frontiers of Brain Science, New York:
       Penquin Books, 2007.

[16]   L. B. Merabet and A. Pascual-Leone, "Neural reorganization
       following sensory loss," *Nature Reviews Neuroscience,* vol. 11,
       no. 1, pp. 44-52, 2010.

[17]   T. Elbert, C. Panev, C. Wienbruch, B. Rockstroh and E. Taub,
       "Increased Cortical Representation of the fingers of the left
       hand in String Players," *Science,* vol. 270, pp. 305-307, 1995.

[18]   B. Milner, "Les troubles de la mémoire accompagnant des
       lésions hippocampiques bilatérales," *Physiol. Hippocampe
       Cent. Natl. Rech. Sci.,* pp. 257-272, 1962.

[19]   C. Xie, "Understanding the Human Brain: A Dedicated
       Lifetime Pursuit: Interview with Dr. Brenda Milner," *McGill
       Journal of Medicane,* vol. 9, no. 2, pp. 165-172, 2006.

[20]   W. B. Scoville and B. Milner, "Loss of Recent Memory After
       Bilateral Hippocampal Lesions," *Journal of Neurol. Neurosurg.
       Psychiat.,* vol. 20, no. 11, 1957.

[21]   H. Ebbinghaus, Memory: A Contribution to Experimental
       Psychology, 1885.

[22]   W. James, Talks to Teachers on Psychology and to Students on
       Some of Life's Ideals, 1901.

[23]   R. Bork and E. Bjork, A new theory of disuse and an old theory
       of stimulus fluctuation, Hillsdale, NJ: Erlbaum, 1992.

[24] T. Dray and C. A. Manogue, "Spherical Coordinates," *The College Mathematics Journal,* vol. 34, no. 2, pp. 168-169, 18 October 2003.

[25] D. Rohrer and K. Taylor, "The Effects of Overlearning and Distributed Practice on the Retention of Mathematics Knowledge," *Applied Cognitive Psychology,* vol. 20, pp. 1209-1224, 2006.

[26] C.-A. E. Moulton, A. Dubrowski, H. MacRae, B. Graham, E. Grober and R. Reznick, "Teaching surgical skills: What kind of practice makes perfect," *Annals of Surgery,* vol. 244, pp. 400-409, 2006.

[27] H. Bahrick, L. Bahrick, A. Bahrick and P. Bahrick, "Maintenance of foreign language vocabulary and the spacing effect," *Psychological Science,* vol. 19, no. 11, pp. 316-321, 1993.

[28] N. J. Cepeda, E. Vul, D. Rohrer, J. T. Wixted and H. Pashler, "Spacing effects in learning a temporal ridegline of optimal retention," *Psychologicl Science,* vol. 19, no. 11, pp. 1095-1102, 2008.

[29] D. Godden and A. Baddeley, "Context-Dependent Memory in Two Natural Environments: On Land and Underwater," *British Journal of Psychology,* p. 35, 1975.

[30] S. M. Smith, A. Glenberg and R. A. Bjork, "Environmental Context and Human Memory," *Memory and Cognition,* vol. 6, p. 342, 1978.

[31] S. M. Smith, "Background Music and Context-Dependent Memory," *The American Journal of Psychology,* vol. 98, no. 4, pp. 591-603, 1985.

[32] R. Mehta, R. Zhu and A. Cheema, "Bad? Exploring the Effects of Ambient Noise on Creative Cognition," *Journal of Consumer Research,* vol. 39, pp. 784-799, 2012.

[33] Kerr and Booth, "Specific and Varied Practice of Motor Skills," *Perceptual Motor Skills ,* vol. 46, p. 395, 1978.

[34] K. Hall, D. Domiongues and R. Cavazos, "Contextual interference effects with skilled baseball players," *Perceptual and motor skills,* vol. 78, no. 3, pp. 835-841, 1994.

[35]   Kornell and Bjork, "Learning Concepts and Categories, "Is Spacing the "Enemy of Induction"?,"," *Psychological Science,* vol. 19, p. 585, 2008.

[36]   D. Rohrer and I. Taylor, "The Shuffling of Mathematical Problems Improves Learning," *Instructional Science,* vol. 35, pp. 481-498, 2007.

[37]   K. Taylor and D. Rohrer, "The Effects of Interleaved Practice," *Applied Cognitive Psychology,* vol. 24, pp. 837-848, 2010.

[38]   R. Rhodes, The Making of the Atomic Bomb: 25th Anniversary Edition, New York: Simon & Schuster, 2012.

[39]   H. Poincare, "Mathematical Creation," *Monist,* vol. 20, pp. 321-333, 1910.

[40]   G. Wallas, The Art of Thought, 1926.

[41]   U. N. Sio and T. C. Ormerod, "Does Incubation Enhance Problem Solving? A Meta-Analytic Review," *Psychological Bulletin,* vol. 135, no. 1, pp. 94-120, 2009.

[42]   H. Roediger and J. Karpicke, "Test-Enhanced Learning," *Psychological Science,* vol. 17, p. 250, 2006.

[43]   E. Abbott, "On the analysis of the factors of recall in the learning process," *Psychological Monographs,* vol. 11, pp. 159-177, 1909.

[44]   A. Gates, "Recitation as a factor in memorizing," *Archives of Psychology,* vol. 6, no. 40, 1917.

[45]   H. F. Spitzer, "Studies in Retention," *The Journal of Educational Psychology,* vol. 30, no. 9, pp. 641-656, 1939.

[46]   M. A. McDaniel, P. K. Agarwal, B. J. Huelser, K. B. McDermott and I. Henry L. Roediner, " Test-Enhanced Learning in a Middle School Science Classroom: The Effects of Quiz Frequency and Placement," *Journal of Eduucational Psychology,* vol. 103, no. 2, pp. 399-414, 2011.

[47]   P. Agarwal, J. Karpicke, S. Kang, H. Roediger and K. McDermott, "Examining the testing effect with open- and closed-book tests," *Applied Cognitive Psychology,* vol. 22, pp. 861-876, 2008.

[48]   S. Kang, K. McDermott and H. Roediger, "Test format and corrective feedback modify the effect of testing on long-term

retention," *European Journal of Cognitive Pscyhology,* vol. 19, pp. 528-558, 2007.

[49]   K. B. Lyle and N. A. Crawford, "Retrieving Essential Material at the End of Lectures Improves Performance on Statistics Exams," *Teaching of Psychology,* vol. 38, no. 2, pp. 94-97, 2011.

[50]   C. O. Fritz, P. E. Morris, R. A. Bjork, R. Gelman and T. D. Wickens, "When further learning fails: Stability and change following repeated presentation of text," *British Journal of Psychology,* vol. 91, pp. 493-511, 2000.

[51]   A. Butler and H. Roediger, "Feedback enhances the positive effects and reduces the negative effects of multiple-choice testing," *Memory & Cognition,* vol. 36, pp. 604-616, 2008.

[52]   J. L. Little and E. L. Bjork, "Pretesting with Multiple-choice Questions Facilitates Learning," in *Proceedings of the 33rd Annual Conference of the Cognitive Science Society* .

[53]   K. A. Ericsson, R. T. Krampe and C. Tesch-Romer, "The Role of Deliberate Practice in the Acquisition of Expert Performance," *Psychological Review,* vol. 100, pp. 363-406, 1993.

[54]   A. L. Duckworth, T. A. Kirby, E. Tsukayama, H. Berstein and K. A. Ericcson, "Deliberate Practice Spells Success: Why Grittier Competitors Triumph at the National Spelling Bee," *Social Pshychological and Personality Science,* vol. 2, no. 2, pp. 174-181, 2011.

[55]   J. D. Karpicke, A. C. Butler and H. L. Roediger III, "Metacognitive strategies in student learning: Do students practice retrieval when they study on their own?," *Memory,* vol. 17, no. 4, pp. 471-479, 2009.

[56]   A. A. Callender and M. A. McDaniel, "The limited benefits of rereading educational texts," *Comtemporary Educational Psychology,* pp. 30-41, 2009.

[57]   T. Mayatsu, K. Nguyen and M. A. McDaniel, "Five Popular Study Strategies: Their Pitfalls and Optimal Implementations," *Perspective on Psychologicl Science,* vol. 13, no. 3, pp. 390-407, 2018.

[58]   A. Amer, "The effect of knowledge-map and underlining training on the reading comprehension of scientific texts," *English for Specific Purposes,* vol. 13, pp. 35-45, 1994.

[59]   D. Leutner, C. Leopold and V. D. Elzen-Rump, "Self-regulated learning with a text-highlighting strategy: A training experiment," *Zeitschrift fur Psychologie,* vol. 215, pp. 174-182.

[60]   C. Yue, B. Storm, N. Kornell and E. Bjork, "Highlighting and its relation to distributed study and students' metacognitive beliefs," *Educational Psychology Review,* vol. 27, pp. 69-78, 2015.

[61]   R. Lorch, E. Lorch and M. Klusewitz, "Effects of typographical cues on reading and recall of text," *Comtemporary Education Psychology,* vol. 20, pp. 51-64, 1995.

[62]   J. Blanchard and V. Mikkelson, "Underlining performance outcomes in expository text," *The Journal of Educational Research,* vol. 80, pp. 197-201, 1987.

[63]   S. Nist and K. Kirby, "The text marking patterns of college students," *Reading Psychology,* vol. 10, pp. 321-338, 1989.

[64]   D. Dumke and G. Schafer, "Verbesserung des lernens aus texten durch trainiertes unterstrichen [Improving text learning by trained underlining].," *Psychologie in Erziehung und Unterricht,* vol. 33, pp. 210-219, 1986.

[65]   T. Schnell and D. Rocchio, "A comparison of underlining strategies for improving reading comprehension and retention," *Reading Horizons,* vol. 18, 1978.

[66]   T. Miyatsu, K. Nguyen and M. A. McDaniel, "Five Popular Study Strategies: Their Pitfalls and Optimal Implementations," *Perspectives on Psychological Science,* vol. 13, no. 3, pp. 390-407, 2018.

[67]   W. Fass and G. Schumacher, "Effects of motivation, subject activity, and readability on the retention of prose materials," *Journal of Educational Psychology,* vol. 70, pp. 803-807, 1978.

[68]   R. Kulhavy, J. Dyer and L. Silver, "The effects of notetaking and test expectancy on the learning of text material," *The Journal of Educational Research,* vol. 68, pp. 363-365, 1975.

[69] J. Rickards and G. August, "Generative under- lining strategies in prose recall," *Journal of Educational Psychology,* vol. 67, pp. 860-865, 1975.

[70] S. M. Mannes and W. Kintsch, "Knowledge Organization and Text Organization," *Cognition & Instruction,* vol. 4, no. 2, pp. 91-115, 1987.

[71] M. A. McDaniel, G. O. Einstein, P. K. Dunay and R. E. Cobb, "Encoding difficulty and memory: Toward a unifying theory," *Journal of Memory and Language,* vol. 25, pp. 645-656, 1986.

[72] D. M. Oppenheimer, C. D. Yauman and E. B. Vaughan, "Fortune Favors the Bold (and the Italicized): Effects of Disfluency on Educational Outcomes," in *Proceedings of the Annual Meeting of the Cognitive Science Society*, 2010.

[73] M. Gladwell, Outliers, New York: Little, Brown & Company, 2008.

[74] R. Hogarth, Educating Intuition, Chicago, IL: University of Chicago Press, 2001.

[75] A. Gullich, B. N. Macnamara and D. Z. Hambrick, "What Makes a Champion? Early Multidisciplinary Practice, Not Early Specialization, Predicts World-Class Performance," *Perspectives on Psychological Sciance,* vol. 17, no. 1, pp. 6-29, 2022.

[76] O. Malamud, "Discovering One's Talent: Learning From Academic Specialization," *Industrial and Labor Relations Review,* vol. 64, no. 2, pp. 375-405, 2011.

[77] O. Malamud, "Breadth versus Depth: The Timing of Specialization in Higher Education," *Labour,* vol. 24, no. 4, pp. 359-390, 2010.

[78] D. Epstein, Range, Why Generalists Triumph in a Specialized World, New York: Riverhead Books, 2019.

[79] A. Vance, Elon Musk: Tesla, SpaceX, and the Quest for a Fantastic Future, Ecco, 2015.

[80] H. Pashler, M. McDaniel, D. Rohrer and R. Bjork, "Learning Styles: Concepts and Evidence," *Psychological Science in the Public Interest,* vol. 9, no. 3, pp. 105-119, 2009.

[81]   L. Massa and R. Mayer, "Testing the ATI hypothesis: Should multimedia instruction accommodate verbalizer-visualizer cognitive style? Learning and Individual Differences," *Learning and Individual Differences,* vol. 16, pp. 321-336, 2006.

[82]   F. Constantinidou and S. Baker, "Stimulus modality and verbal learning performance in normal aging," *Brain and Language,* vol. 82, pp. 296-311, 2002.

[83]   J. Baker and K. Jordan, "The influence of multisensory cues on representation of quantity in children," in *Math cognition Vol 1: Evolutionary origins and early development of basic number processing,* Oxford, Oxford University Press, 2015, p. Ch. 11.

[84]   H. Broadbent, T. Osborne, D. Mareschal and N. Z. Kirkham, "Withstanding the test of time: Multisensory cues improve the delayed retention of incidental learning," *Developmental Science,* 2018.

[85]   J. L. Villegas, E. Castro and J. Gutiérrez, "Representations in problem solving: A case study with optimization problems," *Electronic Journal of Research in Educational Psychology,* vol. 7, no. 1, pp. 279-308, 2009.

[86]   P. J. Sampson, "Promoting Engagement in Larger Classes," *New Horizons,* 2015.

[87]   P. D. Mueller and D. Oppenheimer, "The Pen is Mightier Than the Keyboard: Advantages of Longhand Over Laptop Note Taking," *Psychological Science,* vol. 25, no. 6, pp. 1159-1168, 2014.

[88]   A. R. Luria, The mind of a mnemonist: a little book about a vast memory, Cambridge: Harvard University Press, 1987.

[89]   J. S. Durmer and D. F. Dinges, "Neurocognitive Consequences of Sleep Deprivation," *Seminars in Neurology,* vol. 25, no. 1, pp. 117-129, 205.

[90]   N. Kleitman, Sleep and Wakefulness, Chicago: Chicago University Press, 1963.

[91]   M. Walker, Why We sleep, New York: Scribner, 2017.

[92] E. Aserinsky and N. Kleitman, "Regularly occurring periods of eye motility and concomitant phenomena during sleep," *Science,* vol. 118, pp. 273-274, 1953.

[93] E. Aserinsky, "The Discovery of REM Sleep," *Journal of the History of Neurosciences,* vol. 5, no. 3, pp. 2113-2227, 1996.

[94] W. Dement and N. Kleitman, "The Relation of Eye Movements during Sleep to Dream Activity: An Objective Method for the Study of Dreaming," *Journal of Experimental Pschology,* vol. 53, pp. 339-346, 1957.

[95] T. A. Nielson, "A review of mentation in REM and NREM sleep: "Covert" REM sleep as a possible reconciliation of two opposing models," *Behavoral and Brain Sciences,* vol. 23, pp. 793-1121, 2000.

[96] A. Takashima, K. Petersson, F. Rutters, I. Tendolkar, O. Jensen, M. Zwarts, B. McNaughton and G. Fernandez, " Declarative memory consolidation in humans: a prospective functional magnetic resonance imaging study," *Proceedings of the National Academy of the United States of America,* vol. 103, pp. 756-761, 2006.

[97] S. Gais, G. Albouy, M. Boly, T. ng-Vu, A. Darsaud, M. Desseilles, G. Rauchs, M. Schabus, V. Sterpenich, G. Vandewalle, P. Maquet and P. Peigneux, "Sleep transforms the cerebral trace of declarative memories," *Proceedings of the National Academy of Sciences of the United States of America,* vol. 104, pp. 18778-18783, 2007.

[98] B. A. Mander, S. Santhanam, J. M. Saletin and M. P. Walker, "Wake deterioration and sleep restoration of human learning," *Current Biology,* vol. 21, no. 5, pp. R183-R184, 2011.

[99] J. M. Saletin, A. N. Goldstein and M. P. Walker, "The Role of Sleep in Directed Forgetting and Remembering of Human Memories," *Cerebral Cortex,* vol. 21, pp. 2534-2541, 2011.

[100] M. Scullin, M. McDaniel, D. Howard and C. Kudelka, "Sleep and testing promote conceptual learning of classroom materials.," in *25th Anniversary Meeing of the Associated Professional Sleep Societies LLC*, Minneapolis, MN, 2011.

[101] U. Wagner, S. Gais, H. Haider, R. Verleger and J. Born, "Sleep Inspires Insight," *Nature,* vol. 427, pp. 352-355, 2004.

[102] S. Mednick, K. Nakayama and R. Stickgold, "Sleep-dependent learning; a nap is as good as a night," *Nature Neuroscience,* vol. 6, pp. 697-698, 2003.

[103] C. Smith and D. Smith, "Ingestion of ethanol just prior to sleep onset impairs memory for procedural but not declarative tasks," *Sleep,* vol. 26, no. 2, pp. 185-191, 2003.

[104] L. Allen, Wff'n'Proof: The game of modern logic, New Haven: Aototalic Institutional Materials Publishers, 1966.

[105] J. J. Iliff, M. Wang, Y. Liao, B. A. Plogg, W. Peng, G. A. Gundersen, H. Benveniste, G. E. Vates, R. Deane, S. A. Goldman, E. A. Nagelhus and M. Nedergaard, "A Paravascular Pathway Facilitates CSF Flow Through the Brain Parenchyma and the Clearance of Interstitial Solutes, Including Amyloid β," *Science Translational Medicine,* vol. 4, no. 147, 2012.

[106] A. Louveau, I. Smirnov, T. J. Keyes, J. D. Eccles, S. J. Rouhani, J. D. Peske, N. C. Derecki, D. Castle, J. W. Mandell, S. L. Kevn, T. H. Harris and J. Kipnis, "Structural and functional features of central nervous system lymphatics," *Nature,* vol. 523, pp. 337-341, 2015.

[107] A. Aspelund, S. Antila, S. T. Proulx, T. V. Karlsen, S. Karaman, M. Detmar, H. Wiig and K. Alitalo, "A dural lymphatic vascular system that drains brain interstitial fluid and macromolecules," *Journal of Experimental Medicine,* vol. 212, no. 7, pp. 991-999, 2015.

[108] R. D. Osoria, E. Pirraglia, L. F. Aguera-Ortiz, E. H. During, H. Sacks, I. Ayappa, J. Walsleben, A. Mooney, A. Hussain, L. Glodzik, B. Frangione, P. Martinez-Martin and M. J. d. Leon, "Greater Risk of Alzheimer's Disease in Older Adults With Insomnia," *Journal of the American Geriatic Society,* vol. 59, no. 3, pp. 559-562, 2011.

[109] A. S. P. Lim, L. Yu, M. Kowgier, J. A. Schneider, A. S. Buchman and D. A. Bennett, "Modification of the Relationship of the Apolipoprotein E ε4 Allele to the Risk of Alzheimer Disease and Neurofibrillary Tangle Density by Sleep," *JAMA Neurology,* vol. 70, no. 12, pp. 1544-1551, 2013.

[110] L. Xie, H. Kang, Q. Xu, M. J. Chen, Y. Liao, M. Thiyagarajan, J. O'Donnell, D. J. Christensen, C. Nicholson, J. J. Iliff, T. Takano, R. Deane and M. Nedergaard, "Sleep Drives Metabolite Clearance from the Adult Brain," *Science,* vol. 342, no. 6156, pp. 373-377, 2013.

[111] C. Everson, B. Bergmann and A. Rechtschaffen, "Sleep deprivation in the rat: III. Total Sleep Deprivation," *Sleep,* vol. 12, no. 1, pp. 13-21, 1989.

[112] M. Walker and R. Stickgold, "It's Practice, with Sleep, that Makes Perfect: Implications of Sleep-Dependent Learning and Plasticity for Skill Performance," *Clinics in Sports Medicine,* vol. 24, no. 2, pp. 301-317, 2005.

[113] K. Louie and M. A. Wilson, "Temporally Structured Replay of Awake Hippocampal Ensemble Activity during Rapid Eye Movement Sleep," *Neurology,* vol. 29, pp. 145-156, 2001.

[114] P. Peigneux, S. Laureys, S. Fuchs, F. Collette, F. Perrin, J. Reggers, C. Phillips, C. Degueldre, G. D. Fiore, J.¨. l. Aerts, A.¨. Luxen and P. Maquet, "Are Spatial Memories Strengthened in the Human Hippocampus during Slow Wave Sleep?," *Neuron,* vol. 44, pp. 535-545, 2004.

[115] E. Wamsley and R. Stickgold, "Virtual maze learning enhanced by a short daytime nap containing only NREM sleep," *Sleep,* vol. 31, p. A386, 2008.

[116] E. J. Wamsley, M. Tucker, J. D. Payne and J. A. B. R. Stickgold, "Dreaming of a Learning Task is Associated with Enhanced Sleep-Dependent Memory Consolidation," *Current Biology,* vol. 20, pp. 850-855, 2010.

[117] E. J. Wamsley and R. Stickgold, "Dreaming of a learning task is associated with enhanced memory consolidation: Replication in an overnight study," *J. of Sleep Res.,* 2019.

[118] C. S. Dweck, Mindset: The New Psychology of Success, New York: Random House, 2006.

[119] A. Binet, L'étude expérimentale de l'intelligence, 1903.

[120] J. R. Flynn, "The Mean IQ of Americans: Massive Gains 1932 to 1978," *Psychological Bulletin,* vol. 95, pp. 29-51, 1984.

[121] K. Woodlett and E. A. Maguire, "Acquiring the 'knowledge' of London's layout drives structural brain changes," *Current Biology,* vol. 21, pp. 2109-2114, 2011.

[122] E. Maguire, D. Fadian, I. Johnsrude, C. Good, J. Ashburner, R. Frackowiak and C. Frith, "Navigation-related structural change in the hippocampi of taxi drivers," *Proceedings of the National Academy of Sciences,* vol. 97, no. 8, pp. 4398-4403, 2000.

[123] C. Mueller and C. Dweck, "Intelligence praise can undermine motivation and Performance," *Journal of Personality and Social Psychology,* vol. 75, pp. 33-52, 1998.

[124] J. Eccles, A. Wigfield and U. Schiefele, Motivation to Succeed in Handbook of Child Psychology vol. 3, New York: Wiley, 1998.

[125] H. Grant and C. Dweck, "Clarifying Achievement Golas and Their Impact," *Journal of Personality and Social Psychology,* vol. 85, no. 3, pp. 541-553, 2003.

[126] W. Mischel and E. Ebbesen, "Attention in delay of gratification," *Journal of Personality and Social Psychology,* vol. 16, pp. 329-337, 1970.

[127] W. Mischel, Y. Shoda and M. Rodriguez, "Delay of gratification in children," *Science,* vol. 244, no. 4907, pp. 933-938, 1989.

[128] W. Mischel, The Marshmallow Test: Mastering Self-Control, New York: Little, Brown Spark, 2014.

[129] A. F. Arnsten, "Stress signalling pathways that impair prefrontal cortex structure and function," *Nature Reviews Neuroscience,* vol. 10, no. 6, pp. 410-422, 2009.

[130] R. B. Cialdini, Influence: The Psychology of Persuasion, Harper Buisiness, 1984.

[131] M. Oaten and K. Cheng, "Longitudinal gains in self-regulation from regular physical exercise," *British Journal of Health Psychology,* vol. 11, pp. 717-733, 2006.

[132] R. Baumeister, D. Tice and K. Vohs, "The Strength Model of Self-Control," *Current Directions in Psychological Science,* vol. 6, no. 16, pp. 351-355, 2007.

[133] A. Duckworth, Grit: The Power of Passion and Perseverence, New York: Scribner, 2016.

[134] "Darwin Correspondence Project, "letter no. 7032"," [Online]. Available: ttps://www.darwinproject.ac.uk/letter/?docId=letters/DCP-LETT-7032.xml.

[135] W. James, "The Energies of Men," *Science,* vol. 25, no. 635, pp. 321-332, 1907.

[136] K. A. Ericsson, "Why Expert Performance is Special and Cannot be Extrapolated from Studies of Performance in the General Population: A Response to Criticisms," *Intelligence,* vol. 45, no. 1, pp. 81-103, 2014.

[137] J. Brouwers, V. d. Bosscher and P. Sotiriadou, "An Examination of the Importance of Performances in Youth and Junior Competition as an Indicator of Later Success in Tennis," *Sport Management Review,* vol. 15, pp. 461-475, 2012.

[138] R. S. Siegler and G. B. Ramani, "Playing Board Games Promotes Low-Income Children's Numerical Development," *Development Science,* vol. 11, pp. 655-661, 2008.

[139] K. Rimfeld, Y. Kovas, P. S. Dale and R. Plomin, "True Grit and Genetics: Predicting Academic Achievement From Personability,"," *Journal of Personality and Social Psychology,* vol. 111, no. 5, pp. 780-789, 2016.

[140] R. Eisenberger, "Learned industriousness," *Psychological Review,* vol. 99, no. 2, pp. 248-267, 1992.

[141] C. J. Loomis, Tap Dancing to Work: Warren Buffett on Practically Everything, 1966-2012: A Fortune Magazine Book, New York: Portfolio/Penquin, 2012.

[142] B. Bloom, Developing Talent in Young People, New York: Ballantine Books, 1985.

[143] A. Wrzensiewski, C. McCauley, P. Rozin and B. Schwartz, "Jobs, Careers, and Callings: People's Relations to Their Work," *Journal of Research Personality,* vol. 31, pp. 21-33, 1997.

[144] D. Park, E. Tsukayama, A. Yu and A. Duckworth, "The Development of Grit and Growth Mindset During

Adolescence," *Journal of Experimental Child Psychology,* vol. 198, 2020.

[145] J. Fredricks and J. Eccles, "Is extracurricular participation associated with beneficial outcomes: Concurrent and longitudinal relations?," *Developmental Psychology,* vol. 42, pp. 698-713, 2006.

[146] M. Gardner, J. Roth and J. Brooks-Gunn, "Adolescents' participation in organized activities and developmental success 2 and 8 years after high school: Do sponsorship, duration, and intensity matter?," *Developmental Psychology,* vol. 44, no. 3, pp. 814-830, 2008.

[147] W. W. Willingham, "Extracurricular Work Spurs Success in College," Educational Testing Service and the College Board, 1985.

[148] C. J. L. Murray, "The State of US Health, 1990-2010: Burden of Diseases, Injuries, and Risk Factors," *Journal of the American Medical Association,* vol. 310, no. 6, pp. 591-606, 2013.

[149] L. Mosconi, J. Murray, W. Tsui, M. D. Y. Li, S. Williams, E. Pirraglia, N. Spector, R. Osorio, L. Glodzik, P. McHugh and M. d. Leon, "Mediterranean Diet and Magnetic Resonance Imaging-Assessed Brain Atrophy in Cognitively Normal Individuals at Risk for Alzheimer's Disease," *Journal of Prevention of Alzheimer's Disease,* vol. 1, pp. 23-32, 2014.

[150] L. Mosconi, "Nature's Bounty: Saving the Brain with Food," *Psychology Today,* 2018.

[151] C. T. McEvoy, H. Guyer, K. Langa and K. Yaffe, "Neuroprotective Diets Are Associated with Better Cognitive Function: The Health and Retirement Study," *Journal of the American Geriatrics Society,* vol. 65, no. 8, 2017.

[152] L. Mosconi, Brain Food: The Surprising Science of Eating for Cognitive Power, New York: Penquin Random House, 2018.

[153] C. Edmonds, R. Crombie and M. R. Gardner, "Subjective thirst moderates changes in speed of responding associated with water consumption," *Frontiers of Human Neuroscience,* 2013.

[154] E. Mahoney, J. Kun, M. Smieja and O. Fang, "Review—Point-of-Care Urinalysis with Emerging Sensing and Imaging Technologies," *Journal of the Electrochemical Society,* vol. 167, 2020.

[155] A. Simopoulos, "Evolutionary aspects of diet, the omega-6/omega-3 ratio and genetic variation: nutritional implication for chronic disease," *Biomedicaine & Pharmacotherapy,* vol. 60, no. 9, 2006.

[156] A. Simopoulos, "Evolutionary aspects of diet, the omega-6/omega-3 ratio and the Brain," *Molecular Neurobiology,* vol. 44, no. 2, pp. 203-2115, 2011.

[157] A. H. Stark, M. A. Crawford and R. Reifen, "Update on alpha-linolenic acid," *Nutritional Reviews,* vol. 66, no. 6, pp. 326-332, 2008.

[158] I.-J. Jensen, K.-E. Eilertsen, C. H. A. Otnaes, H. K. Maehre and E. O. Elevoli, "An Update on the Content of Fatty Acids, Dioxins, PCBs, and Heavy Metals in Farmed, Escaped and Wild Atlantic Salmaon," *Foods,* vol. 9, no. 12, 2020.

[159] G. Weinstein, A. S. Beiser, S. H. Choi, S. R. Preis, T. C. Chen, D. Vorgas, R. Au, A. Pikula, P. A. Wolf, A. L. DeStefano, R. S. Vasan and S. Seshadri, "Serum Brain-Derived Neurotrophic Factor and the Risk for Dementia," *JAMA Neurology,* vol. 71, no. 1, pp. 55-61, 2014.

[160] S. Peng, J. Wuu, E. Mufson and M. Fahnestock, "Precursor form of brain-derived neurotrophic factor and mature brain-derived neurotrophic factor are decreased in the pre-clinical stages of Alzheimer's disease," *Journal of Neurochemistry,* vol. 82, no. 5, pp. 1412-1421, 2005.

[161] J. V. Pottala, K. Yaffe, J. G. Robinson, M. A. Espeland, Robert Wallace and W. S. Harris, "Higher RBC EPA+DHA Corresponds with Larger Total Brain and Hippocampal Volume: WHIMS-MRI Study," *Neurology,* vol. 82, no. 5, pp. 435-442, 2014.

[162] D. J. Bos, B. Oranje, E. S. Veerhoek, R. M. V. Diepen, J. M. Weusten, H. Demmelmair, B. Koletzko, M. G. d. S.-v. d. Velden, A. Eilander, M. Hoeksma and S. Durston, "Reduced Symptoms of Inattention after Dietary Omega-3 Fatty Acid

Supplementation in Boys with and without Attention Deficit/Hyperactivity Disorder," *Neuropsychopharmacology,* vol. 40, no. 10, pp. 2298-2306, 2015.

[163] K. Sheppard and C. Cheatham, "Omega-6 to Omega-3 Fatty Acid Ratio and High-Order Cognitive Functions in 7- to 9-year-olds," *American Journal of Clinical Nutrition,* vol. 98, no. 3, pp. 659-667, 2013.

[164] A. V. Witte, L. Kerti, H. M. Hermannstädter, J. B. Fiebach, S. J. Schreiber, J. P. Schuchardt, A. Hahn and A. Flöel, " Long-chain omega-3 fatty acids improve brain function and structure in older adults," *Cerebral Cortex,* vol. 24, no. 11, pp. 3059-3068, 2014.

[165] A. Sala-Vila, R. d. l. Torre, D. Corella and M. A. Martinez-Gonzalez, "Mediterranean Diet and Age-Related Cognitive Decline: A Randomized Clinical Trial," *JAMA Internal Medication,* vol. 175, no. 7, pp. 1125-1132, 2015.

[166] C. Amadieu, S. Lefèvre-Arbogast, C. Delcourt, J.-F. Dartigues, C. Helmer, C. Féart and C. Samieri, "Nutrient biomarker patterns and long-term risk of dementia in older adults, Alzheimer's and Dementia," *Alzeimer's and Dementia,* vol. 13, no. 19, pp. 1126-1132, 2017.

[167] B. M. Volk, L. J. Kunces, D. J. Freidenreich, B. R. Kupchak, C. Saenz, J. C. Artistizabal, M. L. Fernandez, R. S. Bruno, C. M. Maresh, W. J. Kraemer, S. D. Phinney and J. S. Volek, "Effects of step-wise increases in dietary carbohydrate on circulating saturated fatty acids and palmitoleic acid in adults with metabolic syndrome," *PLoS One 9,* vol. 9, no. 11, 2014.

[168] A. Wu, R. Molteni, Z. Ying and F. Gomez-Pinilla, "A Saturated-Fat Diet Aggravates the Outcome of Traumatic Brain Injury on Hippocampal Plasticity and Cognitive Function by Reducing Brain-Derived Neurotrophic Factor," *Neuroscience,* vol. 119, pp. 365-375, 2003.

[169] G. Bowman, L. Silbert, D. Howieson, H. Dodge, M. Traber, B. Frei, J. Kaye, J. Shannon and J. Quinn, "Nutrient Biomarker Patterns, Cognitive Function, and MRI Measures of Brain Aging," *Neurology,* vol. 78, no. 4, pp. 241-249, 2012.

[170] I. Björkhem and S. Meaney, "Brain Cholesterol: Long Secret Life Behind a Barrier," *Arteriosclerosis, Thrombosis, and Vascular Biology,* vol. 24, no. 5, pp. 806-815, 2004.

[171] M. Lenoir, F. Serre, L. Cantin and S. H. Ahmed, "Intense Sweetness Surpasses Cocaine Reward," *PLoS One,* vol. 2, no. 8, 2007.

[172] A.-N. Samaha, "Sugar now or cocaine later?," *Neuropsychopharmacology,* vol. 46, no. 2, pp. 271-272, 2021.

[173] N. Cherbuin, P. Sachdev and K. Anstey, "Higher normal fasting plasma glucose is associated with hippocampal atrophy: The PATH Study," *Neurology,* vol. 79, no. 10, 2012.

[174] S. E. Kanoski and T. L. Davidson, "Western diet consumption and cognitive impairment: links to hippocampal dysfunction and obesity," *Physiology & Behavior,* vol. 103, no. 1, pp. 59-68, 2011.

[175] H. Bruehl, V. Sweat, J. Hassenstab, V. Polyakov and A. Convit, "Cognitive Impairment in Nondiabetic Middle-Aged and Older Adults Is Associated with Insulin Resistance," *Journal of Clinical and Experimental Nueropsychology,* vol. 32, no. 5, pp. 487-493, 2010.

[176] R. Agrawal and F. Gomez-Pinilla, "'Metabolic syndrome' in the brain: deficiency in omega-3 fatty acid exacerbates dysfunctions in insulin receptor signalling and cognition," *Journal of Physiology,* pp. 2485-2499, 2012.

[177] P. K. Crane, R. Walker, R. A. Hubbard, G. Li, D. M. Nathan, H. Zheng, S. Haneuse, S. Craft, T. J. Montine, S. E. Kahn, W. McCormick, S. M. McCurry, J. D. Bowen and E. B. Larson, "Glucose Levels and Risk of Dementia," *New England Journal of Medicine,* vol. 369, no. 6, pp. 540-548, 2014.

[178] G. Vistolli, D. De Maddis, A. Cipak, N. Varkovic, M. Carini and G. Aldini, "Advanced glycoxidation and lipoxidation end products (AGEs and ALEs): an overview of their mechanisms of formation," *Free Radical Research,* vol. 47, 2013.

[179] K. Yaffe, K. Lindquist, A. Schwartz, C. Vitartas, E. Vittinghoff, S. Satterfield, E. Simonsick, L. Launer, C. Rosano, J. Cauley and T. Harris, "Advanced Glycation End Product

Level, Diabetes, and Accelerated Cognitive Aging," *Neurology,* vol. 77, no. 14, pp. 1351-1356, 2011.

[180] J. T. Dwyer and J. Peterson, "Tea and flavonoids: where we are, where to go next," *American Journal of Clinical Nutrition,* vol. 98, 2013.

[181] E. E. Devore, J. H. Kang, M. M. B. Breteler and F. Grodstein, "Dietary intakes of berries and flavonoids in relation to cognitive decline," *Annals of Neurology,* vol. 72, no. 1, pp. 135-143, 2012.

[182] A. M. Brickman, U. A. Khan, F. A. Provenzano, L.-K. Yeung, W. Suzuki, H. Schroeter, M. Wall, R. P. Sloan and S. A. Small, "Enhancing Dentate Gyrus Function with Dietary Flavanols Improves Cognition in Older Adults," *Nature Neuroscience,* vol. 17, no. 12, pp. 1798-1803, 2014.

[183] L. P. v. d. Heide, A. Kamal, A. Artola, W. H. Gispen and G. M. J. Ramakers, "Insulin Modulates Hippocampal Activity-Dependent Saynaptic Plasticity in a N-Methyl-D-Aspartate Receptor and Phosphatidyl-Inositol-3-Kinase-Dependent Manner," *Journal of Neurochemistry,* vol. 94, no. 4, pp. 1158-1166, 2005.

[184] J. Blumberg and G. Bock, "The Apha-Tocopherol, Beta-Carotene Caner Prevention Study in Finland," *Nutritional Review,* vol. 52, no. 7, pp. 242-245, 1994.

[185] Y.-I. Kim, "Does a high folate intake increase the risk of breast cancer?"," *Nutritional Review,* vol. 64, pp. 468-475, 2006.

[186] H. Chen, M. Iinuma, M. Onozuka and K.-Y. Kubo, "Chewing Maintains Hippocampus-Dependent Cognitive Function," *International Journal of Medical Science,* vol. 12, no. 6, pp. 502-509, 2015.

[187] G. P. Dias, T. Murphy, D. Stangl, S. Ahmet, B. Morisse, A. Nix, L. J. Aimone, J. B. Aimone, M. Kuro-O, F. H. Gage and S. Thuret, "Intermittent fasting enhances long-term memory consolidation, adult hippocampal neurogenesis, and expression of longevity gene Klotho," *Molecuilar Psychiatry,* vol. 26, pp. 6365-6379, 2021.

[188] M. P. Mattson, "Challenging Oneself Intermittently to Improve Health," *Dose Response,* vol. 12, pp. 600-618, 2014.

[189] M. C. Morris, C. C. Tangney, Y. Wang, F. M. Sacks, L. L. Barnes, D. A. Bennett and N. T. Aggarwal, "MIND diet slows cognitive decline with aging," *Alzheimers and Dementia,* vol. 11, no. 9, pp. 1015-1022, 2015.

[190] J. Corley, "Adherence to the MIND diet is associated with 12-year all-cause mortality in older adults,"," *Public Health Nutrition,* vol. 25, no. 2, pp. 1-10, 2020.

[191] I. Benzie and Y. Szeto, "Total antioxidant capacity of teas by ferricreducing/antioxidant power assay," *Journal of Agricultural Food and Chemistry,* vol. 47, pp. 633-636, 1999.

[192] R. Llinas, I of the Vortex: From Neurons to Self, Cambridge, MA: MIT Press, 2002.

[193] A. J. Cerrillo-Urbina, A. García-Hermoso, M. Sánchez-López, M. J. Pardo-Guijarro, J. L. S. Gómez and V. Martínez-Vizcaíno, "The effects of physical exercise in children with attention deficit hyperactivity disorder: a systematic review and meta-analysis of randomized control trials," *Child Care, Health and Development,* vol. 41, no. 6, 2015.

[194] Y. Netz, R. Tomer, S. Axelrad, E. Argov and O. Inbar, "The Effect of a Single Aerobic Training Session on Cognitive Flexibility in Late Middle-Aged Adults," *International Journal of Sports Medicine,* vol. 28, pp. 82-87, 2007.

[195] J. P. Guilford, P. R. Christensen, P. R. Merrifield and R. C. Wilson, Alternate Uses: Manual of Instructions and Interpretations, Orange, CA: Sheridan Psychological Services, 1978.

[196] J. H. Kwon, K. M. Moon and K.-W. Min, "Exercise-Induced Myokines can Explain the Importance of Physical Activity in the Elderly: An Overview," *Healthcare,* vol. 8, no. 4, p. 378, 2020.

[197] S. Wrigley, D. Arafa and D. Tropea, "Insulin-Like Growth Factor 1: At the Crossroads of Brain Development and Aging," *Frontiers of Cellular Neuroscience,* vol. 11, no. 14, 2017.

[198] S. C. Danzer, K. R. C. Crooks, D. C. Lo and J. O. McNamara, "Increased Expression of Brain-Derived Neurotrophic Factor Induces Formation of Basal Dendrites and Axonal Branching in Dentate Granule Cells in Hippocampal Explant Cultures," *Neuroscience,* vol. 22, no. 22, pp. 9754-9763, 2002.

[199] H. v. Praag, G. Kempermann and F. H. Gage, "Running Increases Cell Proliferation and Neurogenesis in the Adult Mouse Dentate Gyrus," *Nature Neuroscience,* vol. 2, no. 3, pp. 266-270, 1999.

[200] C. Dufouil, E. Pereira, G. Chêne, M. M. Glymour, A. Alpérovitch, E. Saubusse, M. Risse-Fleury, B. Heuls, J.-C. Salord, M.-A. Brieu and F. Forette, "Older age at retirement is associated with decreased risk of dementia," *European Journal of Epidemiology,* vol. 29, no. 5, pp. 353-361, 2014.

[201] M. Fotuhi, Boost Your Brain: The New Art and Science Behind Enhanced Brain Performance, HarperOne, 2014.

[202] S. J. Colcombe, K. I. Erickson, P. E. Scalf, J. S. Kim, R. Prakash, E. McAuley, S. Elavsky, D. X. Marquez, L. Hu and A. F. Kramer, "Aerobic Exercise Training Increases Brain Volume in Aging Humans," *The Journals of Gerontology; Series A,* vol. 61, no. 11, pp. 1166-1170, 2006.

[203] R. L. Rogers, J. S. Meyer and K. F. Mortel, " After reaching retirement age physical activity sustains cerebral perfusion and cognition," *Journal of the American Geriatric Society,* vol. 38, no. 2, pp. 123-128, 1990.

[204] P. Zientarski, "Neuroscience Meets Social and Emotional Learing Podcast #121," 7 April 2021. [Online]. Available: https://youtu.be/UHYNEhxkxfE.

[205] J. J. Ratey and E. Hagerman, Spark: The Revolutionary New Science of Exercise and the Brain, New York: Little, Brown Spark, 2008.

[206] A. Fedewa and S. Ahn, "The Effects of Physical Activity and Physical Fitness on Children's Achievement and Cognitive Outcomes: A Meta-Analysis," *Research Quarterly for Exercise and Sport,* vol. 82, no. 3, pp. 521-535, 2011.

[207] T. J. Schoenfeld, P. Rada, P. R. Pieruzzini, B. Hsueh and E. Gould, "Physical Exercise Prevents Stress-Induced Activation of Granule Neurons and Enhances Local Inhibitory Mechanisms in the Dentate Gyrus," *The Journal of Neuroscience,* vol. 33, no. 18, pp. 7770-7777, 2013.

[208] A. G. Brellenthin, K. M. Crombie, C. J. Hillard and K. F. Koltyn, " Endocannabinoid and Mood Responses to Exercise in Adults with Varying Activity Levels," *Medicine and Science in Sports and Exercise,* vol. 49, no. 8, pp. 1688-1696, 2017.

[209] T. R. Lago, A. Hsiung, B. P. Leitner, C. J. Duckworth, N. L. Balderston, K. Y. Chen, C. Grillon and M. Ernst, "Exercise modulates the interaction between cognition and anxiety in humans," *Cognition and Emotion,* vol. 33, no. 4, pp. 863-870, 2019.

[210] M. Audiffren and N. André, "The exercise–cognition relationship: A virtuous circle," *Journal of Sport and Health Science,* vol. 8, no. 4, pp. 339-347, 2019.

[211] L. G. Breuning, Habits of a Happy Brain, Avon, MA: Adams Media, 2015.

[212] A. Hodes and D. Lichtstein, "Natriuretic hormones in brain function," *Frontiers in Endocrinology,* vol. 5, no. article 201, pp. 1-13, 2014.

[213] B. K. Hölzel, J. Carmody, M. Vangel, C. Congleton, S. M. Yerramsetti, T. Gard and S. W. Lazar, "Mindfulness Practice Leads to Increases in Regional Brain Gray Matter Density," *Psychiatry Research: Neuroimaging ,* vol. 191, no. 1, pp. 36-43, 2011.

[214] E. Luders, N. Cherbuin and F. Kurth, "Forever Young(er): potential age-defying effects of long-term meditation on gray matter atrophy," *Neuroimaging,* vol. 5, 2015.

[215] B. Newberg, N. Wintering, M. R. Waldman, D. Amen, D. S. Khalsa and A. Alavi, "Cerebral Blood Flow Differences Between Long-Term Meditators and Non-Meditators," *Consciousness and Cognition,* vol. 19, no. 4, pp. 899-905, 2010.

[216] J. B. West and A. W. Luks, Respiratory Physiology: The Essentials, Philadelphia: Wolters Kluwer, 2008.

[217] J. Shields, "Lymph, lymph glands, and homeostasis," *Lymphology,* vol. 25, no. 4, pp. 147-152, 1992.

[218] J. G. Allen, P. MacNaughton, U. Satish, S. Santanam, J. Vallarino and J. D. Spengler, "Associations of Cognitive Function Scores with Carbon Dioxide, Ventilation, and Volatile Organic Compound Exposures in Office Workers: A Controlled Exposure Study of Green and Conventional Office Environments," *Environmental Health Perspectives,* vol. 124, no. 6, 2016.

[219] K. Breuer and U. Satish, "Emergency management simulations: an approach to the assessment of decision-making processes in complex dynamic crisis environments," in *From Modeling to Managing Security: A Systems Dynamics Approach,* Norway:Høyskoleforlaget AS, Norway:Høyskoleforlaget AS - Norwegian Academic Press, 2003, pp. 145-156.

[220] N. N. Taleb, Antifragile: Things That Gain from Disorder, New York: Random House, 2012.

[221] M. Goyal, S. Singh, E. M. S. Sibinga, N. F. Gould, A. Rowland-Seymour, R. Sharma, Z. Berger, D. Sleicher, D. D. Maron, H. M. Shihab, P. D. Ranasinghe, S. Linn, S. Saha, E. B. Bass and Ha, "Meditation Programs for Psychological Stress and Well-being A Systematic Review and Meta-analysis," *JAMA Internal Medicine,* vol. 174, no. 3, pp. 357-368, 2014.

[222] G. E. Kelly, "Lecture attendance rates at university and related factors," *Journal of Further and Higher Education,* vol. 36, no. 1, pp. 17-40, 2014.

[223] D. Kahneman and A. Tversky, "Prospect Theory: An Analysis of Decision under Risk," *Econometrica,* vol. 47, no. 2, pp. 263-291, 1979.

[224] J. Ra and S. Marken, "Life in College Matters for Life After College," Gallup, 6 May 2014. [Online]. Available: https://news.gallup.com/poll/168848/life-college-matters-life-college.aspx.

[225] P. Felten and L. M. Lambert, Relationship-Rich Education How Human Connections Drive Success in College, Baltimore: Johns Hopkins University Press, 2020.

[226] "The Gallup-Purdue Index 2015 Report The Relationship Between Student Debt, Experiences and Perceptions of College Worth," 2015. [Online]. Available: https://www.gallup.com/services/185924/gallup-purdue-index-2015-report.aspx?_ga=2.138418102.405238504.1660482581-1743764383.1653758571.

[227] "A "Fit" Over Rankings Why College Engagement Matters More Than Selectivity," October 2018. [Online]. Available: https://ed.stanford.edu/sites/default/files/challenge_success_white_paper_on_college_admissions_10.1.2018-reduced.pdf.

Appendix A: Brain Energy Calculations

Using Positron-emission spectroscopy (PET) scanners, the amount of glucose and oxygen being used in the brain can be measured, which is the amount of energy the brain is consuming. This energy consumption has been measured for many different species of rodents and primates; it has been found that all neurons, regardless of their size, use 5.79×10^{-15} moles of glucose per minute [2].

There are 686 Kcal per mole of glucose. So,

$$\left(5.79 \times 10^{-9} \, \frac{\text{mole glucose}}{\text{neuron min}}\right)\left(686 \, \frac{\text{Kcal}}{\text{mole glucose}}\right)\left(60 \, \frac{\text{min}}{\text{hr}}\right)\left(24 \, \frac{\text{hr}}{\text{day}}\right)$$

$$= 5.72 \times 10^{-9} \, \frac{\text{Kcal}}{\text{neuron} - \text{day}}$$

With 86 billion neurons in the human brain

$$(5.72 \times 10^{-9} \, \frac{\text{Kcal}}{\text{neuron} - \text{day}})(86 \times 10^{9} \, \text{neurons}) = 492 \, \frac{\text{Kcal}}{\text{day}}$$

The human brain requires 492 Kcal per day. The average woman requires 2,000 Kcal/day and the average man 2,500 Kcal/day. So, the brain uses between 20% and 25% of the fuel we consume each day.

Talking in terms of calories can be a little confusing.

1 Kilocalorie = 1 Calorie = 1,000 calories = 4,184 J

So, 1 large Calorie is equal to 1,000 small calories. Usually when you see the energy stated for a food they are talking about large Calories even if they use the lower-case c.

In terms of Joules (J) the brain uses

$$\left(492 \ \frac{\text{kcal}}{\text{day}}\right)\left(4{,}184 \ \frac{\text{J}}{\text{kcal}}\right) = 3.31 \text{ x } 10^6 \ \frac{\text{J}}{\text{day}}$$

A watt is the energy consumption in J/s, so

$$\left(3.31 \text{ x } 10^6 \ \frac{\text{J}}{\text{day}}\right)\left(\frac{1 \text{ day}}{24 \text{ hr}}\right)\left(\frac{1 \text{ hr}}{60 \text{ m}}\right)\left(\frac{1 \text{ m}}{60 \text{ s}}\right) = 38.3\frac{\text{J}}{\text{s}} = 38.3 \text{ Watts}$$

Your brain's energy consumption is comparable to a not very bright incandescent light bulb.

When you concentrate regions of your brain do consume more energy, but this increase is small compared to the baseline energy consumption.

Appendix B: Boolean Algebra and Digital Circuits

Let a 1 represent a true statement and a 0 representing a false statement. As an example of the And operation, let A stand for doing your homework and B stand for doing a chore. You are allowed to go to the movies if you finished both your homework And your chore. Then the And operation between A and B, written as AB = C, will result in C = 1 (true) you went to the movies only if you completed your homework (A=1) and completed your chore (B=1). The And operation is expressed with this table, which is called a truth table.

A	B	C = AB
0	0	0
0	1	0
1	0	0
1	1	1

As an example of the Or operation, again let A stand for doing your homework and B stand for doing a chore. This time you are allowed to go to the movies if you have completed your homework Or you completed your chore. The Or operation is written as A + B = C and expressed with this truth table.

A	B	C = A + B
0	0	0
0	1	1
1	0	1
1	1	1

The following is the truth table for the not operation.

A	$C = \overline{A}$
0	1
1	0

Working with circuits that contained electronic switches at Bell Labs, Claude Shannon realized he could implement these Boolean logic functions with switching circuits. An open switch would represent a 0 and a closed switch would represent a 1.

In figure A.1 is the implementation of the And operation. This circuit is called an And gate. The variables A and B control whether the two switches are open or closed. If the variable A is 0 (false) the switch is open. If the variable A is 1 (true) the switch is closed. To have a complete circuit, and turn on the LED, both switches must be closed.

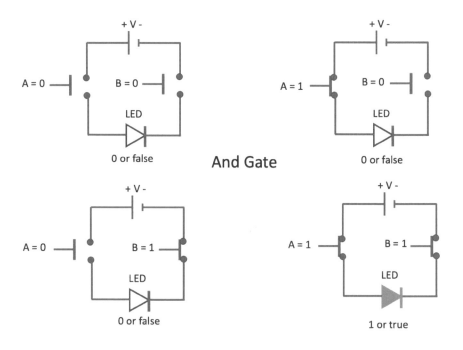

Figure A.1 Implementation of the And operation with switches

In figure A.2 is the implementation of the Or operation. This circuit is called an Or gate. Again, the variables A and B control whether the two switches are open or closed. If the variable A is 0 (false) the switch is open. If the variable A is 1 (true) the switch is closed. A complete circuit will occur, and turn on the LED, if either switch is closed.

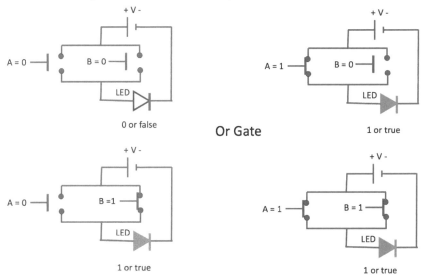

Figure A.2 Implementation of the Or operation with switches

In figure A.3 is the implementation of the Not operation. This circuit is called a Not gate or inverter. Again, the variable A controls whether the switch is open or closed. If the variable A is 0 (false) the switch is open and the LED lights (1). If the variable A is 1 (true) the switch is closed shorting the LED, so it does not light.

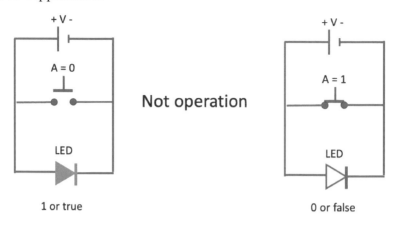

Figure A.3 Implementation of the Not operation with switches

Boolean algebra is a way to solve complex logic problems with the Boolean logic operations of And, Or, and Not. Shannon would apply Boolean algebra to the relay (electronic switching) circuits at Bell Labs to obtain circuits with far fewer components to accomplish the same function.

Let's look at some of the rules for Boolean algebra. Any of these rules can be verified by creating a truth table, as I will do for rule 5 below.

$A + \bar{A} = 1$, it is always true you did, or you did not do your homework. (rule 1)

$A\bar{A} = 0$, you cannot both do and not do your homework. (rule 2)

$A + AB = A$ (rule 3)

$A + \bar{A}B = A + B$, (rule 4)

$AB + AC = A(B+C)$, we prove this rule with the following truth table. The fourth column, $AB + AC$, is the same as the fifth column, $A(B + C)$, proving the rule. (rule 5)

A	B	C	AB +AC	A(B+C)
0	0	0	0	0
0	0	1	0	0
0	1	0	0	0
0	1	1	0	0
1	0	0	0	0
1	0	1	1	1
1	1	0	1	1
1	1	1	1	1

Let's look at an example to see how Shannon would apply Boolean algebra to simplify a circuit. The circuit has four inputs, M, H, P, and A. The output of the circuit is N. The following table shows the output for all combinations of inputs.

M	H	P	A	N
1	1	1	1	1
1	1	1	0	1
1	1	0	1	1
1	1	0	0	1
1	0	1	1	1
1	0	1	0	0
1	0	0	1	0
1	0	0	0	0
0	1	1	1	0
0	1	1	0	0
0	1	0	1	0
0	1	0	0	0
0	0	1	1	0
0	0	1	0	0
0	0	0	1	0
0	0	0	0	0

In the truth table, N is a 1 when MHPA or MHP$\overline{\text{A}}$ or MH$\overline{\text{P}}$A or MH$\overline{\text{P}}$$\overline{\text{A}}$ or M$\overline{\text{H}}$PA are true. N is then the Or of these 5 conditions,

$$N = MHPA + MHP\bar{A} + MH\bar{P}A + MH\bar{P}\bar{A} + M\bar{H}PA \quad\quad (A.1)$$

Now we will utilize some of the above rules we have for Boolean algebra.

Using rule 5 factor MHP out of the first two terms and MH$\bar{P}$ out of the third and fourth terms,

$$N = MHP(A + \bar{A}) + MH\bar{P}(A + \bar{A}) + M\bar{H}PA$$

Using rule 1 that $(A + \bar{A}) = 1$ we get

$$N = MHP + MH\bar{P} + M\bar{H}PA$$

Using rule 5, factor out of the first two terms MH,

$$N = MH(P + \bar{P}) + M\bar{H}PA$$

Using rule 1

$$N = MH + M\bar{H}PA$$

Factoring out M,

$$N = M(H + \bar{H}PA)$$

Using rule 4

$$N = M(H + PA)$$

or

$$N = MH + MPA \quad\quad (A.2)$$

Implementing equation (A.1) requires 3 Not gates, 5 four input And gates, and one 5 input Or gate. Implementing equation (A.2), obtained from performing Boolean algebra on equation (A.1), only requires one three input And gate, one two input And gate, and one two input Or gate. Applying Boolean algebra, Shannon showed how to design to get the simplest circuits to perform a switching task.

Appendix C: Problems from Chapter 6

Problem 1

I had a program manager, Max Yoder, from the Office of Naval Research who used to like to say, "think outside the dots." If someone asked, "Don't you mean "think outside the box?"" he would get a gleam in his eye and show them this problem.

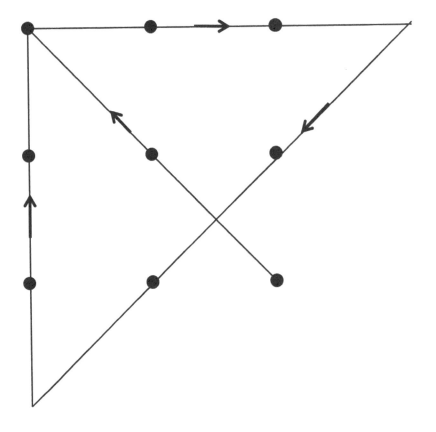

Problem 2

It usually takes incubation to get the insight not to think in two-dimensions for the arrangement of the sticks, but to think in three-dimensions.

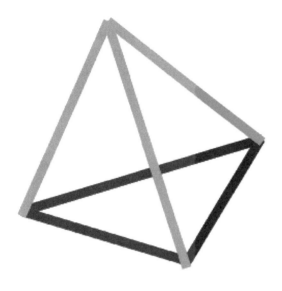

Problem 3

Mt. Everest was still the tallest mountain in the world even before it was discovered.

Suggested Reading

I took a wholistic approach with this book touching on all the learning techniques I know to utilize when learning, the mental attributes you should develop to help you succeed, and how to maintain the health and functioning of your brain. I could not go into the detail that the following books do on these topics. I can highly recommend the following books.

Make It Stick by Peter Brown, by Henry L. Roediger, and Mark A. McDaniel

Why We Sleep: Unlocking the Power of Sleep and Dreams, by Matthew Walker

How We Learn: The Surprising Truth About When, Where, and Why It Happens by Benedict Carey

Mindset: The New Psychology of Success by Carol Dweck

Grit: The Power of Passion and Perseverance by Angela Duckworth

Peak: Secrets from the New Science of Expertise by Anders Ericsson and Robert Pool

Spark: The Revolutionary New Science of Exercise and the Brain by John J. Ratey and Eric Hagerman

Brain Food: The Surprising Science of Eating for Cognitive Power by Lisa Mosconi

The Human Advantage: A New Understanding of How Our Brain Became Remarkable, by Suzana Herculano-Houzel

About the author

Michael R. Melloch is a professor of electrical and computer engineering at Purdue University. He has also served as Assistant Dean for the College of Engineering and Associate Head for Education for the School of Electrical & Computer Engineering. Before joining the faculty at Purdue, he held positions as a design engineer at Intel Corporation and as a member of the technical staff in the Central Research Laboratories of Texas Instruments, Inc. He has published more than 300 scientific articles. He is a Fellow of the IEEE, the American Physical Society, the AVS, and the Optical Society of America. He has received every teaching award at the school, college, and university level at Purdue University. *The Keys to Learning: Unlocking Your Brain's Potential* is his first book.

Acknowledgment

I would like to thank my maternal grandmother who instilled in me the value of education even before I started school. My parents, Lottie and Ray, who sacrificed everything for their children. My wife Lyn and daughter Kate for their support. This book is much more readable thanks to Lyn's editing. For all the students I have had in class over the years, probably close to 4,000, this book is for you and for my future students.

Review Request

I hope you have enjoyed this book and found the content useful.

I'd love if you could write a review!

Acetylcholine 19, 161, 170

Adenosine 106, 109

Advanced glycation end products (AGES) 166

Allocortex 24

Altman, Joseph 19, 20

Alzheimer's 104, 118, 149, 154, 156, 158, 166, 167, 170, 171, 179

Amygdala 24, 104, 105, 146, 183, 184, 186, 191

Angiogenesis 124

Aserinsky, Eugene 111

Atrial Natriuretic Peptide (ANP) 184

Autonomic nervous system (ANS) 190, 191

Axon 12 – 15, 18, 21, 24, 25, 150, 159, 177, 178

Bahrick 50, 51

Berlin Philharmonic 86, 93

Berlin University of the Arts 86

Binet, Alfred 123

Bliss Point 162

Blood-brain barrier 10, 153, 158, 159, 169, 177, 184, 188

Boole, George 35

Boolean algebra/logic 35, 36, 96, 243 – 249

Brain Derived Neurotropic Factor (BDNF) 156, 158, 177, 179, 182, 184

Buffett, Warren 128, 141, 144, 201

Caffeine 109, 149

Cerebral cortex 12, 24, 41, 44, 46

Cerebral spinal fluid (CSF) 10, 25, 118

Cerebrum 23, 24

Chess 33 – 35, 85, 87, 93, 130, 135, 138, 195

Chronotypes 108

Choline 160, 161, 170

Chunking, Chunks 32, 33

Circadian rhythm 106 – 109

Cis bond 150, 158

Corpus callosum 23

Cortisol 192, 193

Cram 43, 44, 66, 104, 113, 217

Creativity 36, 116, 121, 122, 214

Curse of knowledge 47

Deliberate practice 86 – 88

Dement, William 111

Dementia 149, 156, 157, 163, 166, 168, 178

Dendrite 12 – 15, 21, 24, 124, 156, 177

Desirable difficulties 92

Diabetes 162, 163, 165, 166, 179, 193

Dreaming 66, 110 – 112, 115, 116, 120, 121, 139, 202

Duckworth, Angela 88, 137, 138, 140, 207, 209

Dweck, Carol 122, 125 – 127

Ebbinghaus, Hermann 40 – 43, 74

Edison, Thomas 121, 140

Ehrlich, Paul 10

Epinephrine 160, 177, 183, 184, 191, 192

Ericsson, Anders 31, 37, 86 – 88, 93

Faloon, Steve 31 – 33, 93

Fatal familial insomnia 119

Fatty acid 150 – 154

Flynn Effect 123

Flynn, James 123

Forgetting curve 40, 41, 74

Four Bahrick study 50

Frankenstein 66

Gallup 199, 201, 207, 216

Gallup-Purdue 199, 201, 203, 207, 216

Gladwell, Malcolm 93

Glial cells 11, 12, 24, 25

Glycemic index 167, 168

Glycemic load 167, 168

Glycogen 164, 168, 170, 176, 192

Glymphatic system 118, 149, 166, 167, 188

Glucose 10, 118, 148, 162 – 168, 176, 177, 182, 192, 241

Grades 31, 52, 81, 82, 88, 113, 146, 147, 183, 205, 217

Grit 88, 96, 125, 130, 131, 133, 135 – 141, 144 – 147, 156, 209, 214 – 217

Gyrification 24, 186

Heart Rate 175, 179, 180, 183, 184, 190, 192

Heart Rate Variability (HRV) 190, 191

Herculano-Houzel, Suzanna 11, 252

High density lipoproteins (HDL) 158 – 160

High-Fructose Corn Syrup (HFCS) 162, 163, 165

Hippocampus 20, 23 – 25, 39, 41 – 43, 105, 112 – 114, 119, 120, 124, 125, 132, 156, 166, 170, 177, 178, 182, 186, 192, 213, 214

Incubation 43, 48, 66 – 70, 77, 78, 82, 90, 99, 116, 135, 145, 213, 215, 251

Insulin 162, 164 – 168, 177

Intelligent quotient (IQ) 123 – 126

Irving, John 140

James, William 20, 43, 44, 73, 138, 142, 143

Jobs, Steve 36

King, Stephen 139

Kleitman, Nathaniel 106, 107, 111

Latticework of mental models 35, 44, 67, 75, 76, 93, 94, 115, 141, 214

Lawler, Phil 180

Learning Readiness Phys Ed (LRPE) 181, 182

Learning styles 98, 99

Long-term depression (LTD) 14

Long-term potentiation (LTP) 14, 43, 44, 75, 78, 113, 116, 192

Low density lipoproteins (LDL) 158 – 160

Marshmallow test, 131 – 133

McCartney, Paul 68, 116

Memory 20, 23, 26 – 28, 30 – 33, 38 – 45, 48, 49, 54, 56, 73, 75, 76, 82, 99, 102, 103, 112 – 115, 119, 120, 125, 136, 160, 161, 166, 167, 178, 183 – 185, 196

Memory

Explicit, conscious (facts and events) 27, 39, 40, 166

Implicit, subconscious (procedures) 27, 39, 40

Retrieval strength 44, 45, 48, 60, 113

Working 31 – 33

Mendeleev, Dimitri 66

Mental models 15, 22, 26 – 28, 31 – 33, 35 – 38, 44, 45, 47, 60, 63, 67, 70, 75, 76, 78, 82, 85, 91, 93 – 97, 112, 115, 116, 141, 175, 182, 195, 198, 213, 214

Microsleep 101, 105

Milner, Brenda 39, 40

MIND Diet 171 – 174

Mindset 9, 122 – 128, 130, 132, 134 – 137, 139, 140, 144 – 146, 178, 195, 199, 212, 214, 217, 252

Mindset

Entity Theory 122

Fixed 122, 123, 125 – 128, 136, 137, 214

Growth 122 – 128, 134 – 136, 139, 140, 144 – 146, 195, 199, 214, 217

Incremental Theory 122

Molaison, Henry (Patient H.M.) 23, 39, 105, 113, 119

Monounsaturated fatty acid 150 – 153, 157

Muscle spindles 183

Munger, Charlie 35, 94

Musk, Elon 96, 97

Myelin 14, 15, 25, 150, 157, 159

Myelination 14, 15

Myokine 176, 177, 179, 182

Naperville 180– 182

Neocortex 24, 113, 114, 213, 214

Neuron 11 – 16, 18 – 21, 23, 25, 43, 44, 46, 75, 99, 109, 118, 124, 125, 148, 150, 154, 156, 158, 160, 166, 170, 175, 177 – 179, 182, 184, 186, 192, 241

Neurogenesis 19, 20, 170, 177, 178

Neuroplasticity 15, 16, 18 – 20, 25, 26, 165, 166, 170, 177

Neurotransmitters 13, 14, 19, 112, 115, 160, 161, 167, 168, 170, 175, 177, 178, 182, 183, 192

Nobel Prize 18, 21, 96, 130, 141

NREM 109 – 113, 119, 120

Occipital lobe 17, 18, 24

Pancreas 163 – 165, 168

Parietal lobe 24, 187

Patient H.M. 23, 39, 105, 113, 119

Polyunsaturated Fatty Acid (PUFA) 150 – 158, 160, 165, 166, 170, 172, 173

Poincaré, Henri 67

Prefrontal cortex 15, 104, 105, 115, 132, 134, 146, 183, 187

Purdue University 8, 26, 53, 146, 199, 201, 203, 205, 207, 209, 216, 253

Ramón y Cajal, Santiago 21

REM 109 – 112, 115 – 117, 120, 186

Richards, Keith 68, 69

Richardson, Bruce 106, 107

Sarcopenia 179

Saturated fatty acid 150 – 153, 157, 158, 160, 170

Self-control 130 – 135, 146, 156, 214, 215

Shannon, Claude 35, 67, 96, 244, 246, 247, 249

Shelley, Mary 66

Shereshevsky, Soloman 102, 103

Sleep

Chronotype 108

Cycle 110, 111

Dreaming 110 – 112, 115, 120, 121

REM 109 – 112, 115 – 117, 120, 186

NREM 109 – 113, 119, 120

Paralysis 112

Spindles 109, 110, 113, 114, 120

Stages 109 – 112, 114, 121

Stanford University 36, 122, 131, 216

Study

Background sound 54 – 56

Blocked 44, 48 – 50, 59, 60, 62, 64

Interleaving 44, 58, 59, 62 – 64, 89, 90, 94, 213, 214

Purposeful 19, 31, 33, 34, 37, 38, 72, 77, 81, 82, 85 – 91, 93 – 95, 97, 125, 195, 199, 206, 215, 216

Self-testing 73, 77, 82, 89 – 91, 215

Spaced 39, 43, 44, 47 – 50, 52, 55, 58 – 61, 64 – 66, 69, 70, 72, 74, 75, 78, 82, 92, 113, 119, 130, 213

Testing 57, 60, 68, 72 – 74, 77, 78, 83, 87, 89, 92, 215

Varied locations

Spaced study 39, 44, 48, 50, 60, 78, 130, 213

Steinbeck, John 68

Suprachiasmatic nucleus 107

Synapse 13, 14, 16, 18, 43, 44, 75, 124, 184, 192

Synaptic Cleft 13, 14

Synesthesia 102, 103

Szilard, Leo 66, 67

Temporal lobes 24

Terminal bouton 12 – 14

Trans bond 158

Trans fatty acid 152, 156, 158 – 160, 172, 173

Triglyceride 152, 154, 160, 164, 166

Violin 16, 36, 37, 85 – 87, 93, 94, 130, 135, 141

Von Helmhotz, Hermann 66

Wallas, George 67, 68

Walker, Matthew 119 – 121, 252

Zero Hour 181

Made in United States
Troutdale, OR
08/20/2024